Living Eng

R A Banks

HODDER AND STOUGHTON
LONDON SYDNEY AUCKLAND TORONTO

Acknowledgments

The author and publishers would like to thank the following for permission to reproduce copyright material in this book:

For Hilaire Belloc (an extract from 'The Mowing of a Field' from *Hills and the Sea*) – A D Peters and Co. Ltd; for Richard Church (five short extracts from *Over the Bridge* and one extract from *Calm October*) – Laurence Pollinger Ltd and the Estate of Richard Church; for Neil Gunn (an extract from *The Silver Darlings* published by Faber) – Faber and Faber Ltd; for L P Hartley (the short story 'A High Dive' from *The Complete Short Stories of L P Hartley* © 1973 published by Hamish Hamilton) – the Executors of the Estate of the late L P Hartley and Hamish Hamilton Ltd; for Laurie Lee (an extract from *Cider with Rosie* published by The Hogarth Press) – Mr Laurie Lee and The Hogarth Press Ltd; for George Orwell (three short extracts from *Shooting an Elephant* and an extract from *Animal Farm* published by Secker and Warburg) – the Estate of the late Sonia Brownell Orwell and Martin Secker and Warburg Ltd; for C P Snow (an extract from *The Affair*) – Macmillan Publishers Ltd, London and Basingstoke, and Charles Scribner's Sons, New York (copyright © 1960 C P Snow and reprinted with permission); for Dylan Thomas (an extract from *Portrait of the Artist as a Young Dog* published by Dent) – J M Dent and Sons Ltd; for Philip Ziegler (an extract from *The Black Death* published by Collins) – William Collins Sons and Co. Ltd; for an extract from *Hansard* of 13 March 1979 and an extract from *A Language for Life* (The Bullock Report, 1975) – Her Majesty's Stationery Office; for a leader from *The Times* of 28 November 1981 – Times Newspapers Ltd; University of London School Examinations Department for permission to reuse questions which have previously appeared in GCE O-level papers; Oxford University Press for permission to quote from H W Fowler's *A Dictionary of Modern English Usage* (second edition, 1965).

Every effort has been made to trace copyright holders; any rights not acknowledged here will be acknowledged in subsequent printings if notice is given to the publisher.

British Library Cataloguing in Publication Data
Banks, R. A.
  Living English.
  1. English language
  I. Title
  420   PE1072

ISBN 0 340 24997 8

First published 1983

Third impression 1987

Copyright © 1983 R A Banks

Cover photograph by Keith Gibson

Printed and bound in Great Britain for
Hodder and Stoughton Educational,
a division of Hodder and Stoughton Ltd,
Mill Road, Dunton Green, Sevenoaks, Kent,
by Page Bros (Norwich) Ltd

Phototypeset in 10 on 11pt Monophoto Baskerville
by Butler and Tanner Ltd, Frome and London

Contents

Acknowledgments   ii

Introduction   v

Abbreviations   vi

1   Living English   1

2   'Correct' English   3
    Exercises 1–2   12

3   Punctuation   15
    Exercises 3–12   31

4   Spelling   34
    Exercises 13–22   43

5   Grammar   46
    Exercises 23–63   108

6   Spoken and Written English   119
    Exercises 64–78   128

7   Vocabulary   137
    Exercises 79–90   142

8   Composition   145
    Exercises 91–103   170

9   Summary; Summary and Directed Writing; Précis   179
    Exercises 104–8   188

10   Comprehension   194
    Exercises 109–15   211

11   Figures of Speech   232
    Exercises 116–25   242

12   Common Errors   245
    Exercises 126–30   262

Selected Bibliography   264

Key to the Exercises   265

Index   279

For Mary-Lou

Introduction

The emphasis throughout this book is on the *living* aspects of English. At times, in order to explain its present vitality, it has been necessary to look briefly at its origins and to examine in detail its current forms. The language is constantly developing, changing, and adapting to new ideas and fashions; similarly the study of English is constantly growing, revising its approaches, and modifying its conclusions.

The study of the English language is complex and not the least difficulty in writing this book was that of deciding how much traditional description to retain and how much new terminology to use. Certainly the newest approaches to areas such as Composition, Comprehension, Summary, and Directed Writing are included and there are sections on Grammar, Spelling, and Punctuation which set out to describe current modern usage. These sections should provide clear and full accounts for easy reference.

The book is intended to help candidates prepare for public examinations such as GCE, CSE, 16+ and Commercial and Technical Certificates. It will also prove useful, too, for the general reader who wishes to have available an easy reference book for grammatical, punctuation, and spelling usage. Sections at the ends of chapters provide some exercises for students who wish to reinforce their knowledge and develop their control over the language. Throughout current usage has been the final referee as well as the rule-maker.

Throughout the preparation of this book my wife, Mary-Lou, has continually given her encouragement and support. I am also deeply grateful to Mrs Daphne Meeking who gave unstintingly of her help in typing the final script.

Sunbury-on-Thames, 1983   R A Banks

Abbreviations

A	adverb
AP	adverb particle
C	complement
oC	objective complement
sC	subjective complement
G	gerund
O	object
dO	direct object
iO	indirect object
NP	noun phrase
P	preposition
S	subject
V	verb
iV	intransitive verb
tV	transitive verb

In definitions based on dictionary entries, and in Chapter 12, Common Errors, the following abbreviations are used:

adj.	adjective
adv.	adverb
n.	noun
pers.	personal
poss.	possessive
prep.	preposition
pron.	pronoun
v.i.	intransitive verb
v.t.	transitive verb

1
Living English

1:1

Classical Latin and Ancient Greek are sometimes referred to as 'dead' languages; English, French, Spanish, Italian and German are described as 'living' languages. The distinction lies in the fact that a 'dead' language is one that has stopped developing, whereas a 'living' language is one that is continuing to change and grow.

1:2

Just how much English has changed and grown can be seen by comparing two versions of the Lord's Prayer in English, one written about the year 1000 AD and the other published in 1976:

Fæder ure þu þe eart on heofonum; Si þin nama gehalgod to be cume þin rice gewurþe ðin willa on eorðan swa swa on heofonum. urne gedæghwamlican hlaf syle us to dæg and forgyf us ure gyltas swa swa we forgyfað urum gyltendum and ne gelæd þu us on costnunge ac alys us of yfele soþlice

(from a manuscript in Corpus Christi College, Cambridge)

Our father in heaven,
may your holy name be honoured;
may your kingdom come;
may your will be done on earth as it is in heaven.
Give us today the food we need.
Forgive us the wrongs we have done, as we forgive the wrongs that others have done to us.
Do not bring us to hard testing
but keep us safe from The Evil One.

(The Good News Bible, 1976)

1:3

English has changed throughout the centuries, often as a result of social, political and scientific developments—the influence of Roman civilisation, the introduction of Christianity, the Viking and Norman invasions, the Reformation and the Renaissance, wars, emigration, and immigration.

Wars lead to movement of peoples; economic factors bring about the migration of men and women from one part of the country to another and from one land to another; better transport, travel abroad, the telephone, radio, television, communication satellites, newspapers, intermarriage erode political frontiers. Scientific inventions, micro-chip revolutions, advances in medicine or manufacturing processes, new material or geographical discoveries, science, developments in ideas—all require new expressions. Such changes alter the demands on a language and the way it is used. The changes come about in a variety of ways. It is easiest to illustrate some of them in terms of changes of vocabulary, but there have been major changes, too, in grammar and the sounds of words.

(i) A word common to many languages will take on meanings particular to the regions where it is used: *e.g.* the word corresponding to *beech* in English is used in other countries to refer to 'oak', 'elder', or 'elm'.

(ii) A word in one language may change its meaning under the influence of another language: *e.g.* the word 'dream' in English once meant 'joy' but it came to have its present meaning because of a Viking word *draumr*. The word *friend* meant 'kinsman' to the Vikings and this is the meaning of the word today in some parts of Scotland and the United States of America.

(iii) Sometimes a word in a language is pushed out completely by a word from another language: *e.g.* *take* and *sky* (Old Norse) pushed out 'niman' and 'wolcen' (Old English).

(iv) English is still able to make new words by combining others in order to express new ideas: *e.g.* *teenage, newsprint, Beatlemania, discotheque, foot-fault, typewriter, pizzaland, station-wagon.*

(v) As part of its living development, English has borrowed words from languages spoken elsewhere in the world: *e.g. abbot, school,* and *elephant* (from Latin); *kangaroo, wombat,* and *boomerang* (from Australia); *confetti, stiletto, spaghetti* (from Italy); *shampoo, tandoori* (through Urdu); *juggernaut, tomato* (from Spanish and Aztec); *robot* (from Czechoslovakia); *thug, cushy, loot* (from India); *shish-kebab* (from Turkey); *pyjamas, check-mate* (from Iran); *taboo* (from Tonga); *chop-suey, kow-tow* (from China).

A search through a good etymological dictionary (one which gives the origins of words) will reveal many hundreds more.

(vi) English also invents and/or adopts new words to meet a new situation or to describe a new invention: *e.g. computer, silicon-chip, caterpillar-track, biro, deepfreeze, beefburger, bulldozer, spaghetti-junction, motorway, creosote.*

1:4

The living language of English, it can be argued, is perhaps the most important world language. It is widely used in international, commercial, and political circles throughout the world. It is flexible and changes easily in response to developments in all fields of human activity—learning, economics, politics, and science, to name just a few. More people speak Chinese than English, it is true, but the position of English as a world language is unchallenged.

2
'Correct' English

The notion of 'correct' English seems to imply that somewhere there is a list of rules drawn up by an authority and that a student has only to learn and obey them in order to write or speak fluently and clearly. No such list exists; the student has to learn a different approach for him or herself.

Appropriateness

2:1

This book does not aim to deal with notions of 'correctness'; it is a book which sets out to suggest approaches which will lead a student to recognise in written forms of English what is 'appropriate' and to develop such control over the use of language that he or she can write in a clear, lively, and appropriate way. The student will need to read, listen to, and study a wide range of 'varieties' of English and to bear constantly in mind the purpose of the language and the audience for whom it is intended.

2:2

Consider the following passages carefully. The variety of English in each is clearly different. Analyse the nature of each passage and try to determine the features of its language which make it different from the others. Some of the questions you should ask yourself are these:

(i) What kind of person is using the language?
(ii) What is the general 'context' in which the language is being used?
(iii) At what kind of reader is the passage aimed?
(iv) How is the content of the passage helped (or hindered) by its expression?
(v) What does the writer's (or speaker's) choice of vocabulary contribute to the passage's overall effect? How does it do this?
(vi) What do you notice about the way the sentences are constructed and punctuated? Does this help or obstruct meaning?

(a) At 29 you're open to change and ready to consider new ideas. You're not so worried about your future that you find it necessary to be chained to a desk simply to clean your boss's shoes.
And, with the average age of a ship's company at 22, you're more likely to be in sympathy with the attitudes and ideas of the people who work for you.

What it amounts to is that we get the best possible man to be in control of our vastly complex and expensive equipment, and you get the best possible chance to use your abilities before you're too old to enjoy them.

It makes sense to us.

We hope it makes sense to you.

(**b**) Slide the split retainer on the accelerator pump control rod, with the dishing towards the hooked end of the rod. The spring is then passed over the hooked end of the rod and compressed, allowing the piston to be located on the rod. The assembly is positioned in the carburettor and the split retainer pressed into place.

(**c**) Her delicate looks, her provocative ways both fascinated and irritated William, whose awkward, tongue-tied manner had a violent nature, and he followed her like a great cat padding after some half-frightened, half-teasing excited little bird that he knows some day he will finally catch. And Ellen, inexperienced and too highly strung, sometimes feared the future and longed for a more light-hearted lover.

(**d**) Assessments . . . under Schedule A (income from property) or D (profits, interest, etc.) made or prepared before the Chancellor's autumn statement will not have taken the proposed changes into account. But they will be taken into account where appropriate, either when the assessment is adjusted on the settlement of an appeal or, if there is no appeal, by the issue of a notice of amended assessment.

(**e**) The man in the alpaca coat leaned against the doorpost. He was grinning. He seemed pleased with life. He said: 'Ain't you the little pip? You hate yourself, don't you? Go an' do this an' go an' do that! You tell me something . . . Why?'

Callaghan said: 'That's a good question. It should be answered. There are several answers. Here's one of them.' He blew a cloud of tobacco smoke into the man's face.

(**f**) When I was three I had a great passion for frogs. Whenever I saw one I would shut the dog in, because I was afraid that she would eat them. One day I saw a frog under our plum tree and being unable to pull the dog away ran for a jar to put the frog in. I ran all the way to our house (a good 150 yards), collected an old fish bowl and ran back to the frog. About eight yards from the house I fell over and broke the bowl.

(**g**) There is—thank goodness—no absolute standard by which to judge the value of a work of art. There may be such irrefutable standards for a brand of petrol or an egg-beater, but there is no litmus you can dip into a poem to test its value by the paper's change of colour. You do have the acid test of time and in the end it will burn out most of the rubbish. But a poet must have been dead for about fifty years, or lived so long that he's as good as posthumous for this test to be relevant.

(*h*) Bromine occurs chiefly as the bromides of potassium, sodium and magnesium usually in association with larger proportions of the chlorides of those metals. Since the bromides are much more soluble in water than the chlorides, a liquid rich in bromides is left by crystallising out the chlorides. Treated in this way, the mother liquors from the Stassfurt deposits in Germany, after the removal of a large proportion of the potassium chloride, contain about $\frac{1}{4}$% of bromide and the bromide is obtained by allowing this solution to come into contact with chlorine, which displaces the bromide.

(*i*) 'Three pounds.'
'Reds or whites? Anything else?'
'I've got no carrots left. Give us a couple of pounds.'
'Any fruit?'
'What are those oranges like? Not those. The ones over there.'
'Beautiful. Sweet. Thin skins.'
'I'll have a couple.'
'You're pushing the boat out, ain't you? Give the old man a treat.'

(*j*) The branch cracked and a flame of amethyst and red coiled up and straightened out so that side of her face away from the sun was glowing and her eyes gleamed. She came again from the recesses and put on more wood so that the fire gave them a brilliant display of flame and sparks. She began to work the wet clay with her fingers, tidying the edges so that now the fire sat in the middle of the shallow dish.

Levels of Meaning

2:3

The term *register* is frequently used to refer to the level on which spoken or written language is being employed. The register is often determined by the context or situation in which the speaker or writer finds or imagines himself or herself to be; obviously it is necessary to be aware of what is 'appropriate' or 'inappropriate' in order to employ the right register. Love-letters, a letter from a bank manager to a client with an overdraft or from a solicitor to a criminal in prison, letters written to *The Times* or *The Sun*, and letters complaining about loud aircraft noise to the manager of the public relations department at a major international airport will all demand appropriate 'registers'. Similarly a description of a sunset, or of an encounter with a ghost, or of a visit to a disco will require an appropriate level of language usage.

Sometimes a speaker or writer will deliberately use the wrong register, one quite inappropriate to the context in order to create a humorous or satirical or embarrassing effect.

The greater your awareness of, and control over, the different registers of English, the more effective your own use of language will be.

Conventions

2:4

Being aware of what is 'appropriate' in written English depends, too, on being able to recognise certain conventions that are used. Varieties of English (*e.g.* 'legal', 'official', 'scientific', 'literary', 'journalistic') follow patterns of approach, vocabulary, structures, and punctuation that have grown into conventions, perhaps over many years. Probably we never need to acquire control over more than a few such varieties, but it is useful to be able to recognise them and to be sensitive to the way they are being used. Whatever the variety, *the clear communication of meaning on the right level* should be the aim of the writer; he or she should be able to operate within the traditions of the chosen variety of English and avoid becoming unintentionally obscure.

2:5

In considering some of the conventions used, it is helpful to bear in mind the following headings: (i) Approach; (ii) Vocabulary; (iii) Structures; (iv) Punctuation.

(i) Approach

It is perhaps the prime aim of 'legal' English to avoid ambiguities at all costs; it does not set out to entertain, persuade, sell, shock, or attack. The more precise, clear, and unencumbered it is, the better English it will be. It is important that the terms of a will, for example, should unambiguously set out what its writer intends; a contract must be incapable of being misunderstood or misinterpreted. Such English tends to rely on words and formulas rather than on punctuation to establish meaning.

On the other hand it is often the method of 'political' writing deliberately to avoid a too precise use of the language. Journalists and commentators have long memories and delight in quoting a politician's speech, often out of context, many months later in order to embarrass him; if his remarks are capable of several interpretations the politician can still persuade the uncritical reader without leaving himself vulnerable to a shrewd interviewer later on.

'Literary' English sometimes draws its strength from the fact that it can be interpreted on several levels of meaning; comparisons, colourful, imaginative words, experiments in new structures to surprise, amuse, analyse, or persuade often abound. In such language a deliberately 'ambiguous' use of English can enrich, rather than obscure, meaning. (NOTE: *Ambiguous* can mean 'of double meaning' as well as 'obscure'.)

The approach that a writer is using can be discovered by a close and careful analysis of what he has written.

(ii) Vocabulary

Conventions have arisen within some varieties of English which demand the use of specialised vocabulary to avoid ambiguities or unnecessary length. Scientific, legal, and commercial varieties often use jargon to achieve this concise expression. The word 'jargon' has sometimes assumed the meaning of 'slang' or 'confused talk' but it should be properly defined as 'the terminology of a profession, art, group, etc.' (*Chambers Twentieth Century Dictionary.*)

It is appropriate within certain contexts to make use of jargon. A legal document may contain words and phrases such as *hereinafter, hereby assigns, precedent to the right of the insured to recover hereunder,* or an account of a scientific experiment may use such vocabulary as *agitate, saturate, effervesce, evolution, determination,* in very specific senses.

Those who write on language itself very often fall back on the jargon of their subject to explain their meaning concisely to those within their own set:

e.g. In initial sequences of voiceless consonants followed by voiced semi-vowels (= glides), the voicing of the semi-vowel may be slightly delayed by assimilation to the preceding voiceless consonant.

(C. K. Thomas, *An Introduction to the Phonetics of American English*, second edition, 1958)

This is writing that is appropriate to the context; it is 'good' English only in so far as it communicates its meaning to its specialised audience. The writer did not intend that everyone should immediately understand what he wrote. His vocabulary is as appropriate to his subject matter and his audience as that of English intended to make an immediate appeal to everyone: *Keep off the grass*; *Drinka pinta milka day*; *No Entry*.

When you are writing, choose vocabulary which conveys your meaning clearly and economically to the particular readers for whom you are writing.

(iii) Structures

Two structures can be recognised in most writing:

Simple: the arrangement of simple statements beside each other. Often the statements are not joined by any conjunctions at all but are separated merely by full stops or semi-colons; sometimes they are simply joined by *and, but,* or *or.*

Complex: the arrangement of statements so that they depend on each other. They are often joined by conjunctions such as: *because, although, if, unless, so that, until, on condition that.*

(a) Children often use simple structures to narrate events:

I got up and went downstairs. I had my breakfast and then had a wash. I got dressed and went to school. I was late and my teacher told me off.

Books of instructions and some scientific textbooks use structures like these in order to make the processes seem simple:

Weigh a small dry test-tube. Introduce a small piece of marble and weigh again. Set up the apparatus. Weigh the whole apparatus. Then loosen the cork. The small tube will then slip down.

This is hardly elegant writing but it is clear and appropriate. Sometimes, however, writers deliberately choose simple structures, to suggest strong emotions, drama, direct experience, or basic, deeply-felt reactions. For example, examine the following passage which describes the experience of a short-sighted boy as he emerges from an optician's shop and sees the world for the first time through his new pair of spectacles:

> The lamplight! I looked in wonder at the diminishing crystals of gas-flame strung down the hill. Clapham was hung with necklaces of light, and the horses pulling the omnibuses struck the granite road with hooves of iron and ebony. I could see the skeletons inside the flesh and blood of the Saturday-night shoppers. The garments they wore were made of separate threads.
>
> (Richard Church, *Over the Bridge*)

This is writing that uses simple structures but is clear, appropriate, and elegant.

(**b**) Legal documents make little pretence at elegance but they often need to use more *complex* constructions in order to be clear:

> Memorandum of an agreement between —— hereinafter called the Author, which expression shall where the context admits include the author's executors, administrators and assigns, as one part and —— hereinafter called the Publisher, which expression shall where the context admits include the Publisher's executors and assigns or successors in business as the case may be.

Occasionally structures such as these can lead the writer into paths which confuse the readers. Consider the following notice which appeared in the shops of a well-known chain of retailers:

> *Trades Description Act 1968*
>
> Reduced tickets indicate that the goods to which they relate were previously offered at a higher price but not that they were so offered for a period of not less than 20 days within the preceding six months.

What produces the difficulty in understanding this explanation? It partly lies in the placing of 'not' in front of the second 'that', a key word in this passage. (The double negative, the mixing of *that* and *which*, and the mention of 'twenty days within the preceding six months' also demand that the shopper, surrounded by her children and laden with shopping, should spend several minutes understanding the message—even if she had the time.) This notice is neither clear nor appropriate nor elegant.

Nevertheless, writing which uses *complex* structures can be very effective indeed in conveying mood, altering pace, and producing an imaginative response:

> The lamp-lighter was a half-fairy figure, always followed by a number of children who danced about him and shouted with glee when he stopped at a lamp, flipped open a little glass trap-door at the bottom of the lantern, pushed

his brass-topped pole into it, and kindled a fish-tail flame that flashed into life with a pop like a bursting balsam-seed.

(Richard Church, *Over the Bridge*)

The choice of appropriate structures for your writing will allow you to indicate mood, vary pace, convey shades of meaning, change attitude, and regulate the response you want your reader to have. It is an art that will well repay the learning.

(iv) Punctuation

Later in this book you will find a complete section on punctuation (pp. 15–33) which explains its major conventional uses. At this point in the discussion of what is 'appropriate' in the writing of English, it is important to bear in mind that the use of punctuation marks can have a subtle yet significant effect on meaning. Take, for example, the following two sentences:

The detective followed the man who had picked up the watch.
The detective followed the man, who had picked up the watch.

The words are the same in both and yet the insertion of a single comma has changed the sense: the first suggests that the man whom the detective followed was the one who had picked up the watch—he ignored everyone else, presumably; the second suggests that the detective followed the man (rather than the woman), who had incidentally picked up the watch. The first may also imply that the detective followed the man *because* he had picked up the watch and the second may imply that there was only *one* man to follow.

Punctuation is important. If you use commas where full stops are undeniably required the reader will be unable to follow what you are trying to say; your ideas will run into each other in confusion and become garbled. This is, perhaps, the most common fault found in the work of unsuccessful candidates at examinations in English Language. It demonstrates very clearly that the writer has no conception of what an English sentence is and that he or she has scant regard for the reader.

Consider the following passage; can you understand what the writer is saying?

Passengers travelling by a service noted calls by request must inform the guard sometimes at the previous stopping station or when joining the local train at a changing point passengers from a provincial station should give adequate notice at the station or in the case of an unstaffed halt by an appropriate hand signal to the driver.

With punctuation the sense becomes clearer:

Passengers travelling by a service noted 'Calls by Request' must inform the guard, sometimes at the previous stopping station or when joining the local train at a changing point. Passengers from a provincial station should give adequate notice at the station or, in the case of an unstaffed halt, by an appropriate hand signal to the driver.

(*ABC Rail Guide*, 1976)

But even now it is difficult to follow without a precise knowledge of the context; yet the punctuation has cleared up some of the confusion for the reader.

There is an extreme view, sometimes held by lawyers, that if documents require punctuation to make their meaning clear, then the expression of the law is unsound. Many insurance policies deliberately leave out all punctuation marks except capital letters; even these documents need to note where one statement ends and the next begins:

> The Insured shall give written notice to the Company as soon as possible after the occurrence of any accident with full particulars thereof Every letter claim writ summons and process shall be forwarded to the Company on receipt Written notice shall also be given to the Company immediately the Insured shall have knowledge of any prosecution or inquest in connection with any accident for which there may be liability under this Policy No admission offer promise payment or indemnity shall be made or given by or on behalf of the Insured without the written consent of the Company which shall be entitled to take over and conduct in the name of the Insured for its own benefit any claim and shall have full discretion in the conduct of any proceedings and in the settlement of any claim.
>
> (Alliance Assurance Co., Ltd, *Personal Liability Insurance*)

But imagine the following passage without any punctuation marks!

> In the Nuts (Unground) (Other than Groundnuts) Order, the expression nuts shall have reference to such nuts, other than groundnuts as would, but for the Amending Order, not qualify as nuts (Unground) (Other than Groundnuts) by reason of their being nuts (Unground).
>
> (Quoted by R. Quirk, *The Use of English*, second edition, 1968)

2:6

In this chapter it has been suggested that students should approach their study of the English Language from the following standpoints: (i) from an awareness of what is appropriate within a context for a particular purpose; (ii) from an understanding of the different levels of meaning on which a language operates; and (iii) from a recognition of what conventions surround and help written English.

2:7

It is not especially helpful to come to such a study with notions of what constitutes 'correctness' in the English Language other than these. For example, it is sometimes asserted and readily assumed that 'infinitives should not be split' and 'sentences should not end with a preposition'. In his discussion of these 'rules', an earlier writer (G. H. Vallins, *Better English*, 1953) managed to concede that 'an occasional modest split with a single adverb only may be justified' and the late Sir Winston Churchill, when reproached for ending sentences with prepositions, is reported to have shown up the stupidity of such a 'rule' by saying 'This is the sort of English up with which I will not put.'

2:8

Control over the language is best learnt by using it in active situations. English is a living language in the sense that it is continuing to change and the sensitive user of it will be ready to respond to these changes rather than resist them because of some rigid prescribed 'rules'. That is not to say that 'anything goes'. If the sense of what is written is garbled and confused, and the expression is inappropriate to the context or heedless of the conventions of the written language, then it is likely to be 'bad' English.

Students often need to remind themselves that they must have open minds (but not vacant ones) when they examine and use language. To be aware of what is happening to the language today provides a useful moving-off point to develop a control over *living* English.

EXERCISES

1 Write a passage of about 150 words on *one* of the following topics; make sure that you use an appropriate 'register' for the subject you choose:

1 A conversation between a boy and a girl as they wait at a bus-stop on their way to a party on their first date.

2 An account given to a policeman of a serious road accident which you have just witnessed.

3 The opening of a short story or a novel on a science fiction topic.

4 A criticism written for a newspaper of a film you saw last night on television. (Make it clear which paper you are writing for.)

5 A polite but firm letter to a neighbour to tell him that his dog's barking stops you from getting a good night's sleep.

6 An account for your own personal diary of an embarrassing meeting you had recently with somebody you wanted to forget.

7 A letter to a disc-jockey congratulating (or criticising) him or her on the way the programme is introduced.

8 A persuasive note to a friend explaining why he or she should jump at the opportunity to lend you twenty pounds.

9 A description of a poignant incident within your family written for a relative now living in Australia.

10 An account of an embarrassing meeting with a foreigner written *either* for one of your own fellow-countrymen *or* for a native of the foreigner's home country.

2

1 Write *two* accounts for young teenagers of how to play a disc on a modern turntable which has its own separate tuner amplifier:

   (*a*) *In the first* assume that the teenagers have a working knowledge of technical terms, such as amplifier, bass control, speed-selector, pick-up cartridge, stylus, record-size selector, etc.

   (*b*) *In the second* assume that the teenagers are about to use the apparatus for the very first time and have no such knowledge.

2 Rewrite the following paragraph in simpler terms (but without losing its essential meaning) so that an elderly, but not well-educated person could readily understand it:

The tax etc. is payable on the due date whether you appeal or not unless you apply to postpone payment of all or part of it. If you appeal against the assessment and consider that the amount charged is likely to exceed the ultimate liability, you may apply to the Inspector to postpone payment of part or all of the tax etc. pending settlement of the appeal. Any such application should show

   (*a*) why you think the amount charged is likely to be excessive; and

   (*b*) what amount you propose to be postponed.

3 Consider possible ways in which the following passage might be punctuated; bear in mind that the way you punctuate it will help to determine its meaning:

Hed been coming from milking it was early first light and he was just passing joness pond hed stopped for a minute to chuck a stone at a rat he got tuppence a tail when he caught one down by the lily weeds he suddenly saw something floating it was spread out white in the water hed thought at first it was a dead swan or something or at least one of joness goats but when he went closer he saw staring up at him the white drowned face of miss flynn her hair was loose which made him think of a swan and she wasnt wearing a stitch of clothes her eyes were wide open and she was staring up through the water like somebody gazing through a window well hed got such a shock he dropped one of his buckets and the milk ran into the pond hed stood there a bit thinking thats miss flynn and there was no one but him around then hed run back to the farm and told them about it and theyd come and fished her out with a hay rake hed not waited to see any more not he hed got his milk to deliver

4 Write an account in about 150 words of an encounter with a ghost. Set out deliberately to use *either* simple structures (statements separated by full stops or semi-colons or joined by *and*, *but* or *or*) *or* complex structures (longer, interdependent statements joined by words such as *when*, *where*, *since*, *as*, *because*, *that*, *which*) but whichever style you choose, use it to create an atmosphere of dramatic fear and uncertainty.

5 Draw up a short statement (about 100 words) for the press made by a politician who really believes that standards of education have been falling, although he does not wish to admit it publicly for political reasons.
Or
Draw up a short reply (about 100 words) made by a doctor who has been criticised by a journalist for leaving the National Health Service to set up in private practice, although still maintaining a belief in the idea of a state system of medical treatment for all.

6 Write the advertising copy for a new, mass-produced motor-car which aims to persuade the public to buy it in preference to a similar model of about the same price sold by a competitor. (Bear in mind that claims must not be false or so exaggerated that they contravene the Trade Description Acts.)

7 Some of the language in the following passage is intentionally 'ambiguous', in the sense that it sometimes deliberately carries more than one meaning. Consider some of the 'ambiguities' here which contribute to its total effect and try to describe some of the different levels of meaning found in them:

The swift December dusk had come tumbling clownishly after its dull day and, as he stared through the dull square of the window of the schoolroom, he felt his belly crave for its food. The stare began to crumble and a cloud of fine stardust fell through space. The dull light fell more faintly upon the page whereon another quotation began to unfold itself slowly and to spread abroad its widening tail.

8 The passage below sets out to mean the exact opposite of what it says. Rewrite it so that its meaning and its expression correspond without the

use of irony. (NOTE: '*irony:* the conveyance of meaning—generally satirical—by words whose literal meaning is the opposite'; *Chambers Twentieth
Century Dictionary*)

She could hardly have done a better job. It is not everyone who can take
a slice of fine, tender steak and turn it into an old boot merely by using a
frying-pan; but, then, she had this happy knack, an art she was born with
and no school could teach her. You might say she was a natural genius.

9 Make a list of expressions which young people (say, those under twenty)
use today as part of their everyday vocabulary but which their parents
rarely use. Similarly make a list of common expressions which your
parents used (and continue to use) when they were young. Consider the
lists and try to discover what determines the nature of the expressions and
their survival.

10 Make a list of *twenty* technical terms or phrases used in a particular
profession or trade (*e.g.* medicine, the law, teaching, car-repairing,
dress-making, cooking) and set out beside each an explanation which the
non-expert can understand.

3
Punctuation

Punctuation marks arose originally to help written texts to be read aloud clearly and accurately. By the end of the seventeenth century the names we now give to punctuation marks (comma, colon, semicolon, full stop) had become established and quotation marks, exclamation marks, and dashes had made their way firmly into the written language. These punctuation marks are now conventional signs to help the reader establish the sense easily. Writers neglect them at their peril; without them (or if they are carelessly used) the readers will lose their way and communication will break down.

Current Usage

The Full Stop

3:1

The full stop is used:
    (i) At the end of a complete statement (or utterance) which is neither an exclamation nor a question.

    e.g. He saw an elephant among the trees.
           He asked me if I had seen it.
           Yes. An elephant.

    (ii) After abbreviations.

    e.g. B.A. (= Bachelor of Arts)
           F.R.C.O. (= Fellow of the Royal College of Organists)

           e.g. (= *exempli gratia*, for example)

           N.B. (= *nota bene*, note well)

NOTE   It is often the practice to omit the full stop if the last letter of the abbreviated word is given:

    e.g. Mr (= Mister)
           Dr (= Doctor)
           Messrs (= Messieurs)

The full stop is the most important of the punctuation marks. Its omission, when its use is undeniably required, will confuse the reader; ideas will career wildly into each other and the meaning intended by the writer will not be communicated to the reader.

Consider the following passages and observe how the sense is obscure if the full stops are omitted or how the sense changes according to where the full stops are placed:

A The sun rose as night was swept away with the wind from the south hope was renewed

B The sun rose, as night was swept away. With the wind from the south hope was renewed.

C The sun rose. As night was swept away with the wind from the south, hope was renewed.

D The sun rose, as night was swept away with the wind from the south. Hope was renewed.

The Comma

3:2

Commas are frequently overused. It is as well always to consider the effect on the sense and construction of a sentence that their inclusion or omission would have. Consider the following:

I saw my friend Janet.

I saw my friend, Janet.

The first sentence implies that I have several friends, but the one that I saw was Janet. The omission of the comma allows 'Janet' to *define* which friend it was that I saw.

The second sentence may imply that I have only one friend and that her name happens to be 'Janet'. The inclusion of the comma allows the word 'Janet' merely to *qualify* the word 'friend'. It might also mean that the speaker is addressing Janet when he or she says, 'I saw my friend.'

Commas are both an aid to sense and to ease of reading. They are sometimes used in long sentences to break up words into sections where the sense allows a pause to be taken. It is better to underuse them than to overuse them.

The conventional uses of the comma are:

(i) To separate two descriptions, set side by side, of the same object or person; the second of the two descriptions adds to the meaning of the first and is parallel to it. (Technically, the second statement is said to be '*in apposition to*' the first.)

e.g. Mr Brown, *the grocer*, sells butter.
I saw my friend, Janet.

(ii) To separate the items or elements in a list.

e.g. At the grocer's shop I bought some eggs, bacon, sugar, tea, and biscuits.

NOTE Some writers would not insert the comma before the final *and* but others would argue that because it separates 'tea' from 'biscuits' as elements in a list it should be there. Look, however, at the final comma in the following list, where it is essential:

For breakfast I ate some cereals, toast, and eggs and bacon.

The final pair of items here ('eggs and bacon') may be seen as a single element; to have omitted the comma after 'toast' would have obscured the sense by running 'toast' and 'eggs and bacon' together.

(iii) To mark off the name or title of a person being addressed.

e.g. *Mr Jones*, what is the trouble?
I'd much rather, *John*, you told me the truth.
Doctor, I have had a pain in my chest for quite a time.

(iv) Following introductory words which introduce direct speech or a direct question.

e.g. He said, 'I know that I should have come earlier.'
The doctor asked, 'Why did you hesitate?'

(v) To separate short clauses which list actions, moods, events, and so on.

e.g. The man rose, left the room, slammed the door, and made his way into the street.

(vi) To indicate a statement interpolated within a sentence. Commas here effectively bracket off the interpolation.

e.g. It was obvious, *all things considered*, that he had done the wrong thing.

(vii) To separate, or mark off, a phrase which stands apart from the rest of a sentence.

e.g. *The decision taken*, there was no going back.
His mind growing confused, he made his way through the streets.

(viii) To indicate where words have been deliberately omitted but need to be understood.

e.g. The doctor could pursue his own ideas; I, mine.

(ix) To mark off a series of statements in the same sentence.

e.g. He knew *what he had to do*, *where he had to go*, and *when he should take the next step*.
He was a man *who was essentially nervous*, *who felt threatened*, and *who saw his life of no use*.

(x) To mark off a statement which qualifies the meaning of a word. (The omission of the comma here would alter the sense by changing the qualification into a clear definition.)

e.g. He stumbled into the house, *which was his home*. (This implies that there was only one house and this house happened to be his home.)
(*Qualifying*)

But
He stumbled into the house which was his home. (This implies that there were many houses but the one into which he stumbled was his home.) (*Defining*)

(xi) To mark off from the rest of the sentence a qualifying statement indicating such things as time, place, or manner *or* which introduce a condition or a concession.

e.g. *When he realised that*, he knew he had to make a quick decision. *If he had the courage*, he would be able to act decisively. *Provided he did not weaken*, he could carry out his plan.

The Semicolon

3:3

The semicolon marks off one part of a sentence from another much more sharply than a comma. It is particularly useful to divide a long sentence into self-contained sections. The semicolon is used:

(i) To separate a series of complete statements which, nevertheless, belong to a longer whole statement.

e.g. He was ill; he now knew it; he would go to the doctor's.

NOTE The semicolons here give to the three short statements a dramatic note which would not be present if the first were replaced by a comma and the second by a conjunction, such as *and*; indeed, to change the statement in this way would weaken it so much that it would become almost meaningless.

(ii) To introduce a sharp contrast between complete statements which are closely related.

e.g. He knew what he should do; yet he could not do it.
He trusted the doctor; he distrusted himself.

NOTE The semicolon is particularly useful to make this kind of contrast before linking words such as *therefore, otherwise, still, yet, for, nevertheless*.

(iii) To break up a long sentence which would otherwise be overwhelmed by a confusion of commas.

e.g. He would do it, if he could; for, after all, he had the time.

The Colon

3:4

The colon is used:

(i) To introduce a list which follows immediately.

e.g. He studied the use of the following punctuation marks: full stops, semicolons, colons, question marks, etc.

(ii) To introduce examples which illustrate or expand an idea and which follow immediately.

e.g. He counted his treasures: gold, silver, diamonds, and books.

(iii) To introduce a quotation which follows immediately.

e.g. Hamlet once contemplated his own death: 'To be or not to be ...'

(iv) To introduce an explanation which follows immediately.

e.g. This is what to do: pour the yellow liquid into the green one and then get out—fast.

(v) To introduce a speech which follows immediately.

e.g. He rose to his feet, cleared his throat, and began: 'Unaccustomed as I am to public speaking, I should like to say ...'

(vi) To divide two sharply contrasting statements.

(NOTE A semicolon sometimes has this function, too: see **3:3**(ii).)

e.g. Speech is silver: silence is golden.
The river ran downhill: he made his way slowly up the path.

The Question Mark
3:5

The question mark had its origin in an awareness not of grammar but of rhetoric: it indicated where the voice was to turn upward to indicate that a question was being asked. The full stop which forms part of this punctuation mark shows that a statement (in this case, a question) has come to an end.
The question mark is used:

(i) To mark the end of a direct question.

e.g. Where did you go?
How are you today?

NOTE It is not used in an indirect question:

e.g. *He asked where you went. He wonders how I am.* Remember, however, that the context can easily turn such statements into direct questions themselves.

(ii) To show that statements within a given context are to be taken as direct questions.

e.g. *Question marks are not used in indirect questions?*
No, they are not.
He asked where you went? You may well be surprised!
He wonders how I am? I never knew he cared!

The Exclamation Mark
3:6

The exclamation mark, like the question mark, is mainly a rhetorical sign; it shows where a statement is used as an interjection or carries very strong emotion. The full stop which forms part of this punctuation mark shows that a statement (in this case, an exclamation) has come to an end.

e.g. Good gracious! You must certainly not go there!
Oh dear! I thought that you might say that.

After this last sentence an exclamation mark is also possible but, if it is added, it will inject strong emotion into the utterance. This is one of the occasions in the use of punctuation where a sign does not merely follow the sense and structure but can determine meaning. The context will usually make it clear when the emotion in a statement is strong enough to warrant the use of an exclamation mark.

The Apostrophe
3:7

The apostrophe is one of the most interesting punctuation marks in English but it is very often misused. Misunderstandings abound and it is not uncommon to find on notices displayed in shops simple plurals of nouns that are wrongly given an apostrophe -*s*:

e.g. Sign in a men's hairdresser's: *No Boy's Today*
Notice in a greengrocer's shop: *Tomatoe's 30p a pound.*

The apostrophe is used:
(i) To denote the possessive form of the noun.
All nouns, singular and plural, take an *apostrophe* +*s* to show the possessive case:

e.g. The boy's book
The men's hats

There are two main groups of exceptions which merely take an apostrophe without the final -*s*:
(*a*) Plural nouns which already end in -s:

e.g. The boys' books
The princesses' tiaras

(*b*) Singular nouns that already contain so many 's' sounds (sibilants) that the addition of a further -*s* would be ugly:

e.g. Ulysses' travels
Jesus' sayings
Artaxerxes' exploits

(ii) To mark the omission of a letter or group of letters in a word.

> *e.g. don't* (= do not); *I'd* or *I'ld* (= I should); *it's* (= it is)
> (Be particularly careful to distinguish *it's* (= it is) from *its* (= belonging to it) where *its* is a possessive *pronoun* and so does not take an apostrophe any more than *his* or *hers* does.)
>   Normally the omission marked by an apostrophe is of a single letter only (*don't, isn't, wouldn't*) but sometimes words which have letters omitted at two places within themselves show the omission conventionally at one place only (*shan't*=shall not, *can't*=can not). In Victorian times the contracted spellings of *though* and *through* (*thorough*) were shown as *tho'* and *thro'* or *thru'* (*thoro'*) and were used by Tennyson; they are still occasionally found today.

(iii) To form the plurals of letters, figures, and contractions consisting of initial letters.

> *e.g.* Dot your i's and cross your t's.
> There are three 4's in twelve.
> In the 1930's there was much unemployment.
> How many M.P.'s are there in the House?

> The use of the apostrophe in such cases is often confusing. It is now the convention to omit the use of the apostrophe here but to italicise single letters before adding the final *s*: *es*, *gs*, but 4s, the 1930s, M.P.s and so on.

>   Where the reader is likely to be confused the apostrophe is, nevertheless, retained: *is* and *i's*.

(iv) Current practice omits the apostrophe in the following cases in spite of what has been said above:
Certain words where the initial letters are omitted:

> *e.g. bus* (for *omnibus*), *phone* (*telephone*), *car* (*autocar*)

> Some place names:

> *e.g. Land's End* but *Golders Green*; *St James's Park* but *St Helens*. (Notice, too, the omission of the full stop in the abbreviation *St*=Saint.)

> Some well-known proper nouns:

> *e.g. Woolworths, Sainsburys, Marks and Spencers, Hodders*, and many others.

Parentheses (Brackets and the Double Dash)

3:8

(i) Most frequently brackets are used to mark off within a sentence a word, comment, explanation or statement without which the sentence would otherwise be grammatically complete. It should be possible to take out the brackets and what they contain and then read the sentence without feeling that it is incomplete. Sometimes, instead of brackets two dashes are used; what is placed between the dashes will, however, remain an interpolation. If there is a distinction to be made between the use of brackets and the use of dashes it is probably that dashes mark off the interpolation less sharply from the rest of the sentence than brackets.

Compare, for example, the following:

> He managed (such was his skill) to build his own house.
> He managed—such was his skill—to build his own house.
> He had enough money (he was rich) to buy the bicycle.
> He had enough money—he was rich—to buy the bicycle.

(ii) Brackets are also used to add information, to amplify a comment without interrupting its general flow.

e.g. They were all there (John, Margaret, Timothy, and Sarah) and the party was complete.
He had enough money (ninety pounds) to buy the bicycle.

(iii) Brackets are used, too, to provide a comment or a gloss on a statement; what is contained within the brackets should be taken as an 'aside' when they are used in this way. It is often effective to use brackets like this to convey humour, satire, or irony.

e.g. She thought she was beautiful. (It was a pity about her squint.)
He said he needed fifty pounds. (That's what he said last time.)
The old man seemed full of life. (It depends how you define 'life'.)

Square brackets [ ] are used to indicate comments, corrections, explanations, or other comments not in the original text but added later by the writer or by an editor:

e.g. The poem was written in 1972, although it referred to events which took place two years before. [*Editor's note:* see the poet's Autobiography, p. 10.]

The Dash

3:9

It is not acceptable to use dashes in a slovenly manner to avoid having to decide whether a full stop is required or not. They are most effectively used to achieve a deliberately specific effect.

(i) To indicate a change in the direction of a comment:

e.g. She was wearing a top hat—I noticed her immediately.

(A full stop instead of a dash here would have separated the two statements too harshly and omitted the slightly humorous link between them.)

(ii) To provide an antithetical (or contrasting) comment within a sentence:

e.g. Everything—except the mummy—left the auction room hurriedly.

(Commas instead of the dashes would not have produced a sharp enough contrast to make the point sufficiently dramatic.)

(iii) To indicate hesitant or faltering speech:

e.g. 'I—er—I should like to—er—emphasise that—that public speakers should—er—should always speak—talk clearly.'

(iv) To mark a sudden breaking-off of a statement, often for dramatic effect:

e.g. 'If I were you, I should get off the camel, unless—'
'He knew this was his last chance to live or—'
'He struggled to the edge of the cliff, looked over, and jumped—'

(v) To suggest a sudden start to a statement, perhaps by way of interruption:

e.g. —Oh, I don't agree with you for one minute when you say so confidently that there is life before death.

(vi) To mark off a parenthesis, perhaps less emphatically than brackets: see **3:8** (i).

(vii) To pull together items in a list or a number of loosely strung words in order to resume the direction of a sentence:

e.g. Tom, Dick, and Harry—they were three fine lads.

Kicking in the stomach, twisting arms, stamping on a fallen opponent, gouging eyes—these are not the actions of a gentleman playing rugby.

The dash—used sensitively—can add a dimension to the meaning of a sentence over and above the sum total of the weight of the words. The order, the balance, the nature of the vocabulary used give dimension, too, but the nuances, the humour, the point, the comment implicit in a sentence can often be brought out by the careful use of the dash. It is a punctuation mark that is the more effective for being used sparingly: when it appears it needs to pack its own punch.

Inverted Commas (quotation marks, single and double)
3:10

The use of these punctuation marks and the 'correct' forms they should take provide printers, proof-readers and grammarians with ample opportunities to display their authority. Fowler's comment in *Modern English Usage* (1926) makes its points firmly and appeals to the reader's sense of reason: 'There is no universally accepted distinction between the single form ('...') and the double ("..."). The more sensible practice is to regard the single as the normal ... To reverse this is clearly less reasonable.' G. H. Vallins in *Good English* (1951), however, abhors them: 'One of the simplest and most beneficial reforms in English usage would be their total abolition. They are a nuisance to the writer who ... is often puzzled to determine their correct relationship with other stops; an irritation to the reader, who does not need them, although he may imagine he does.'

However, publishers have their 'house styles' and they usually determine how the conventions should operate for their own publications. What follows is a summary of the practices more usually found in books, serious newspapers, and magazines.

(i) Where only one set of quotation marks is needed the single are usually preferred to the double. They are used to mark off the exact words used by a speaker or a writer:

e.g. He said, 'I never know how to use quotation marks.'
Vallins argued that quotation marks 'are a nuisance to the writer'.

The placing of the final full stop in these examples is interesting. In the first, the full stop marks both the end of the statement in single inverted commas and the end of the whole sentence beginning *He said* ... It is unnecessary to use *two* full stops here and the normal practice is to allow the one inside the closing inverted comma to do the work of both. In the second example, the words within the inverted commas do not constitute a complete sentence but are merely six quoted words used by a writer; the full stop, therefore, might be placed after the quotation to indicate the end of the whole sentence beginning *Vallins argued* ... For the sake of uniformity, however, many publishing houses place a single full stop within the final inverted comma, whatever the situation.

(ii) Where a direct statement, question, or exclamation is given in the form of the actual words used and this statement, question, or exclamation includes another that is quoted (as in the examples in (i) above), double inverted commas are used to mark off the quotation within the statement, question, or exclamation:

e.g. The weeping child said, 'I never said, "What a big nose you have!" to auntie.'

or The angry auntie said, 'Do I have to ask little Sally once more, "Will you say you are sorry to auntie?"'

but, The angry auntie said, 'Do I have to ask little Sally, "Will you say you are sorry to auntie?" once more?'

The game of punctuating such sentences can continue endlessly; it provides ample amusement for several wet afternoons. For a student, however, it is important to think out the function of punctuation marks such as these, to use them as clearly as possible within the conventions, and to be consistent.

(iii) Inverted commas are used to mark a word or phrase outside the predominant variety of English being used:

e.g. To argue that economically, politically, and socially it would be better for Great Britain to leave the common market is 'bosh'.
The normally restrained and decorous young lady was 'over the moon' when she was given the new pony.

(iv) Inverted commas are used to mark a quotation from an article, a book, a poem, a magazine and so on:

e.g. 'To be or not to be' is a quotation from *Hamlet*. Hamlet looked upon himself as 'a rogue and peasant slave' because he could not take the necessary action to solve his problem.

(v) Titles of books and periodicals or the names of ships are sometimes put within inverted commas; it is usually more convenient to under-line them to indicate that in print the words would be italicised. This device enables the writer to avoid the complications of double in-verted commas within single inverted commas where a title is used in direct speech:

e.g. He asked, 'Have you read *The Times*?'

is preferable to the following, because it seems clearer:

He asked, 'Have you read "The Times"?'

Similarly:

The fishing-boat's skipper asked his look-out, 'How did you miss seeing *The Queen Elizabeth* before she ran us down?'

is preferable to

The fishing-boat's skipper asked his look-out, 'How did you miss seeing "The Queen Elizabeth" before she ran us down?'

A problem sometimes arises in quoting the title of a newspaper or magazine which begins with the definite article (*The*) or the indefinite article (*A*). Where the article forms part of the title it is better to retain it, unless it produces obvious clumsiness:

e.g. The leading articles in *The Guardian* please some but annoy others.

but

A *Guardian* leading article is often deliberately provocative.

Italics (indicated in handwriting and typewriting by underlining)

3:11

In 1501 Aldus Manutius produced a sloping type for use in his printing; this type became known as *Italic*. Writers who are preparing a manuscript for printing show words to be italicised by underlining them. Although italic script is a device used for printing, underlining can be used by writers effectively in order to:

(i) avoid the confusing over-use of double inverted commas within single inverted commas; it is often clearer and more convenient to underline titles, words used outside the predominant variety of English, and short quotations:

e.g. The judge asked the accused one-armed man, 'Did you not see the notice which said, *Do not feed the Animals?*'

(ii) stress a word or short phrase:

e.g. I cannot really say that I *like* eating cold porridge.
I positively abhor eating *cold, lumpy porridge.*

It is important not to make use of excessive underlining. Fowler in *A Dictionary of Modern English Usage* gives a timely warning:

To italicise whole sentences or large parts of them as a guarantee that some portion of what one has written is really worth attending to is a miserable confession that the rest is negligible.

Hyphens

3:12

All punctuation marks should be used to indicate meaning; clearly the presence, absence, or placing of a hyphen in the following noun phrase determines its sense:

a sweet shop girl
or a sweet-shop girl
or a sweet shop-girl

On the other hand, to omit the hyphen from 'a walking-stick' is unlikely to confuse a reader since we all know that sticks do not normally walk, and yet clearly the relationship between 'walking' and 'stick' is different, say, from the relationship between 'walking' and 'man' in the phrase 'a walking man'. In order to demonstrate this difference in grammatical relationship it is conventional to mark it by using or not using a hyphen:

e.g. a walking-stick

but a walking man

In the phrases 'a running river' and 'a running man' the word *running* acts as an adjective in both: *i.e.* it describes the way the river runs and does not suggest that the river is *for running* in the same way that a 'walking-stick' suggests that the stick is *for walking*.

(i) Hyphens should be used, therefore, to convey a significance in the relationship of one word to another or others. For example, examine the differences in meaning between:

(*a*) animal-lovers *and* animal lovers;

(*b*) eleven-year-old children *and* eleven year-old children;

(*c*) the one-armed man *and* the one armed man;

(*d*) a red-hot poker *and* a red, hot poker;

(*e*) the first-night performance *and* the first night performance;

(*f*) a far-sighted person *and* a far, sighted person;

(*g*) the comprehensive-school building *and* the comprehensive school-building;

(*h*) a French-cheese salesman *and* a French cheese-salesman;

(*i*) a novel-reader *and* a novel reader;

(*j*) a dry-cleaned jacket *and* a dry, cleaned jacket.

(ii) Hyphens are used to form compound nouns or adjectives, especially where such compounds are newly-coined, not fully established as compounds, or carry a specific meaning:

e.g. *teddy-boys, punk-rockers;*
pub-crawling, high-rise, pre-school;
nuclear-disarmament, flower-power;

(iii) Hyphens often separate elements in a compound word which would look awkward (perhaps because of a clash of vowels or a danger of confusing consonants) or be difficult to read or pronounce if it were written as a single word:

e.g. *socio-economic; co-opt* (although *disservice* presents apparently no problems); *hi-fi; anti-ecclesiastical; retro-active* (although this word is often accepted as an unhyphenated compound, *retroactive*).

Part of the problem with such words lies in the difficulty that the reader might have in distinguishing the syllables or parts of words if hyphens are not used.

(iv) Hyphens may be used to split words at the end of lines (because of lack of space) in order to carry them forward to the next line. It is customary, however, to divide words in British English at an appropriate morphological point: *e.g. posit-ion* rather than *posi-tion*.

Often this morphological break (*i.e.* the point at which a unit with its own division of meaning within the word ends) coincides with the syllabic break (*i.e.* the point at which the part of a word uttered by a single effort of the voice ends): *e.g. resent-ment.*

(v) Hyphens are a convenient way of joining together several words to form a new useful compound. Germanic languages (including English) have used this compounding of words to form new ones throughout the centuries. Modern German does it less self-consciously than Modern English, perhaps. *For example*, a German word for 'submarine' is *Unter/see/boot*, or for 'shock' or 'collision' *Gegen/einander/stoszen*, or for 'in-need-of-support' *unter/stützungs/bedürftig*.

Modern English uses hyphens to suggest the more hesitant compounding of words: *e.g. rule-of-thumb, never-to-be-forgotten*, the *once-and-for-all result*. Sometimes it dispenses with them after a time: *e.g.* the *whodunnit*, a *roundabout, radiography*—but *radio-activity* (perhaps because of the clashing of vowels).

Capital Letters
3:13

These are used to mark:
   (i) the beginning of a sentence;

   (ii) the beginning of direct speech within a sentence:

   e.g. He said, '*T*he elephant has just left the house', and his family wondered what he could possibly mean.

   (iii) a proper name—of a person or place:

   e.g. The mother decided to name her baby *A*nastasia *H*yacinth *S*mith;
The plane flew low over *N*ether *W*allop, *M*iddle *W*allop, and *U*pper *W*allop before crashing in the river.

   (iv) the names of objects which are clearly trade-names, distinguishing proprietary names, or the distinctive names of types of machines, plants, animals, etc.:

   e.g. She switched on the *B*endix washing-machine;
He drank a glass of *R*ibena;
The sky was full of *S*pitfires, *S*tukas, and *M*esserschmitts;
When you were in Africa were you bothered by the dreaded *C*hilopoda? No, I stamped on such creatures.

   (v) days of the week and months of the year:

   *e.g. M*onday, *T*uesday, *W*ednesday; *J*anuary, *F*ebruary, *M*arch.
  (NOTE In French the equivalent words use small letters; German uses capitals, however.)

   (vi) the names of languages and nationalities:

   *e.g. E*nglish, *F*rench, *I*talian; *J*apanese flowers, *G*erman sausages.

(vii)   treaties, acts of parliament, organisations, assemblies, and important historical events:

  e.g. The *V*ersailles *T*reaty;
    The *A*ct of *S*uccession;
    The *T*rades *U*nion *C*ongress;
    The *C*onfederation of *B*ritish *I*ndustry;
    The *W*orld *H*ealth *O*rganisation;
    The *F*rench *R*evolution.

(viii)   titles of books, papers, and journals, radio or television programmes, and the names of ships:

  e.g. *L*iving *E*nglish; *T*he *T*imes; *H*amsters *T*oday;
    *T*op of the *P*ops;
    *T*he *A*rchers;
    *T*he *A*rk *R*oyal.

NOTE   In (vii) and (viii) the first word has a capital but afterwards conjunctions, prepositions, and articles have small letters.

(ix)   the personal pronoun '*I*' and the poetic, vocative of address '*O*':

  e.g. He came in as *I* went out;
    O Caesar, why did you come to die here?

(x)   nouns which represent personified abstract ideas:

  e.g. The green-eyed monster, *J*ealousy, looked through the door, but *G*reed soon drew him away.

(xi)   titles of people:

  e.g. *T*he *D*uke of *E*dinburgh; *T*he *P*early *K*ing of *B*ermondsey; *T*he *M*ayor of *L*lanarmon-*D*yffryn-*C*eiriog.

(xii)   abbreviations of the names of organisations:

  e.g. *NATFHE*, the *NUT*, *PAT*, and the *AMMA* have all considered joining the *TUC*.

Paragraphing and Indenting
3:14

The paragraph is defined in *Chambers Twentieth Century Dictionary* as:

  'a short passage, or a collection of sentences with unity of purpose'.

Its structure and use have been described and discussed elsewhere in this book (see pages 147–8).

(i)   Until recent times the beginning of a paragraph was marked by the indentation of the first line: *i.e.* it was spaced back from the main body of writing by about three or four letters. It has become increasingly the practice, however, in the typing of business letters to abandon this custom, but paragraphs are still almost always indented in printed books.

(ii) In setting out dialogue in direct speech, writers and printers usually mark a change of speaker by indenting the first word of the speech:

e.g. The door creaked open to reveal a man dressed in thigh-length boots, green trousers, a lace shirt and a three-cornered hat. The younger son spoke first:

> 'Gad, Sir, you must be ...'
> 'I most certainly am!'
> The ladies and gentlemen could not believe what they heard.
> 'Well, come in; you can't stay on the doorstep all night,' said Lord Dimwit.
> 'I had no intention of doing that,' replied the visitor.

(iii) Passages of verse or prose quoted which are more than two or three lines in length are indented and given without the use of quotation marks:

e.g. The opening of *The Pilgrim's Progress* describes the way in which John Bunyan fell asleep and dreamed:

> As I walked through the wilderness of this world, I lighted on a certain place where was a den, and laid me down in that place to sleep; and as I slept, I dreamed a dream. I dreamed, and behold, I saw a man clothed with rags ...

In this way he hints to his reader that his story will be imaginative and carry at times the atmosphere of a nightmare.

English is a living language and its conventions about punctuation are open to change brought about by practice, but it is a foolish student who tries to justify his own peculiar punctuation merely because he and one or two other uninformed people decide to write eccentrically.

EXERCISES

3 Punctuate the following passage and then write a brief series of notes commenting on and justifying what you have done:

running down the street i saw jack swinging from a lamppost lit by gas and swaying in the wind what are you doing i demanded i thought i would turn it up a bit he replied but it was clear he would fall off i cried this very minute he came down with a crash and started singing auld lang syne

4 Punctuate each of the following sentences *twice* to bring out *two* possible meanings determined by your punctuation:

1 he says i am to sing the second verse i ask why
2 the film she saw was a strange one
3 the house i had seen that night was clearly haunted
4 everyone ran to the houses collapsed in a heap i heard the hurricane vanishing into the distance
5 i can describe to you my rubbish he replied i dont want to know
6 higginbottom the lawyer you know the man i saw
7 can you give me the details i need to know for my work you see
8 how fast did the rabbits run in the field by the hedge or near the trees
9 off you go quickly before i see you never cheat
10 can you do it at once if i pay you six pence i believe you said so

5 How can you alter the sense of the following by changing the punctuation?

1 I assure you it is true. I am never wrong.
2 John, the baker's son, Fred, and I saw it before it blew up. It was a fantastic sight!
3 He thought he saw her getting off the bus. He looked once more but she had gone.
4 What is it that you can never understand? The purpose of life is obvious.
5 We went to the Safari Park before last Wednesday, to be precise.
6 What more is there to say, now that I have admitted it? Brown must be involved!
7 If we offend, it is with our good will.
That you should think, we come not to offend,
But with good will. To show our simple skill,
That is the true beginning of our end.
Consider then we come but in despite.
We do not come as minding to content you,
Our true intent is. All for your delight,
We are not here. That you should here repent you,
The actors are at hand; and, by their show,
You shall know all that you are like to know.
(Shakespeare, *A Midsummer Night's Dream*, V, i, 108–17)
8 Would you prefer the soldier to kill you or the general?

9 How can you believe that there are fairies at the bottom of your garden? I assure you there are not.

10 I finished my work and returned the day after I intended to go on holiday.

6 Bearing in mind that the way you use punctuation helps to determine meaning, set out the following passage correctly punctuated; the passage contains some dialogue. (Be prepared to justify the meaning that your punctuation will give to the passage.)

> jean rawlings the headmasters secretary is sitting at her desk a knock is heard as a nervous little boy enters hidden behind a huge pile of exercise books he stammers almost inaudibly asking whether he can see the headmaster he nearly falls over the carpet no you cant at the moment he is busy er when er can i see him you mean what for jenkins the prefect sent me with these books to show him they are a disgrace i think he is always picking on us for no reason at all he tells us off whenever he can all right if you want to leave them there where you can see a space ill make clear thats all you want if you can come back tomorrow when the headmaster is free he will want to see you to thank you and watch how you go as the boy falls over the carpet and upsets the pile of books

7

1 Write a sentence (between 10 and 15 words in length) which is capable of carrying two different meanings according to how it is punctuated. (Do not alter the words or their position.)

2 Using about 300 words, write a piece of dialogue between two people who are having an argument about a mutual friend. If you wish, you may continue the introduction given below and/or imitate the way the conversation is set out. Whatever you do, be consistent in the layout you adopt and punctuate your work accurately:

BILL   You can't believe a word she says.
LINDA   Your trouble is that she won't go out with you.
BILL   I've never asked her . . . and, what's more, I'm not likely to.
LINDA   She's one of the cleverest, kindest, and most thoughtful people I know—and she's modest, too.

8 Write a letter to your local public librarian asking him to obtain five books for you as soon as possible. Explain to him the urgency and give him the full titles and the authors' names. Keep your letter short but polite and clear. Take great care with your punctuation.

9 Write a brief, factual statement for inclusion in your local newspaper of the leisure activities available in your area at the weekend, under the headings: *Friday, Saturday, Sunday*.

You should set out the facts in short note form, giving such details as what will take place, times, venues, and people organising the events and taking part. Some of the information may be given in list form, if you wish.

(The purpose of this exercise is to see how effectively and accurately you can control the use of the following items of punctuation: underlining (*itali-cising*), brackets, dashes, colons, semicolons, capital letters, commas and full-stops. Check your work against the descriptions of punctuation usage given earlier in this chapter.)

10 Imagine that your bedroom has been damaged by fire. Make a short but detailed statement for your insurance company, which includes a brief account of how the fire started and a list of what has been damaged (indicating the extent of the loss or damage to each item). You should also show in your list the approximate price you paid for each item you mention, together with an estimate of how long you have had it. (Punctuate the list with great care.)

11 Most newspapers and some magazines include from time to time an account of a meal taken in a restaurant by a reporter, an account written to inform the readers of what was on offer, how it was presented, the cost involved, and the value of the experience. Usually such reports contain both facts and comments.

Write such a report for your daily newspaper of such a visit you have paid to a restaurant either in this country or abroad. (Give the name of the paper for which the report is intended and punctuate your work carefully. Use an appropriate register.)

12 Write a short contribution to a formal debate on *one* of the following motions:
1 that there should be equal opportunities in all walks of life for men and women;
2 that there are no such things as rights—only responsibilities;
3 that the school-leaving age should be reduced;
4 that everyone should have to learn a foreign language;
5 that most pop music is a noise invented to rob the young of their money and the ability to think.

Your contribution may support or oppose the motion and should be about 300 words in length. Try to use some rhetorical questions effectively and introduce some balance into your arguments. Paragraph and punctuate your work accurately to bring out the arguments you are making clearly.

4
Spelling

4:1

The British are divided into two: those who can spell correctly and those who cannot; the second group is by far the more numerous. The English language presents native readers and writers with immense problems, because its spelling is based partly on etymology (the way the words originated and developed). Most people do not have enough historical or linguistic knowledge to be able to relate modern English spelling to etymology and so they fall back on trying to represent in writing the words as they sound in speech. Such an approach is often doomed before it begins, because it tends to ignore two things: first, words are not pronounced in the same way everywhere in the British Isles and the phonetic speller in Yorkshire ought, therefore, to produce a spelling for a word which is quite different from that of a phonetic speller in the West Country. Even the simple word 'gate' would produce some amazing variations in spelling throughout the country if people were to spell it exactly as they pronounced it. Secondly, words change in pronunciation over the years and English spelling would need to be in a state of constant flux from one decade to the next and one century to the next. Alexander Pope (who died in 1744) rhymed the words *obey* and *tea*, for example, but they certainly do not rhyme today; Pope spelt the rhymed syllables differently, too, since he did not base his spelling on phonetics any more than we do today.

4:2

Consistency in English spelling was not, however, one of its strongest features until comparatively recent times. The scribes who produced the handwritten books for the monastic libraries in Anglo-Saxon England often spelt their English words as they pronounced them; there are even some, although fewer, variations in the way they wrote their Latin words. Variations in the spelling of English at this time have been an invaluable help to scholars who want to find out more about early regional dialects and to discover in what part of the country a particular manuscript might have been produced, or even from what area a particular scribe might have originated. The spelling of words carried traces of evidence about the regional origin of the man, the book he was copying, the monastery in which he was writing, and the area in which he was working.

Today the person who cannot spell accurately according to the conventions set up by printers and maintained by dictionary-makers is considered illiterate. It would take some strong arguments by those wishing to reform English spelling to sweep away at a stroke the evidence of some eight hundred years of the development of our language it contains. So far English has rejected all such attempts.

Spelling 'Rules'

4:3

So-called 'rules' for language always seem to carry a list of exceptions; nevertheless, it is often useful to observe the patterns of usage of a language. The 'exceptions' provide the tests against which the 'rules' can be measured; linguists sometimes refer to the exceptions as 'elsewhere-words' since they show that 'elsewhere' a usage is adopted different from the 'rule'.

Plural of Nouns

4:4

(i) Regular nouns in the plural are spelt by adding an -*s* to the singular form: *e.g.* dog, *dogs*; book, *books*; song, *songs*.

(ii) Some nouns, because of their forms earlier in the language, make their plurals in other ways:

(**a**) by adding -*en*: *e.g.* ox, *oxen*; brother, *brethren* (in a religious context: otherwise, *brothers*).

(**b**) The following nouns ending in -*f*, or -*fe* change the *f* into *v* and add a final -(*e*)*s* to form their plurals: *e.g.* calf, *calves*; elf, *elves*; half, *halves*; hoof, *hooves*; knife, *knives*; leaf, *leaves*; loaf, *loaves*; life, *lives*; self, *selves*; scarf, *scarves*; shelf, *shelves*; thief, *thieves*; wharf, *wharves*; wife, *wives*.

Other words ending in -*f* are regular, *i.e.* they take -*s* to form their plurals: *e.g.* cliff, *cliffs*, proof, *proofs*; handkerchief, *handkerchiefs*; roof, *roofs* (although with these two latter words the pronunciation of their plural endings may be either *fs* or *vz*).

(**c**) Some nouns change the middle vowel of the singular to form the plural: *e.g.* man, *men*; woman, *women*; postman, *postmen*; fireman, *firemen*; gentleman, *gentlemen* (but note, German, *Germans*; Roman, *Romans*); foot, *feet*; tooth, *teeth*; mouse, *mice*; louse, *lice*; goose, *geese*.

(**d**) Singular nouns ending in *a consonant* + *y* change the *y* to an *i* and add -*es* to form the plural: *e.g.* baby, *babies*; lady, *ladies*; penny, *pennies* (although this word also has the plural form *pence*).

(**e**) Singular nouns ending in *a vowel* + *y* form their plurals by adding a final -*s*: *e.g.* chimney, *chimneys*; monkey, *monkeys*.

(**f**) Singular nouns ending in -*ch*, -*s*, -*sh*, and -*x* add -*es* to form the plural: *e.g.* church, *churches*; bus, *buses*; bush, *bushes*; box, *boxes*; tax, *taxes*.

(*g*) Some nouns carry the same form in both singular and plural: *e.g.* sheep, *sheep*; deer, *deer*; salmon, *salmon*; trout, *trout*; grouse, *grouse*; mackerel, *mackerel*; plaice, *plaice*.

(*h*) Singular nouns ending in -*o* often take a final -*es* to form the plural: *e.g.* potato, *potatoes*; tomato, *tomatoes*; hero, *heroes*; echo, *echoes*.

But the following form their plurals merely by adding a final -*s*: bamboo, *bamboos*; embryo, *embryos*; folio, *folios*; kangaroo, *kangaroos*; radio, *radios*; zoo, *zoos*; kilo, *kilos*; photo, *photos*; piano, *pianos*; solo, *solos*; soprano, *sopranos*; Eskimo, *Eskimos*; dynamo, *dynamos*.

(iii) Words that end in a final -*s* in the singular provide special problems:

(*a*) Some of them seem to have a plural form but are used only with a singular verb: *news*, *physics*, *measles*, and—when they refer to a specific science as a subject—*linguistics, mathematics, politics, statistics* (when these do not refer directly to a science they may take a plural verb).

(*b*) Some, however, with a seemingly plural form, may be used with either a singular or a plural verb, according to the context and sense; *athletics*; *gallows*; *headquarters*; *innings*; *kennels*; *series*; *species*.

(*c*) Some with a plural form are used only with plural verbs: *e.g.* *alms*, *binoculars*; *braces*; *eaves*; *glasses*; *knickers*; *pants*; *pliers*; *pyjamas*; *scales*; *scissors*; *shorts*; *trousers*; *spectacles*; *tights*; *tongs*; *tweezers*; *arrears*; *belongings*; *clothes*; *earnings*; *looks*; *odds*; *proceeds*; *remains*; *riches*; *surroundings*; *thanks*; *wages*.

(iv) Nouns derived from classical languages and retaining their recognisable classical forms in the singular:

(*a*) sometimes retain their classical plural forms: *e.g.* radius, *radii*; stimulus, *stimuli*; fungus, *fungi*; nucleus, *nuclei*; tumulus, *tumuli*; genus, *genera*; antenna, *antennae*; medium, *media*; bacterium, *bacteria*; curriculum, *curricula*; larva, *larvae*.

(*b*) sometimes take either the classical plural ending or add a new native English ending: *e.g.* formula, *formulae* or *formulas*; terminus, *termini* or *terminuses*; radius, *radii* or *radiuses*. (*Note:* the plural of 'genius' is usually *geniuses*.)

(*c*) sometimes end in -*is* (singular) but -*es* (plural): *e.g.* basis, *bases*; crisis, *crises*; diagnosis, *diagnoses*; hypothesis, *hypotheses*; oasis, *oases*; neurosis, *neuroses*; thesis, *theses*.

(*d*) sometimes have a singular form ending -*on* but a plural form ending -*a*: *e.g.* phenomenon, *phenomena*; criterion, *criteria*.

(*e*) sometimes have a singular form ending -*ix* but a plural form ending -*ices*: *e.g.* appendix, *appendices*; index, *indices*. (*Indexes* is usually preferred in printed books.)

(v) Some words recently borrowed from foreign languages retain their own foreign singular and plural forms: bureau, *bureaux*; plateau, *plateaux*.

(vi) Where words consist of a number of letters only *or* where letters or numerals are given in their plural forms, it is the convention to add a final *s* without preceding it with an apostrophe: *e.g.* three *es*; IOUs; NBs. See **3:7** (iii).

Prefixes and Suffixes
4:5

It is often useful to examine a word to see how it can be divided into syllables and to isolate its prefixes and suffixes. To establish what is the *prefix* or the *suffix* frequently helps correct spelling.

(i) Prefixes

NOTE Sometimes the prefix is 'assimilated' with the next syllable, *i.e.* the last consonant of the prefix is 'made similar' to the first consonant of the next syllable:

e.g. (**a**) ad- (*cf. ad*umbrate) becomes   *ac-* : *ac*/cident; *ac*/cord;
     (Latin 'to')   *af-* : *af*/fect; *af*/ford;
                                 ag- : *ag*/gression;
                                 al- : *al*/literation; *al*/low;
                                 an- : *an*/nihilate; *an*/nounce;
                                 ap- : *ap*/proximate; *ap*/peal;
                                 ar- : *ar*/rive; *ar*/range;
                                 as- : *as*/similate; *as*/semble;
                                 at- : *at*/tract; *at*/tack.

    dis- (*cf. dis*/affect) becomes *dif-* : *dif*/fer; *dif*/ficult;
    (Latin 'in two'; 'apart')   *dif*/fuse.
    com- (*cf. com*/memorate) becomes *col-* : *col*/late; *col*/lect;
    (Latin *cum* 'with')   *con-* : *con*/nive; *con*/nect;
                                   cor- : *cor*/respond; *cor*/rect.
    in- (*cf. in*/ability; becomes   *il-* : *il*/logical; *il*/legible;
         in/nocent)   *il*/legal;
    (Latin used to form negative)   *im-* : *im*/mortal; *im*/mobile;
                                     im/moderate; *im*/modest;
                                 ir- *ir*/regular; *ir*/relevant;
                                   ir/reparable.
    sub- (*cf. sub*-marine) becomes *suf-* : *suf*/focate; *suf*/fix;
    (Latin 'under')   *suf*/fer;
                                   sug- : *sug*/gest.

(**b**) *dis-*   *dis*/agree; *dis*/appear; *dis*/appoint; *dis*/able;
    (Latin 'in two';   *dis*/solve; *dis*/satisfied; *dis*/arm;
         'apart')   *dis*/colour; *dis*/oblige; *dis*/service;
                     dis/ease; *dis*/sociate; *dis*/sect;

(**c**) *inter-*   *inter*/act; *inter*/cede; *inter*/change;
    (Latin 'between')   *inter*/est; *inter*/regnum; *inter*/rogation;
                     inter/relation; *inter*/rupt.

(**d**) *re-*   *re*/act; *re*/cur; *re*/occur; *re*/quite;
    (Latin 'again';   *re*/produce.
         'back')

(ii) Inflexional endings and suffixes

Additions to ends of words as inflexions to indicate tense, or as markers to show whether a word is an adjective, adverb, or participle, very frequently baffle those who find English spelling difficult. There are some general 'rules' which will help, however.

(**a**) Before inflexions (*e.g. -ed, -ing*), or suffixes (*e.g. -er*) beginning with a vowel, a final consonant in the base form of the word is doubled, provided the vowel in front of the consonant is stressed and spelt with a single letter:

e.g. begín, beginning
refér, referred, referring
occúr, occurred, occurring
sád, sadder

NOTE 1 Where the vowel is not stressed, the final consonant is not doubled before the inflexional ending is added:

e.g. énter, entered, entering
óffer, offered, offering
álter, altered, altering
díffer, differed, differing

NOTE 2 Where the vowel sound (stressed or unstressed) in the base form is spelt with a double letter, the final consonant is not doubled before the inflexional ending is added:

e.g. dréam, dreamed, dreaming
entertáin, entertained, entertaining

EXCEPTIONS

When the base form of the word ends in a vowel spelt with a single letter + a single *c, g, l, m,* or *p,* the final consonant is doubled in British English—even if the vowel in front of it is *not* stressed—before the inflexion is added:

e.g. pánic, panicked, panicking ('ck' = *cc*)
débug, debugged, debugging
trável, travelled, travelling
túnnel, tunnelled, tunnelling
impéril, imperilled, imperilling
wórship, worshipped, worshipping.

(**b**) Where the base form of a word ends in a *consonant + y,* the *y* is changed to an *i* before an inflexion or a suffix not beginning with an *i* (*e.g. -ed*) is added:

e.g. márry, married, marriage
cárry, carried, carriage
álly, allied, alliance
húrry, hurried

Where the ending begins with an *i,* however (*e.g. -ing*), the *y* in the base form is left unchanged.

e.g. cárry, carrying
húrry, hurrying

(**c**) *y* is retained in words ending in a *vowel+y* if the inflexional ending or suffix begins with a vowel:

e.g. *delay, delayed, delaying* *play, playing, player*
 volley, volleyed, volleying *annoy, annoyed, annoyance*
 convey, conveying, conveyance

(**d**) Three verbs which end in a *vowel+y* change the *y* to an *i* before adding the inflexion *-d*, although they keep the *-y* before adding the inflexion *-ing*:

e.g. *say, said, saying*
 lay, laid, laying
 pay, paid, paying

(**e**) Some verbs which end in *-ie*, change these letters to a *-y* before adding the inflexional ending *-ing*, although they retain the *-ie* form before adding *-d*:

e.g. *die, died, dying*
 tie, tied, tying
 vie, vied, vying

A few others, however, which end in a *consonant+y*, change the *-y* to an *-i* before adding the inflexional ending *-ed*, although they retain the *-y* before adding *-ing*.

e.g. *relý, relied, relying*
 cáddy, caddied, caddying
 dený, denied, denying

(**f**) Words which end in *-e* sometimes provide difficulties of spelling when inflexional endings are added. Usually the final *-e* is dropped before the inflexional ending is added:

e.g. *save, saved, saving*
 live, lived, living
 pine, pined, pining

If the words end in *-ee, -ye, -oe* and sometimes *-ge*, however, they drop the final *-e* before adding the inflexional ending *-ed*, but retain the final *-e* before adding the inflexional ending *-ing*:

e.g. *agree, agreed, agreeing*
 decree, decreed, decreeing
 dye, dyed, dyeing (to distinguish the word from 'dying', perhaps)
 hoe, hoed, hoeing
 singe, singed, singeing (to indicate the palatal pronunciation of the 'g' in order to distinguish the word from 'singing', perhaps)
 (but *cringe, cringed, cringing*)

(**g**) Words which end in a single *-e* usually drop this final *-e* before adding the suffixes *-able, -ment*:

e.g. *love, lovable*
  move, movable
  save, savable
  judge, judgment (also *judgement*)
  acknowledge, acknowledgment (also *acknowledgement*)
  value, valuable
  desire, desirable
  abridge, abridgment (also *abridgement*)
  like, likable (also *likeable*)

(*h*) It is difficult sometimes to be certain about the suffixes *-er* or *-or* or *-ar* to denote agents, or those who carry out an action.
The *-er* ending is of French origin (from earlier Latin *-arius*) but it is added to words of both French and native English origin:

e.g. *grocer, officer; baker, driver; propeller*

The *-or* ending is from Latin *-orius*, but it has sometimes been changed in some words to *-er*, by analogy with native 'agent' words:

e.g. *actor, supervisor; convener*

The *-ar* ending (from Latin *-arius*) has virtually dropped from the language:

e.g.   *beggar, bursar, pedlar*

The pronunciation of the vowels in all three suffixes has been reduced to a neutral, unstressed vowel (ə).

(*i*) This reduction of vowel sounds in suffixes to a neutral vowel sound (ə) also provides difficulties with words ending in *-ance, -ence*; *-ant, -ent*:

e.g. *repentance;*   *existence;*   *abundance;*
  repentant;   *existent;*   *abundant;*
  absence;   *relevance;*   *presence;*
  absent;   *relevant;*   *present.*

(*j*) The use of the neutral vowel sound (ə) also causes difficulties for the spelling of the suffixes *-ary, -ory, -ery*:

e.g. *ordinary, exemplary, probationary, preliminary,*
  satisfactory, memory, desultory,
  cemetery, monastery.
NOTE the distinction in meaning between *stationary* and *stationery*.

(*k*) The suffixes *-able* and *-ible* need to be distinguished in spelling but their neutral sound (ə) confuses the matter:

e.g. *contestable, continuable, convenable, capable,*
  contemptible, controvertible, audible, defensible.

(*l*) The spellings *-or, -or-, -our, -our-* provide special problems. Here the history of the English language explains—even if it does not justify—what happened.

Because of the influence of French, the Latin ending *-or* was often spelt *-our* in the late Middle Ages. During the Renaissance, when people delighted in tracing classical origins, the Latin spelling *-or* was given new currency (and American English has retained this form). During the eighteenth century Dr Samuel Johnson approved of spellings such as *terrour, horrour, authour.* Modern British English is, however, inconsistent; it has:

e.g. *honour, humour, vapour, colour, vigour*
but *mirror, horror, stupor.*

When this syllable occurs medially (in the middle of the word) it sometimes retains the *u* and sometimes drops it:

honourable, honorary
colourful, coloration (also *colouration*)
humourless, humorous
vapoury, vaporise

(m) There is often an active discussion about the distinction between the use of the suffixes *-ise, -ize.*

Most printing houses seem to prefer the *-ize* form, irrespective of the origins of the suffixes, in many verbs but Fowler (*Modern English Usage*) suggests that the following words always prefer the *-ise* form:

advertise, chastise, circumcise, comprise, compromise,
demise, despise, devise, disfranchise, disguise,
enfranchise, enterprise, excise, exercise, improvise.
incise, premise, supervise, surmise, surprise.

The origin of the *-ize* form is usually attributed to the Greek *-izo*; it does not seem to matter for Modern English whether the verb with which it is to be used is derived from a Greek stem or not. Oxford University Press (printers of *The Oxford English Dictionary*), Cambridge University Press (noted as printers of the Bible) and *The Times* prefer the spelling *-ize* for most words. Modern French has standardised its verbal endings for such words as *-iser* but *The Oxford English Dictionary* argues that 'there is no reason why in English the special French spelling should be followed'.

4:6

For some reason writers of English still confuse the order of *i* and *e*. The rule that *i* comes before *e* except after *c* to make the sound '*ee*' ($\bar{e}$) works well:

achieve, relieve, niece, deceive;

but (after *c*) *receive, deceive, ceiling, conceive.*
There are *two* exceptions: *counterfeit, seize.*
NOTE Words such as *their, neighbour, leisure, reign, foreign, weird, heir,* do not bear the pronunciation ($\bar{e}$).

4:7

There are some pairs of words which vary their spelling according to their function as either verb or noun:

advise, practise, license, prophesy (Verbs)
advice, practice, licence, prophecy (Nouns)

4:8

-all, -full, -fill, well- sometimes drop one *l* when used in combinations (as prefixes or suffixes) with other words:

overal/overall (as noun, adverb, or adjective), *almost, already, altogether/all together, almighty;*
fulfil, fulness/fullness, spoonful, hopeful, beautiful, welcome, welfare.

American Spelling

4:9

There are some marked differences in spelling conventions for certain words between British English and American English. The main differences are reflected in the following list:

British	American
colour	color
honour	honor
labour	labor
centre	center
meagre	meager
enrol, enroll	enroll
enthral, enthrall	enthrall
fulfil	fulfill
levelled	leveled
skilful	skillful
travelled	traveled
defence	defense
offence	offense
pretence	pretense
axe	ax
cheque	check
kerb	curb
gaol, jail	jail
jewellery, jewelry	jewelry
nett, net	net
pyjamas	pajamas
plough	plow
programme	program
storey	story
through	thru
tyre	tire
wagon, waggon	waggon

EXERCISES

13 Use a dictionary and then write sentences to illustrate the meaning of each of the following words whose spelling is often confused. (Try to bring out in your sentences the distinction in meaning between the words in each pair.) Do *not* change the forms of the words:

1 affect, effect;   **2** census, consensus;
3 complement, compliment;   **4** desert, dessert;
5 its, it's;   **6** loose, lose;
7 peer, pier;   **8** principal, principle;
9 stationary, stationery;   **10** there, their.

14 Rewrite the following passage, correcting all the words that are misspelt. (There are *twenty* of them.)

The general commanded the maneouver to begin as part of the exercise to practice with the new machinary provided by the research comittee for home defence, a goverment organisation. A humourous occurence arose, however, when the principle tank got stuck in a ditch.

The silouete of a young lieutenant appeared in the turret. He looked harrassed and somewhat embarassed as his cumbersome elephant sank into the mud and became more and more seperated from the rest of the auxilary squadron. There seemed to be a mischievious plot working against him. Clambering down to inspect the damage, he caught the woolen sleeve of his jacket on a bolt and tore the whole thing off. A bad enough begining to the battle! The young officer's cavortings around his helpless monster added to the choas and his armless jacket exageratted the bizarreness of the situation. He began to loose his self-control and shouted out unecessary advice to the rest of the crew as they appeared in the turret one by one.

15
1 Give the simple past tenses of the following verbs (*i.e.* use a form ending *-ed*):
(*a*) benefit; (*b*) focus; (*c*) panic; (*d*) profit; (*e*) refer.
2 Form the present participles of the following verbs (*i.e.* use a form ending *-ing*):
(*a*) acquire; (*b*) begin; (*c*) control; (*d*) occur; (*e*) singe; (*f*) queue.

16 Which ten of the following words are misspelt?

1 census; genious; jelous; phosphorus; wonderous;
2 liesure; neighbour; niece; perceive; sieze;
3 benefiting; dyeing; occuring; practising; tunneling;
4 arguement; judgement; mistakeable; noticeable; smokey.

17 Give the plural forms of the following words:

1 calorie;   **2** chimney;   **3** hero;   **4** intricacy;
5 piano;   **6** picnic;   **7** prophecy;   **8** roof;
9 status;   **10** tomato.

18

1 Make a list of *five* nouns ending in **-ance** and *five* ending in **-ence**;

2 Make a list of *five* nouns ending in **-er** and *five* ending in **-or**;

3 Make a list of *five* words ending in **-ary** and *five* ending in **-ory**;

4 Make a list of *five* adjectives ending in **-able** and *five* ending in **-ible**.

19 Rewrite the following passage and substitute the appropriate letter or letters for the dashes:

As a *suc—ful auth—* his *ach—vements* had not been *negl—ble*. He *rec—ved* the *incred—* news with *s—prise*; his *correspond—* with his publisher had never led him to believe that he would be sent three *compl—mentary* copies of the *encyclop—*.

20 Complete the words below, the first letters only of which are shown, to match the dictionary definitions given:

1 din—— *noun, plural*; a small rowing boat, sometimes made of rubber;

2 c—— *noun, singular*; a yawning or gaping hollow; a gap or opening;

3 syn—— *verb, intransitive*; to coincide or agree in time;
verb, transitive; to cause to coincide or agree in time;

4 kno—— *adjective*; intelligent; having a lot of facts in one's head;

5 dip—— *noun, singular*; two vowel sounds pronounced as one syllable;

6 negl—— *adjective*; trivial; unimportant;

7 exag—— *verb, transitive*; to overstate, magnify unduly;

8 forf—— *noun*; a penalty; that to which a right has been lost;
verb, transitive; to lose the right to something because of some fault or crime;

9 super—— *verb, transitive*; to set aside in favour of another; to replace;

10 par—— *adjective*; alongside; extended in the same direction and equidistant.

21 Give a brief account of the difficulties you find in spelling words correctly. What are the main areas which give you special problems? (Illustrate your work with as many examples as you can.)

22 The following passage is taken from Professor Albert Eagle's *Literary Phonetic English; suggested Principles and Practice for English Spelling Reform*, 1955, in which he advocated a new system of spelling for the English Language. Rewrite the passage using traditional spelling but not changing the words or structures themselves:

The living langwidge iz az peaple speak it; and the spelling iz required to be a sensible way of transferring that uzage to paper by the use of phonetic bricks called letters, in summ sensible and fairly consistent way. It iz not at all necessary, az summ spelling reformers hav thaut that thare shood be az many letters, like 'ch' or 'sh', to represent a sound not givven by eny single letter. In the case of the vowels we hav seen that this method haz verry graat advahntages over having az menny different vowel letters az thare ar vowels; for by giving *different* ways of spelling the same sound, it enablez uz to distinguish, on paper, different things whooze names bair the same pronunciation.

5
Grammar

Parts of speech

Nouns

5:1

A **proper noun** is the name of a specific

person	(Plato, Shelley, George)
place	(London, Piccadilly, Paris)
country	(England, France)
month	(March, April)
day	(Tuesday, Wednesday)
journal	(*The Times*, *Punch*)
festival	(Christmas, Easter)

(i) Proper nouns are spelt with capital letters and their use determines whether they are 'proper' nouns. It is possible, for example, for some to be used as common nouns when they do not refer to a specific place, person, and so on, although the initial capital is usually retained:

e.g. There are four or five Wednesdays in a month.
How many Georges are there in this school?
Not all writers become Shakespeares.

(ii) Some proper nouns can be used with the definite article:

e.g. *The Observer, The News of the World* (where *The* is part of the titles); the Thames; the University of London; the Tate Gallery; the Savoy Hotel; the British Museum; the Coliseum;
but Covent Garden, Buckingham Palace, *Punch*.

NOTE Sometimes (usually after genitives/possessives) the definite article may be dropped even when it is part of a title. *e.g.* In today's *Sunday Times* ... He left his *Guardian* in the train.

5:2

A **common noun** is the name given to one example or more of a class of things or to the class as a whole:

e.g. boy, girl, ship, theatre, dog, table, book.

These nouns may be modified by definite or indefinite articles and adjectives to form noun phrases:

> *e.g.* the *ship*, a *ship*;
> the large *ship*;
> the *ship* built in Bristol.

5:3

A **collective noun** is the name of a group of persons, or animals:

> *e.g.* school, army, crowd, family;
> herd, flock, shoal.

(i) They are sometimes divided into the following classes:

> **specific:** committee, gang, majority, government
> **generic:** the clergy, the public, the bar (in the legal sense).

(ii) There is often controversy about whether verbs should be in the singular or the plural after collective nouns; both may be used, but careful users sometimes argue that the difference between the singular and plural uses of the verb indicates a difference in attitude:

> *e.g.* The choir sings (*i.e.* when they are heard as a single unity).
> The choir sing (*i.e.* when they are heard as a number of individuals, perhaps, singing harmoniously within the group).

NOTE Some collective nouns, however (*e.g.* cattle, people, police, vermin), always take a plural verb.

5:4

An **abstract noun** is the name of a state, attitude, or quality:

> *e.g.* peace, kindness, warmth;
> importance, knowledge, education.

These nouns are often formed from verbs or adjectives by the addition of endings.

> *e.g. from verbs:*
> *-age* (breakage); *-al* (betrayal, approval); *-ance* (deliverance, appearance); *-ice* (service); *-ment* (disappointment); *-sion* (expansion, suspension); *-th* (growth); *-tion* (organisation, exploitation); *-ure* (disclosure, failure); *-y* (discovery, recovery).
> *from adjectives:*
> *-dom* (freedom);
> *-ice* (justice); *-ity* (sensitivity, equality);
> *-ness* (greediness, eagerness); *-ship* (hardship);
> *-th* (warmth, length); *-y* (jealousy, accuracy).

5:5

Some nouns have combined with other nouns to form new (compound) nouns:

> *e.g.* cowboy; countryman; bookcase; landmine; woodshed; bedroom; spaceship; skyscraper; taxpayer.

Where the compound is not yet finally established or where the compound might read awkwardly, the elements are joined by hyphens:

> *e.g.* walking-stick; son-in-law; egg-head; cat-o'-nine-tails.

5:6

Some nouns are placed in front of other nouns in order to modify them, although together the combinations have not yet become compound nouns:

> *e.g.* bus driver; telephone kiosk; traffic lights; fire station; market price.

5:7

The addition of certain suffixes to verbs, adjectives or nouns can form new nouns which indicate:

(i) an agent, origin, or occupation:
-er (stealer); *-ar* (bursar); *-er* (Londoner);
-or (actor); *-ant* (attendant); *-ent* (referent);
-ist (jurist); *-ee* (employee); *-eer* (auctioneer);
-ier (fancier, brigadier); *-ian* (Martian, Liverpudlian);
-ist (anarchist); *-man* (Scotsman); *-ster* (gangster).

(ii) smallness or diminutiveness:
-en (maiden); *-et* (turret); *-ette* (cigarette);
-ling (duckling); *-let* (piglet).

(iii) the feminine form of a noun:
-ess (actress, mistress); *-ine* (heroine); *-ix* (executrix).

Pronouns

These are words which may be used instead of, or be substituted for, a noun or nouns.

5:8

Personal Pronouns

These are the only words in English that sometimes have different forms dependent on their function within a sentence: as subject; as direct or indirect object of a verb, or as object of a preposition.

Subject			*Direct/Indirect Object*
Singular	1st person : I		me
	2nd person : you (earlier 'thou')		you (earlier 'thee')
	3rd person : he, she, it		him, her, it
Plural	1st person : we		us
	2nd person : you		you
	3rd person : they		them

e.g. *She and I* refuse. (Subject)
   We   refuse. (Subject)

The policeman stopped *him and me*. (Direct object)
The policeman stopped *us*. (Direct object)

Give *me and her* our presents now. (Indirect object)
Give *us* our presents now. (Indirect object)

Between *him and me* there is little love lost. (Object of a preposition)
Between *us* there is little love lost. (Object of a preposition)

NOTE (a) *Between he and I* is incorrect since the preposition 'between' governs the objective forms of the personal pronoun—*him* and *me*.
(b) After the verb 'to be' personal pronouns used as complements are found in both 'subject' and 'object' forms:

e.g. He saw who it was and it turned out to be *she* (or, in informal usage, *her*).

(General usage makes the forms '*It's me*', '*It was me*', in response to questions such as 'Who's there?' or 'Who did it?' the acceptable ones to use, although strictly the subject form 'I' might be the correct grammatical form to use—in spite of the fact that some grammarians argue that the *me, her, him, them* forms in sentences such as that above are really emphatic uses of personal pronouns.)
(c) *You* can also be used as an indefinite or impersonal pronoun. (See page 53.)

5:9

Possessive Pronouns

These may be used instead of nouns or noun phrases *and* indicate possession. (They are sometimes called 'genitives'.)

(*a*) Singular	*1st person* : mine	
	2nd person : yours (earlier 'thine')	
	3rd person : his, hers, its	
Plural	*1st person* : ours	
	2nd person : yours	
	3rd person : theirs	

NOTE The possessive pronouns ending in -*s* do NOT take an apostrophe.

(*It's* = it is; *its* = the possessive form of *it.*) *Hers, ours, yours, theirs* never take an apostrophe before their final 's'.

(*b*) Some of these possessive pronouns may be used more emphatically by using 'of' to precede them (with the noun itself stated as well):

e.g. 'This car of mine is a problem.' (= '*Mine* is a problem car.')
'This house of ours is a good one.' (= '*Ours* is a nice house *ours* is.')

5:10

Demonstrative Pronouns

These may be used instead of nouns or noun phrases *and*
they point out objects or people referred to.

Singular: this, that

Plural: these, those

This, these refer to objects or people near the speaker; *that, those* refer to objects or people at a distance from the speaker.

NOTE Demonstrative **adjectives** have the same forms as demonstrative pronouns but can easily be distinguished from them because adjectives limit or qualify nouns which accompany them:

e.g. '*That* book is on the table.' (Demonstrative adjective)
'*That* is my book.' (Demonstrative pronoun)
'*These* hats belong to me.' (Demonstrative adjective)
'*Those* belong to you.' (Demonstrative pronoun)

5:11

Emphatic Pronouns

These may be used instead of nouns or noun phrases *and*
they emphasise objects or people referred to.

(*a*) In the footnote to **5:8**, page 49, it was pointed out that in statements such as '*It's me*' or '*It was them*' the forms *me* and *them* are emphatic uses of the personal pronoun.

(*b*) Some emphatic pronouns end in -*self* or -*selves* but they are not to be confused with reflexive pronouns which have identical forms:

Singular
{ *1st person* : myself
2nd person : yourself
3rd person : himself, herself, itself, oneself

Plural
{ *1st person* : ourselves
2nd person : yourself
3rd person : themselves

e.g. 'I *myself* undertook the work.' (Emphatic)
'I washed *myself* before going to work.' (Reflexive)
'They *themselves* made no excuses.' (Emphatic)
'They made no attempt to excuse *themselves*.' (Reflexive)

The function of the word will indicate clearly whether it is an emphatic or a reflexive pronoun.

(*c*) See **5:14** (g), page 52, for a note on intensified (emphatic) uses of interrogative pronouns.

5:12

Reflexive Pronouns

These may be used instead of nouns or noun phrases *and*
they 'reflect' the action of a verb back on to the doer or the subject.
The forms of reflexive pronouns are identical with those of emphatic pronouns with which they should not be confused. (See **5:11** (b), page 50, for the forms of emphatic and reflexive pronouns.)

5:13

Reciprocal Pronouns

These may be used instead of nouns (often proper nouns) *and*
they throw the action back from the verb to one or more subjects:

> *Each other* (for two), *one another* (for more than two).

> *e.g.* The two boxers hit *each other*.
> The members of the football team congratulated *one another*.

5:14

Interrogative Pronouns (see the section on questions, **5:92**, pages 105–7)

These may be used instead of nouns or noun phrases *and*
they are used in direct and indirect questions.

who, whose, whom, which, what

(*a*) Clauses introduced by these interrogative pronouns are illustrated as follows:

> Statement: The boy spilt the tea.
> Direct question: '*Who* spilt the tea?'
> Indirect question: I asked *who* spilt the tea.
> NOTE No question mark is needed in indirect questions.

(*b*) NOTE *Whose, which,* and *what* may also be used as interrogative adjectives (or determiners) (see **5:24**, page 63), but then they are used to qualify a noun which immediately follows them:

> '*Whose* book is that?' (Direct question)

> I don't know *which* street to take. (Indirect question)

(*c*) *Whose* is also used with a possessive sense in a contracted indirect question:

e.g. Here is a book but I don't know *whose*.

Here *whose* = 'whose it is' or 'whose (book) it is'.

(*d*) *Who*, *whom*, and *whose* are used to refer to persons.

(*e*) *Which* may refer to a person (or persons) or to a thing:

e.g. *Which* (boy) spilt the tea? (personal Direct question)
Which (dress) do you prefer? (non-personal Indirect question)
I don't know *which* spilt the tea. (personal Indirect question)
I don't know what happened. (non-personal Indirect question)

(*f*) *What* is used non-personally:

e.g. *What* did you do? (Direct question)
I don't know *what* you did. (Indirect question)

(*g*) An intensifying suffix *-ever* may be added to some interrogative pronouns to make them more emphatic:

e.g. *Whoever* did this?
Whatever have you done?
Whose-ever (sometimes *whosever*) is this mess?

The addition of *-ever* also carries the semantic force (the meaning) sometimes of indicating a choice from a number of possibilities:

e.g. *Whoever* did this? (The suffix emphasises 'who' and at the same time recognises the possibility that one or more of a number of people might have done it.)

Whatever have you done? (Here *-ever* emphasises 'what' and at the same time recognises the possibility that you might have done one or more things.)

Whose-ever (sometimes *whosever*) is this mess? (Here *-ever* emphasises 'whose' but at the same time recognises that the mess might belong to one or more persons)

5:15

Indefinite Pronouns (including Distributive Pronouns and Impersonal Pronouns)

There is a large number of words in English which are used to stand in place of nouns or noun phrases, *and*
to indicate an indefinite or at least undefined, number or mass or quantity.

Usually included, however, in this category of Indefinite Pronouns are some words which:
seem to define by total exclusion or inclusion (*e.g. none, all, everyone, everything*);
indicate a choice between two specifically defined persons or objects (*either, neither*).

(i) *one* (*you/they*) (sometimes called 'Impersonal Pronouns');

(ii) *some, any; none; few, fewer, fewest, several; many, much, more, most; less, least; both, all;*

(iii) *each; either, neither* (sometimes called 'Distributive Pronouns' or 'Partitive Pronouns');

(iv) *someone, anyone, everyone, no-one; somebody, anybody, everybody, nobody; something, anything, everything, nothing.*

(i) **One (You/they)** (equivalent to French *on*, German *man*)

(a) At one time (*e.g.* in Anglo-Saxon times) English had the word *man* (*mon*) to refer to an indefinite, undefined person, or to be used where the speaker or writer deliberately wished to remain non-specific. Today Modern English uses the form *one* (or, in less formal usage, *you*). Often 'one' is used to refer to people in general, the average person, and is the equivalent of 'everyman' or 'everyone'. (*One* is sometimes replaced by *You/They* in this sense.)

e.g. '*One* hesitates to condemn others, since *one* may be guilty oneself.'
'*They* (*You*) stop accusing others because *they* (*you*) feel guilty *themselves* (*yourself*).'

(b) It is not considered elegant, however, to over-use this use of *one*; similarly, constructions which jump within themselves from 'one' to 'we' or 'you' or 'I' are best avoided in Standard English. (American English sometimes jumps from 'one' to 'he/him' or 'she/her'.)

(c) In colloquial speech it is often more acceptable to use 'you'. For instance, if one is asked for directions by a passer-by in the street, it is more normal to reply using 'you' rather than 'one':

'You go to the bottom of the road and you turn right,'

rather than

'One goes to the bottom of the road and one turns right.'

(d) The word *one* may, however, be used very definitely as a numerical pronoun:

e.g. 'You should choose *one* of the two.'

(e) The possessive of *one* as an indefinite (impersonal) pronoun is *one's*:

e.g. 'If one had *one's* own way, one would choose the right road rather than the wrong road.'

(f) The word 'ones' (in the plural) is spelt without an apostrophe and used with the definite article (a determiner) can mean little more than 'those':

e.g. '*The ones* (those) I chose were much better.'

(ii) (a) *Some, any*

Some is used in place of a noun or noun phrase in positive contexts as a pronoun and *any* in negative contexts:

> *e.g.* 'I want *some*';
> 'I don't want *any*.'

The word *any* can be used, however, in positive contexts to refer to a certain (though unspecified) quantity:

> *e.g. Question:* 'Do you like red apples?'
> *Answer:* 'Have you *any*?'
>
> *or* Jack likes only green apples but I like *any*.

(b) *None*

This pronoun is equivalent to:
'no' (adjective, determiner) + noun

> *e.g.* I have no books/I have *none*.
>
> *or* negative + any
>
> *e.g.* I haven't any/I have *none*.
> If there is any difference in meaning between the first sentence given in the above examples and the second, it lies in emphasis: 'I have none' is more emphatic in both cases.
> Careful users of the language prefer to use a singular verb with none:
>
> *e.g.* 'None was to be found' rather than 'None are to be found'.
> 'There was none there' rather than 'There were none there'.

(c) *A few, few, fewer, fewest, several; many, much, more, most; less, least*

These words, when used as pronouns, indicate indefinite quantities and are sometimes referred to, therefore, as 'Indefinite Quantifiers'.

A few indicates a small positive number of people or things; *few* suggests a small negative number, almost equivalent to 'none':

> *e.g.* There were *a few* who believed in spite of their doubts.
> Of all the thousands present *few* believed the preacher.

Fewer and *fewest* refer to comparisons with other numbers:

> *e.g.* Of all the thousands who said they believed, *fewer* than ten were really sincere;
> Many made mistakes, but George made (the) *fewest*.

Several indicates an imprecise number:

> *e.g. Several* applied, but few were chosen.
> Of all the probabilities, *several* were likely.

Many, much

> *e.g.* Although John saw few willow-warblers, I saw *many*.
> Although London had little rain, Geneva had *much*.

In informal use *many* and *much* in these examples might have been replaced by *a lot*, or *lots*, or *plenty*.

More, most refer to comparisons with other numbers or with other quantities (*cf. fewer/fewest* above); in such comparisons the number or amount is indefinite or unqualified:

> *e.g.* I had a hundred pounds but she had *more*.
> I had a hundred pounds, Fred had two hundred, but she had *most*.

(NOTE In this example 'most' is used as a superlative in a comparison involving at least three items.)

> Some prefer war: *more* prefer peace.
> *Most* want to live, although a few would rather die.

Less, least

Again, the amounts are not quantified (*cf. more/most* above) in these pronouns which are often used in comparative or superlative senses:

> *e.g.* John had a lot but Jill had *less*.
> Of all the group Fred had *least* to lose.

(d) Both, all

Both is really an 'identifier' or 'identifying pronoun', since it identifies two people or objects already referred to very precisely; *all* is really a 'quantifier' or 'quantifying pronoun' since it specifies a quantity very precisely, the complete whole, the totality, the entire number:

> *e.g.* Jill was black and Fred was white but *both* were English. (*Both* refers to Jill + Fred.)
> One was a Parisian, another a Norman, a third a Breton but *all* were French.
> *All* have a right to their own views.

NOTE the use of the plural verb here: *cf. none* above which takes a singular.

> *Both* and *all* when used as pronouns may take 'of' when they act as predeterminers', *i.e.* when they determine (limit/define) a noun or pronoun that is to follow:

> *e.g.* *Both* of them were found guilty.

> Distinguish the difference in meaning between

> *e.g.* *Both* of the soldiers were found guilty (which suggests, perhaps, that the two sailors or two airmen were not found guilty),
and
> *Both* were found guilty (which suggests, perhaps, that only the two were on trial).

cf. *All* of the soldiers were found guilty (which suggests, perhaps, that not all the sailors or airmen were found guilty),

and

All were found guilty (which suggests that everyone on trial was found guilty).

Consider, too, the difference in sense that occurs when *both* and *all* are used as pronouns with 'of' and when *both* and *all* are used as adjectives to quality nouns. For instance, what difference in meaning can you see between the following?

Both of the soldiers were found guilty. (Pronoun)

and

Both soldiers were found guilty. (Adjective)

or

All of the soldiers were found guilty. (Pronoun)

and

All soldiers were found guilty. (Adjective)

(iii) (a) *Each* (sometimes called a 'Distributive Pronoun' or sometimes a 'Universal Pronoun')

Each is followed by a singular verb:

e.g. *Each* is followed by a singular verb,
or *Each* is bound to have his own opinion.

(In the first of these examples *each* = the word 'each'; in the second *each* = one or other of, or one of many.)

Each (unlike *everyone/everybody*) refers to an individual person or object already identified:

e.g. I saw both Jack and Jill; *each* was carrying something,
but

Everyone was carrying something (where *everyone* might or might not refer to a previously identified person).

Each may be used with either *his/her/its* or *their* for co-reference:

e.g. *Each* of the soldiers carried *his* own pack,
or

Each of the soldiers carried *their* own packs.

Each may also be used with 'of' to determine (limit/define) a noun or pronoun that is to follow (*cf. both* and *all* in (ii) (d) above, pages 55–6):

e.g. *Each* of the boys won a scholarship.
Each of them was successful.

(b) *Either, neither, any* (sometimes called 'Distributive Pronouns' and sometimes called 'Partitive Pronouns')

Either is used to refer to one of two persons or things (whereas *any* refers to more than two), and

Neither is used as a negative to refer to two or more persons or things (whereas *none/not any* refers to more than two).

e.g. *Either* of the two books would be useful.
Neither was useful after all.

Both *either* and *neither* when used as pronouns are followed by verbs which are singular:

e.g. *Either* of the propositions is likely to be true.
Neither of the propositions was very clear to me.

NOTE Be careful not to confuse *either/neither* when they are used as pronouns and *either . . . or/neither . . . nor* constructions where the words are used as positive or negative correlatives:

e.g. *Either* <u>the soldiers</u> *or* <u>the sailors</u> were the murderers.
(NOTE the plural verb here: subject = 'soldiers'/'sailors'.)
Neither <u>the one</u> *nor* <u>the other</u> was found guilty.
(NOTE the singular verb here: subject = 'the one'/'the other'.)
Neither <u>the doctor</u> *nor* <u>his patients</u> escape death.
(NOTE the plural verb here since, although 'doctor' is singular, 'patients' is a plural word.)

(iv) (*a*) *Someone, anyone, everyone, no-one; somebody, anybody, everybody, nobody; something, anything, everything, nothing*

The addition of *-one*, *-body*, *-thing* forms compound indefinite pronouns from *some*, *any*, *every*, and *no*. The new compounds always bear the stress in pronunciation on the first syllable:
sómeone, éverybody, ánything.

(*b*) All the new compounds (except *no one/no-one* where the two *o*'s in such close proximity would appear ugly) are written as single words and they take singular verbs:

e.g. *Everyone* is pleased to win the pools.
Nothing is harder.

(*c*) The difference in sense should be noted between some of these words, written as compounds and used as indefinite pronouns, and the same words, written separately and used as premodifiers + nouns or numerical pronouns:

e.g. Try to distinguish the different meanings of the words *in italics* in the following sentences:

Everyone is able to read.
There are five books; *every one* is interesting.

Somebody must have committed the murder.
You can't have a murder without *some body* or other.

Anyone can see the difference.
It is hard to see *any one* difference between them.

5:16

Numerical Pronouns

These may be used instead of nouns or noun phrases, *and*
they indicate a number (which may be either definite or indefinite).
  (*a*) For the indefinite/impersonal use of *one* (sometimes replaced by *you/*
      they/them see **5:15** (i), page 53).
  (*b*) When *one* is used to replace a noun it has both a singular form (*one*)
      and a plural form (*ones*):

  e.g. How many books were on the shelf? I saw *one.*
      There were *two* (of them) there yesterday.

5:17

Identifying and Quantifying Pronouns

Such, the former/the latter

These words are used to stand in place of nouns or noun phrases *and*
to identify or quantify a noun or noun phrase to which they refer.
They are, therefore, in a sense demonstratives, since they 'point out'.

(*a*) *Such*

The uses of *such* may be determinate or indeterminate:

  e.g. *Such* was the damage that the trains stopped running.
      (*Such* here quantifies the damage but leaves it indeterminate; the
      damage might or might not have been great but it had the serious
      effect of stopping the trains.)

    When *such* is followed by *as* its use can become determinate:

  e.g. To *such* of the boys as pass, prizes will be awarded.
      (*Such* here followed by its defining words determines which boys
      would receive prizes; *i.e.* it identifies them.)

(*b*) *The former/the latter*

Both these pronouns stand in place of one of two persons, things, ideas,
statements already indicated and are being referred to and indicated.
Both have their own grammatical functions within their own clauses.

  e.g. Beer and cider are both drinks: *the former* is more expensive but *the
      latter* quenches the thirst better.
      (The former = beer; the latter = cider; both are the subjects of their
      own clauses.)
  NOTE *The former* could have been replaced, of course, by 'the first'; *the latter*
      could have been replaced by 'the second' without any serious loss of
      or change in the meaning.

Both these pronouns may refer to preceding noun phrases or clauses rather than to single nouns:

> *e.g.* He could see that he was ill and that he might die; *the former* he could do something about but *the latter* left him in despair.
> (*The former* = 'that he was ill'; *the latter* = 'that he might die'. *The former* is the object of 'about'; *the latter* is the subject of 'left him in despair'.)

5:18

Relative Pronouns

Who, whom, whose, which, that; what

These pronouns have three basic functions:
- (i)   they may be used instead of nouns;
- (ii) they relate their own clauses back to a word or words (the antecedent) in another clause;
- (iii) they have their own parts to play in their own clauses (*e.g.* subject, direct object, object of a preposition).

> *e.g.* The boy, *who* is sitting in the front, works hard.
>   (Subject of the verb 'is sitting')
>
> The boy, *whom* I saw sitting in the front, works hard.
>   (Direct object of the verb 'saw')
>
> The boy, at *whom* I was looking, was working hard.
>   (Object of the preposition 'at')

(a) Who, whom, whose

Who and *whom* refer to persons; the function of the pronoun within its own clause determines which form is to be used:
who (subject); *whom* (direct object, object of a preposition).
   Whose may refer to people, animals, or things:

> *e.g.* The men, *whose* careers I followed, were all successful.
> The cat, *whose* tail was caught in the door, screamed horribly.
> The book, *whose* covers were torn, was worthless.

Who, *whom*, and *whose* represent surviving case forms to indicate the functions of the relative pronoun:

> *e.g.* The boy *who* comes first wins a prize. (Subject)
> The boy *whom* we preferred came last. (Object)
> The dog *whose* paw was injured limped home.
> (*Whose* is in a genitive relationship to 'dog', qualifies 'paw' and functions together with 'paw' as a noun phrase subject of 'was injured'; *whose paw* = 'the paw of which', but *whose* is normally preferred in both written and spoken English as less clumsy.)

> NOTE   In informal speech *who* is frequently used where 'whom' might have been used in written forms of the language.

(b) Which, that

Which is an impersonal relative pronoun which may refer to animals or to things:

e.g. That is the house which I bought.

That is the dog which I bought.

NOTE 1 Although *which* is usually reserved for animals, *who/whom* can be used to refer to them if they are looked upon figuratively as persons:

e.g. This is the dog *who* loves me and whom I love.

NOTE 2 *Which* is also used in preference to *who* with collective nouns which take a singular verb rather than a plural:

e.g. The choir *who* sing *Messiah* are famous.
The choir *which* sings *Messiah* is famous.

That can be used instead of the personal relatives *who* or *whom* in defining relative clauses (see below, pages 61–2, for an explanation of a 'defining' relative clause):

e.g. Who is the man *who* (*that*) did it.
Where is the man *whom* (*that*) you blame?

That can be used instead of the impersonal relative *which* in defining relative clauses (see below, pages 61–2):

e.g. There is the cat *which* (*that*) caught its tail in the door.

It is normally not used instead of *which*, however, when the antecedent is an indefinite pronoun:

e.g. *All*
Everything } *that* I do seems valueless
Anything

or when the antecedent noun is modified by *last, first,* or *next* or a superlative:

e.g. This is the last time *that* I go there.
This is the first hovercraft *that* I have seen.
Where is the next bus *that* I have been waiting so long for.
Which is the best meal *that* you have ever had?

When *which* is used in combination with a preposition to indicate place, time, or reason, the preposition + *which* is often replaced by a relative adverb (*e.g. where, when, why*):

e.g. This is the bus stop *at which* (*where*) I waited so long.
This is the century *in which* (*when*) a cure to cancer will be found.
What is the reason *for which* (*why*) you came?

(c) What

What is frequently used as an equivalent of 'that which':

> *e.g.* '*What* (that which) we need is courage.'
> '*What* (that which) you mean is obvious.'
> 'I can see *what* (that which) you mean.'
> 'I asked *what* (that which) you said.'

5:19

The relative pronoun may be omitted altogether from relative clauses, without any loss of meaning, provided it is not the subject of the clause:

> *e.g.* 'This is the man (*whom*) I accused.' (Direct object)
> *but* 'This is the man *who* did it.' (Subject)
> 'Where is the book (*which*) I was reading.' (Direct object)
> 'Where is the book *which* explains the problem.' (Subject)

Notice that when the relative pronoun to be omitted is governed by a preposition, the order of the words in the sentence will need changing:

Then came the moment for *which* I had been waiting.

becomes

Then came the moment (*which*) I had been waiting for.

5:20

It is important to recognise the difference between a 'defining' and a 'non-defining' relative clause in order to understand the situations where the relative pronoun *that* can be used instead of *who, whom,* or *which.* (*That* may replace them only in defining clauses.)

(i) *Defining Clauses* (also called 'Restrictive Clauses')

> As their name suggests, these 'define' or 'restrict' their antecedent noun, so that the noun takes on a narrowed-down meaning.
> Consider for example the meaning of:
>
> A The man *who* (*that*) *entered the shop* was a thief. (Defining)
> B The man, *who entered the shop*, was a thief. (Non-Defining)
>
> NOTE the punctuation of the two sentences.
> In A the clause defines which man, amongst many perhaps, was the thief; in B the clause states that the man was a thief and gives the additional information that he entered the shop.

(ii) *Non-defining Clauses* (also called 'Non-restrictive Clauses' or 'Qualifying Clauses')

> As their name suggests, these do not define or restrict their antecedent noun's meaning; they merely give additional information. They are

usually marked off from the main statement of the sentence by commas:

e.g. This is the house, *which* is falling down. (Non-defining)
This is the house *which* (*that*) is falling down. (Defining)
The clown, *whom* I admired, finally died. (Non-defining)
The clown *whom* (*that*) I admired finally died. (Defining)
The others *whom* (*that*) I do not admire live on. (Defining)
The others, *whom* I do not admire, live on. (Non-defining)

Adjectives
5:21

An adjective limits or qualifies the meaning of a noun (and sometimes of a pronoun): *e.g.* in the phrase 'clever children' *clever* limits or qualifies the meaning of 'children'. The adjective used in this way before a noun is used *attributively*.

In the sentence 'The children are clever', *clever* still limits or qualifies the meaning of 'children' but it is used in the predicate of the sentence (*i.e.* the rest of the sentence other than the subject) and is used *predicatively*. An adjective used predicatively may limit the subject of the verb (as here) or may limit the object: *e.g.* The boy painted his model *green*.

NOTE An adjective may consist of a single word or a group of words:

e.g. (*a*) The *clever* girl sat at the back of the room.
(*b*) The girl *who was clever* sat at the back of the room.
(*c*) She *who was clever* sat at the back of the room.
(Defining adjectival clause limiting the pronoun 'she')

5:22

Possessive Adjectives

These limit or qualify nouns *and*
indicate possession.
my, your, his, her, its, our, their
NOTE *Its* does NOT take an apostrophe. (*It's* = *it is*.)
Compare these forms of the possessive adjectives with those of possessive pronouns (see **5:9**, pages 49–50).

5:23

Demonstrative Adjectives

These limit or qualify nouns *and*
point out objects or people referred to.
Singular: this, that, the ⎫ *This, these* refer to objects or people near the
⎬ speaker; *that, those* to objects or people at a
Plural: these, those, the ⎭ distance from the speaker.
NOTE Demonstrative **pronouns** (*this, that, these, those*) have the same forms

as demonstrative adjectives but can easily be distinguished from them by their use; demonstrative pronouns are used instead of nouns or noun phrases:

e.g. *That* book is on the table. (Demonstrative adjective)
That is my book. (Demonstrative pronoun)
These hats belong to me. (Demonstrative adjective)
These belong to you. (Demonstrative pronoun)

The is sometimes called **the definite article** since in addition to limiting or qualifying a noun or pronoun it can make the reference more definite:

e.g. *The* prize was awarded to the champion.
Cf. '*A* prize was awarded to the champion', where *a* is the indefinite article. (*An* is usually used before a noun beginning with a vowel.)
The one I chose was unique. (Limits the pronoun *one*.)

5:24

Interrogative Adjectives

These limit or qualify nouns *and*
they are used in direct and indirect questions.

Whose, which, what

e.g. '*Whose* elephant is that?' (Direct question)
'*Which* dress did you finally choose?' (Direct question)
I asked *which* dress she had chosen. (Indirect question)
'*What* cloth do you want for your suit?' (Direct question)
He asked me *what* size I wanted. (Indirect question)

NOTE An intensifying suffix *-ever* may be added to both *which* and *what* to make them more emphatic or to indicate a choice from a number of possibilities:

e.g. '*Whichever* fool upset all this water?'
'*Whatever* cloth you choose will be expensive.'

5:25

Indefinite Adjectives (including *Distributive Adjectives*)

There are a large number of words in English which are used (i) to limit or qualify nouns and (ii) indicate an indefinite, or at least undefined, number or mass or quantity:

some, any; no; few, fewer, fewest, several; many, much, more, most; less, least; both, all.

Usually included, however, in this category are some words which:
—seem to define by total exclusion or inclusion (*e.g. no, all, every*);
—indicate a choice between two specifically defined persons or objects (*either, neither*).

(i) **Some, any** (NOTE *Some* is sometimes called 'the partitive article'.)

   (*a*) *Some* is used to limit or qualify a noun in positive contexts and *any* in negative contexts:

  e.g. I want *some* milk.
        I don't want *any* milk.

   (*b*) The word *any* can be used, however, in positive contexts to refer to a certain (though unspecified) number or quantity:

  e.g. Baa, baa, black sheep, have you *any* wool?
    or Jack likes lager but I like *any* beer.

  No

  e.g. *No* milk today, thank you.
        We have *no* bananas for sale.

(ii) **Few, fewer, fewest, several; many, much, more, most; less, least**

(See *Comparative and Superlative Degrees of Adjectives*, **5:31–5:37**, pages 68–70)
These words, when used as adjectives, indicate indefinite quantities and are sometimes referred to, therefore, as 'Indefinite Quantifiers'.

   (*a*) *Few* indicates a small number of people or things, almost equivalent to 'no':

  e.g. There were *few* candidates to choose from.

   (*b*) *Fewer* and *fewest* refer to comparisons with other numbers:

  e.g. Of the thousands who came to the concert, there were *fewer* musicians than fans.
        George made the *fewest* mistakes that day.

(NOTE   Use *fewer* for number and *less* for quantity or size: *fewer* people, *fewer* books, but *less* sugar, *less* wood.)

   (*c*) *Several* usually indicates an imprecise number:

  e.g. There were *several* guitar-players there who had lost their thumbs.

   (*d*) *Many, much*

  e.g. *Many* players took part and there was *much* noise.

   (*e*) *More, most* refer to comparisons with other numbers or with other quantities (*cf. fewer/fewest* in (*b*) above); in such comparisons the number or amount are indefinite or unquantified:

  e.g. I had *more* blame than anyone else.
        I made the *most* money, nevertheless.

   (*f*) *Less, least*
        Again, the amounts are not quantified (*cf. more/most* in (*e*) above) in these adjectives which are often used in comparative or superlative senses:

e.g. John had lost three hundred pounds but I lost *less* money.
Jill lost the *least* money that day.

(NOTE   Use *less* for quantity or size and *fewer* for number.)

(iii) *Both, all*

Both is really an 'identifier' or 'identifying adjective' since it identifies two people or objects already referred to precisely; *all* is really a 'quantifier' or 'quantifying adjective' since it specifies a quantity very precisely, the complete whole, the totality, the entire number:

e.g. Please open *both* cases for customs inspection.
All baggage must be presented for inspection to the customs.

(For the difference in sense between the use of
both (pronoun) + of/*both* (adjective)
and *all* (pronoun) + of/*all* (adjective),
see **5:15** (ii) (d), pages 55–6.)

(iv) *Each; either, neither*

Each is sometimes called a 'Distributive Adjective' or sometimes a 'Universal Adjective'.
(*a*) *Each* + *noun* (*or pronoun*) is followed by a singular verb:

e.g. *Each* boxer enters the contest undefeated.
Each one hopes to defeat the other.

(*b*) *Each* + *noun* (*or pronoun*) refers to an individual person or object already identified:

e.g. The lettuce and cucumber are both expensive; *each* costs more than twenty pence.

(*c*) *Each* + *noun* (*or pronoun*) may be used with either *his/her/its* or *their* for co-reference:

e.g. *Each* ingredient made *its* own contribution to the final taste.

Either, neither are sometimes called 'Distributive Adjectives'.
(*a*) *Either* + *noun* is used to refer to one of two persons or things (whereas *any* + *noun* refers to more than two), and

(*b*) *Neither* + *noun* is used as a negative to refer to two or more persons or things (whereas *none/not any* + *noun* refers to more than two).

e.g. *Either* choice will lead to problems.
Neither solution will provide the answer.

(*c*) Both *either* + *noun* and *neither* + *noun* are followed by verbs which are singular:

e.g. *Either* question is unanswerable.
Neither question is worth asking.

5:26

Numerical Adjectives

These limit or qualify nouns *and*
indicate a number.

> *e.g.* There were *two* cats, *three* dogs, and *four* men involved in the chase.

5:27

Identifying and Quantifying Adjectives: such; the former, the latter

These limit or qualify nouns *and*
identify or quantify a noun to which they refer:

> *e.g.* *Such* behaviour merits severe punishment.
> *Such* students deserve to succeed.
> Sam and Pete were tomcats; *the former* animal was grey, *the latter* animal was tabby.

5:28

The Definite and Indefinite Articles (also called 'Definite' and 'Indefinite Identifiers'): the; a, an

(i) *The (The Definite Article)*

(*a*) This limits or quantifies or 'identifies' a noun or pronoun and often makes it clear that a speaker or writer is referring to a noun just mentioned *or* one about to be mentioned *or* to a specific context:

> *e.g.* Here are carrots, beans, and onions: take *the* carrots and peel them.
> My recipe is *the* one that won a prize.
> Are you referring to *the* prize awarded annually?

(*b*) Sometimes *the* (pronounced 'thee') is used to refer to a specified person or thing:

> *e.g.* 'Michelangelo lived there.' 'Do you mean *the* Michelangelo?'

(*c*) It is used sometimes as part of a geographical feature, or a place, or a newspaper, or an organisation:

> *e.g.* *The* Thames; *The* Netherlands; *The* Costa Brava;
> *The Hague*; *The Houses of Parliament*; *The Mall*;
> *The Times*; *The Observer*; *The Daily Telegraph*;
> *The Scout Association*; *The Girl Guides*; *The Royal Society of Arts*.

(ii) *A, an (Indefinite Articles)*

(*a*) *A* is used before a noun (which it limits) beginning with a consonant:

> *e.g.* *A* dog; *a* cat; *a* book.

(**b**) *An* is used before a noun (which it limits) beginning with a vowel:

e.g. *An* idea; *an* owl; *an* idiot.

(**c**) Both *a* and *an* are used to refer to a class of thing as a whole:

e.g. *A* book is a form of knowledge.
A carrot is a vegetable.

(**d**) Both *a* and *an* + *a noun* refer to a noun, the exact identity of which is not specified within its class:

e.g. I spoke to *a* boy who happened to be there.
I saw *an* apple on the tree.

(**e**) *A*, *an* often are equivalent to *per* (in commercial English):

e.g. The tomatoes cost thirty pence *a* pound.
He ran at ten miles *an* hour.

5:29

Adjective 'Equivalents'

(i) It must be emphasised that it is the function of a word (single words, phrases, or clauses) which determines which part of speech it is.

e.g. Take the word 'steady':
  (*a*) The test established the difference between the two kinds of men: the *steady* and the unsteady. (Noun)
  (*b*) I managed to *steady* the ship after the wave hit her. (Verb)
  (*c*) My *steady* hand held her under control. (Adjective)

(ii) Similarly, it is the function of a word, phrase, or clause which determines whether it is an adjective or not:
  (*a*) The *happy* man laughed until he cried. (Single word)
  (*b*) The man, *happy as usual*, sang a favourite song. (Phrase)
  (*c*) The man *who is happy* is fortunate indeed. (Defining clause)
  (*d*) The boy, *who seemed happy*, bought a new record. (Non-defining clause)

(iii) NOTE Words like *theatre* or *song*, normally used as nouns, may function adjectivally:

e.g. A *theatre* seat; a *song* bird.

Again, it is the function which determines whether the word is an adjective or not.

(iv) Similarly participles of verbs frequently function as adjectives:

e.g. The *running* brook; the *dancing* light; the *fascinating* play.
The *written* word; the *relaxed* audience; the *worried* parent.

5:30

The Formation of Adjectives

(i) Adjectives are often formed by the addition of a **suffix** to another word which may be slightly adapted. Suffixes frequently used to form adjectives in this way include:

-*able:* lov*able*; drink*able*
-*al:* magic*al*; comic*al*
-*ar:* circul*ar*; angul*ar*, nucle*ar*
-*en:* wood*en*; wooll*en*
-*ic:* scientif*ic*; atom*ic*
-*ish:* fool*ish*; child*ish*
-*ive:* mass*ive*; express*ive*
-*ful:* thank*ful*; wonder*ful*
-*less:* thank*less*; hope*less*
-*like:* life*like*; child*like*
-*ly:* wool*ly*; brother*ly*
-*ous:* marvell*ous*; adventur*ous*
-*y:* muck*y*; sleep*y*.

(ii) The addition of a **prefix** often produces an opposite or negative form of another adjective:

*dis-: dis*approving; *dis*liked
*il-: il*logical; *il*legal
*im-: im*probable; *im*precise
*in-: in*attentive; *in*delicate
*ir-: ir*relevant; *ir*reverent
*un-: un*happy; *un*believing.

5:31

Comparative and Superlative degrees of Adjectives

The **comparative** degree is used to compare one person or thing with another, *or* one group (set) of persons or things with another group (set) of persons or things. Only *two* individual items or sets of items are compared when the comparative degree is used:

e.g. I am *taller* than you.
The girls are *taller* than the boys.

There are two main ways of forming the comparatives of adjectives:

(i) by adding -*er* to words of one or two syllables:

e.g. tall, tall*er*; long, long*er*; short, short*er*; happy, happi*er*; clever, clever*er*; narrow, narrow*er*.

(ii) by modifying the adjective with the word *more*; this is the normal form when the adjective has three or more syllables:

e.g. wonderful, *more* wonderful; beautiful, *more* beautiful; ridiculous, *more* ridiculous.

5:32

The **superlative** degree is used in comparing three or more persons, things, or groups (sets):

e.g. 'He was the tall*est* of the three boys.'
'Here was the larg*est* onion I had ever seen.'

There are *two* main ways of forming the superlatives of adjectives:
(i) by adding *-est* to words of one or two syllables:

e.g. tall, tall*est*; long, long*est*; short, short*est*; happy, happi*est*; clever, clev-er*est*; narrow, narrow*est*.

(ii) by modifying the adjective with the word *most*; this is the normal form when the adjective has three or more syllables:

e.g. wonderful, *most* wonderful; beautiful, *most* beautiful; ridiculous, *most* ridiculous.

5:33

(i) the following exceptions should be noted:

	Comparative	*Superlative*
good	better	best
bad	worse	worst
far	farther ⎫	farthest ⎫
	or further ⎭	*or* furthest ⎭
real	more real	most real
little* ⎫		
small ⎭	smaller	smallest

* The forms *littler* and *littlest* are sometimes used in colloquial English or in dialects.
When *little* refers to quantity (mass) rather than height it has other comparative and superlative forms: *little, less, least*:

e.g. He ate *little* food.
I ate even *less* food.
John ate the *least* food of all.

(ii) The adjective *unique* (because of its meaning) does not have a comparative and a superlative form.

5:34

The adjective *old* has the comparative and superlative forms *older* and *oldest* when used predicatively:

e.g. Jill was fifteen but Jim was *older*.
Jill was fifteen, Jim sixteen, but Mary was *oldest*.

Old can have the alternative comparative and superlative forms *elder* and *eldest* when used attributively *and* to refer to members of a family or social group.

> *e.g.* John was the *elder* (or 'older') brother.
> Mary was the *eldest* (or 'oldest') girl in the class.

On other occasions the forms *older* and *oldest* are used:

> *e.g.* Which is the *older* book of the two?
> Which is the *oldest* book in the library?

5:35

It is worth noting that when the *same* degree of comparison is required (*i.e.* when the sameness of two persons, things, or groups (sets) is being compared) the construction *as + adjective + as* is used:

> *e.g.* This book is *as old as* mine.

5:36

When adjectives are being compared to a lower degree, *less, least* are used instead of *more, most* (or *-er, -est*):

> *e.g.* This book is *less* old than mine.
> This book is the *least* old in the library.

5:37

Very frequently, the sentence can be turned round to use a higher degree of comparison (*more, most* or *-er, -est*) without loss of sense:

> *e.g.* This book is *less* old than mine.
> *or* My book is *older* than yours.
>
> This book is the *least* old in the library.
> *or* All the other books in the library are *older* than this one.

Verbs
5:38

Chambers Twentieth Century Dictionary defines a verb as 'the part of speech which asserts or predicates something'.

5:39

A **verb** is an essential part of a clause; every clause follows the basic structure of:

> a **noun or noun phrase** (*subject*) + a **verb or verbal phrase** (*predicate*)

e.g.   The men   arrived.

The verbal phrase may be either **simple** (consisting of a single word) or **complex** (consisting of a verbal group):

> *e.g.* The men *arrived*. (Simple)
> The men *have arrived*. (Complex)

5:40

If the verb or verbal phrase is accompanied by a subject it is said to be **finite**; if no subject is present or clearly understood the verb is **non-finite**.

(i) *Simple finite parts*

(**a**) *The imperative* (this gives an order or a command)

> *e.g.* *Come* here. (the subject 'you' is understood)
> *Put* the books there.

(**b**) *The simple present tense*

> *e.g.* The boys *come* here every day.
> The girls *take* their books away with them every day.

(**c**) *The simple past tense*

> *e.g.* The boys *came* here yesterday.
> The girls *took* their books away yesterday.

(ii) *Simple non-finite parts*

(**a**) The *infinitive*: this usually has 'to' preceding it as a marker:

> *e.g.* The boys came *to see* me.

With certain modal verbs (see page 72) the infinitive is not preceded by the marker 'to':

> *e.g.* The boys could *see* me easily.
> The girls should *take* their books home.

(**b**) The *present participle* (the *-ing participle*)

> *e.g.* The boys were *watching* me.
> The girls were *taking* their books home.
> (See also **5:52**, pages 86–7.)

(**c**) The *past participle* (the *-ed participle*)

> *e.g.* The boys have *watched* me all morning.
> The girls have *taken* their books home.
> (See also **5:53**, pages 87–8.)

5:41

Modals

There are some verbs which cannot stand on their own as the only verb in a clause (*i.e.* as a **full** verb), but must be used with another verb present or clearly understood; these verbs are called **modals** or **modal verbs**. They express a variety of moods or attitudes towards a possible action (or state).

(i) *will; shall; can; may; would; should; could; might; must; ought.*

e.g. '*Ought* he to do it?' 'He *must* (do it).'

The verbs which follow these *modals* are always in the bare infinitive form (*i.e.* the infinitive without the marker 'to') EXCEPT *ought*, which is followed by an infinitive with 'to':

e.g. 'He must *go* there.'
'He ought to *go* there.'

(ii) Some of these *modal* forms should not be confused with identical forms of the same verbs which act merely as *auxiliaries* (*i.e.* verbs which help other verbs to form tenses). (See **5:42**, page 73.)

e.g. shall: = to be obliged to (a Modal):
'Thou *shalt* not kill.' (Modal)
I *shall* go there tomorrow. (Auxiliary)

e.g. will: = to wish to (a Modal):
'*Will* you have this woman to be your lawful, wedded wife?'
'I *will*.' (Modal)
They *will* go there tomorrow. (Auxiliary)

e.g. may: = to be allowed to (a Modal):
You *may* go there if you wish. (Modal)
I *may* go there tomorrow or somewhere else. (Auxiliary)

Notice the difference in meaning between:

I *will* go and nobody *shall* stop me. (Modals)
I *shall* go and nobody *will* stop me. (Auxiliaries)

(iii) Three other modal usages of verbs should be mentioned here: *used to; need; dare.*

(*a*) *used to:* this modal helps another verb to form a tense and is often referred to as a **modal auxiliary**; it occurs only in the past tense and is always used with an infinitive with a 'to' marker. The action of the verb is given the aspect of being a habitual one:

e.g. He *used to* go there every Wednesday.
He *used* never *to* say such things.

(*b*) *need:* this is used as a modal when it is equivalent to 'must'; it is often used with an infinitive without the marker 'to':

e.g. I hardly *need* remind you of your duty.
You *need* not say anything if you prefer not to.

(*c*) *dare:* this is used as a modal in negative or interrogative contexts; it, too, is often used with an infinitive without the marker 'to':

e.g. I *dared* not tell him the truth. (Negative)
Dare we tell him the truth now? (Interrogative)

5:42

Auxiliaries

(i) There are three verbs which help other verbs to make their passive forms (see **5:45**, pages 77–8) and their tenses, *or* to be used negatively or interrogatively.

These three verbs are called **auxiliaries** or **auxiliary verbs** (after the Latin word *auxilium*, help): *have; be; do.*

> *e.g.* The girls *have* taken their books home. (Present perfect tense)
> The boys *are* watching me. (Present continuous tense)
> The boys *did* not go home yesterday afternoon. (Past tense negative)
> *Do* they *go* home every afternoon? (Present tense interrogative)

NOTE These three verbs may be used as **full** verbs in their own right when they carry their full lexical (dictionary) meaning. When they function in this way they are *not* auxiliaries:

> *e.g.* I *have* ten books in my briefcase.
> I *am* a girl (a boy).
> I *do* my homework every night.

> It is the function, therefore, which determines whether these verbs are full or auxiliary verbs.

(ii) Verbs may be used as auxiliaries when they help other verbs to form their tenses (see **5:43**, pages 73–5) or moods (see **5:44**, pages 75–7).

shall, will, may; should, would, might.

> *e.g.* I *shall* go there tomorrow. (Future simple tense)
> They *will* go there the next day. (Future simple tense)
> They *may* go if they are well. (Subjunctive)
> I *should* do it, if it were possible. (Subjunctive)
> They *would* do it, if the situation arose. (Subjunctive)
> I *might* go, if I had the money. (Subjunctive)

5:43

Tenses

The word 'tense' is derived through French from the Latin word for time (*tempus*); it is the form of a verb used to indicate the time when the verb's action occurs or occurred, or its state exists or existed:

> *e.g.* The man *is* a policeman. (Present)
> The man *saw* a policeman. (Past)

(i) There are two main tenses in English: the **present** and the **past**. These tenses may have *simple* forms (consisting of a single word) or *complex* forms (consisting of a verbal group). In their *complex* forms they may use verbal forms which suggest that the action or state is

continuous (or **progressive**) or that the action or state is finished or **perfect**.

The **future** in English is expressed in a number of ways (see **5:43** (iv), pages 74–5); it may refer to a time in the future seen from the standpoint of the present (the *simple future*) or the future seen from the standpoint of the past (the *future in the past*):

e.g. I *shall go* there tomorrow. (Simple future)
I *was going to go* there when I was interrupted. (Future in the past)

(ii) The *non-finite* forms of the verb have no tense forms of their own. They may be used to help other verbs form present or past forms of tenses. It is for this reason that the *-ing* form is often referred to by modern grammarians as the *-ing participle*.

e.g. The policeman *is walking* along the street. (Present progressive/continuous)
The policeman *was walking* along the street. (Past progressive/continuous)
The policeman *has arrested* the criminal. (Present perfect)
The policeman *had arrested* the criminal. (Past perfect)

(iii) The tenses of a full verb in the third person singular are set out in the following table:

		Continuous/Progressive (using the auxiliary 'be' + the *-ing participle*)	*Perfect* (using the auxiliary 'have' + the *past* (or *-ed*) *participle*)
PRESENT			
	sings	is singing	has sung
	look	is looking	has looked
PAST			
	sang	was singing	had sung
	looked	was looking	had looked

NOTE 1 The auxiliary verb changes according to the present or past aspects of the verb; the participle remains unchanged.

NOTE 2 The Past Perfect tense is sometimes called the *Pluperfect* tense.

(iv) The **future** aspects of the verb are set out in *five* different ways in English and may refer *either* to the future seen from the standpoint of the present (*the simple future*) *or* to the future seen from the standpoint of the past (*the future in the past*)—even if the imagined future never takes place:

(a) Auxiliary *shall* (in first persons singular and plural)/*will* (in second and third persons singular and plural) + infinitive (without the 'to' marker):

e.g. I *shall go* there tomorrow. (Simple future)
They *will go* there tomorrow. (Simple future)
I knew I *should arrive* there soon. (Future in the past)
They saw they *would arrive* late. (Future in the past)

(b) *be going + infinitive* (with the 'to' marker):

e.g. I *am going to see* you tomorrow. (Simple future)
They knew they *were going to see* her the next day. (Future in the past)

(c) *be + infinitive* (with the 'to' marker):

e.g. I *am to see* you tomorrow. (Simple future)
He knew he *was to see* her the next day. (Future in the past)

NOTE This use may also suggest an obligation or a necessity as well as an idea of simple futurity.

(d) *be + ing participle* (NOTE This is the same form as the continuous/progressive form as that used in the present or past tense; in English, however, the context may well indicate that it refers to the future.)

e.g. I *am seeing* her tomorrow. (Simple future)
'He said he *was seeing* her the next day.' (Future in the past)

(e) *the simple present form* (NOTE The context will make its reference to the future clear.)

e.g. 'He *sees* her tomorrow.' (Simple future)
'He knew from his ticket that he *left* the next day.' (Future in the past)

NOTE In all these five forms the use of an adverb (*tomorrow, the next day*) provides the necessary context to enable the verb to contain a 'future' sense. In this way the language is versatile enough to leave native speakers or writers in no doubt about the futurity of the meaning.

(v) Sequence of tenses

(a) In writing or speaking it is considered desirable to keep *either* to the Present tense *or* to the Past tense (in a single form or in a variety of its forms: *e.g.* simple present, present continuous, present perfect, or simple future; *or* simple past, past continuous, past perfect or pluperfect, or future in the past).

(b) Where the sense, however, demands for the sake of accuracy an interchange between the present and the past, the interchange is made correctly:

e.g. I cannot say where we went.
I am telling you what we actually did.

(For the use of tenses in Reported/Indirect Speech, see pages 125–6.)

5:44
Mood

(i) The **modal** verbs and the **modal auxiliary** verbs (see **5:41** and **5:42**, pages 71–3) express mood or attitude to an action or a state represented by a verb:

e.g. He *can* <u>do</u> it. (= ability)

He *must* do it. (=obligation)
I *will* do it. (=willingness, desire)

(ii) The **indicative** mood of the verb is used for:
  (*a*) statements of fact (or suppositions regarded as facts);
  (*b*) questions asking for facts.

e.g. I *read* ten books a year. (Present indicative)
How many *did* you *read* last year? (Past indicative)
I *have read* three so far this year. (Present perfect indicative)
Had you *read* as many this time last year? (Past perfect (pluperfect) indicative)

(iii) The **imperative** mood of the verb is used for:
  (*a*) orders; commands;
  (*b*) requests set out as strong demands.

e.g. *Come* here at once.
Forgive me for troubling you.

The imperative mood is usually set out as a direct order or strong request to another person; it is normally used in the second person; therefore *you* is implicit.
It can be used with the verb *let* as an auxiliary + an infinitive without the marker 'to' with the first person implicit (*I, we*):

e.g. *Let* me do it.
Let's go together.

(iv) The **infinitive** is sometimes referred to as a 'mood' of the verb; it is better to refer to it, perhaps, as a non-finite form of the verb (see **5:40** (ii), page 71).

(v) The **subjunctive** mood is used to express:

(*a*) a supposition which cannot be or which is unlikely to be realised:

e.g. If I *were* you, I should not do it.
If I *win* the pools, I'd retire.

(*b*) a wish or a hope:

e.g. Long *may* she reign!
I hope they *do* it correctly.

(*c*) a condition which has not come about:

e.g. *Were* he here, he would know what to do.
Had he seen it, he would have turned in his grave.
(The conditional '*If* he were here', '*If* he had seen it', is understood.)

(*d*) a proposition or a recommendation following the verbs 'propose' or 'recommend':

e.g. The boss proposed that he *be* promoted.
The board recommended the proposal *be* accepted.

NOTE Because the verbs *should, may, might* can also be used to express doubt or vague possibility, wish or supposition, they are sometimes called 'subjunctive equivalents'. Modern grammarians sometimes prefer to categorise the use of the subjunctive as follows:

1 The *mandative subjunctive*: *i.e.* the form used in clauses beginning with 'that' following a verb in the main clause which suggests recommendation, demand, insistence, and so on.

   e.g. We require that he *be* dismissed.
   They insisted that he *come*.
   They asked that it *be bought*.
   He suggested the politician *speak*.

The use of the subjunctive here is formal; in less formal contexts the subjunctive would be replaced by *should + infinitive*.

2 The *formulaic subjunctive*: *i.e.* the form used in set expressions.

   e.g. *Come* what may, ...
   Be that as it may, ...

The force of the subjunctive here is to suggest 'Let it come ...', 'Let it be as it may ...'

3 The *hypothetical subjunctive*: *i.e.* the form used in clauses which make a condition or a concession or in clauses following verbs such as *wish, suppose*, and so on.

   e.g. I wish I *were* better.
   Suppose he *recover* before the funeral?

Nevertheless, it is clear that the subjunctive form of the verb is often different from the equivalent indicative form and often resembles the base form of the verb (*e.g.* the bare infinitive without the marker 'to'; *or* all the present tense except the third person singular:* I, you, we, they *recover*; *or* the imperative).

5:45

Voice

This term is used to describe whether the subject of a transitive verb (*i.e.* one which takes a direct object, see **5:46**, pages 78–9):

(*a*) does the action of the verb (*the active voice*):

   e.g. I *saw* the policeman.

---

* Note, however, the subjunctive forms of the verb *to be* in *the present tense*:
   I *be*, you *be*, he/she/it *be*, we *be*, they *be*;
or in *the past tense*:
   I *were*, you *were*, he/she/it *were*, we *were*, you *were*, they *were*.

or

(b) suffers or receives the action of the verb (*the passive voice*):

e.g. The policeman *was seen* by me.

(i) The infinitives of most transitive verbs have both **active** and **passive** forms:

e.g. *to see* (active), *to be seen* (passive); *to buy* (active), *to be bought* (passive); *to have hit* (active), *to have been hit* (passive).

NOTE A small number of transitive verbs will not tolerate the transformation into the passive:

e.g. *to have, to lack, to resemble, to suit.*
　　　 I *have* ten thousand books. (Active)
but 'Ten thousand books are had by me' is not English.
　　　 This man *resembles* my brother. (Active)
but 'My brother is resembled by this man' is not English.

(ii) The verb in the **passive** voice consists of *to be* (in one of its tenses or forms) + *a past participle*:

e.g. *to be painted, to be seen, to be bought*

　　　 The picture *was painted* by Matisse.
　　　 The fox *is seen* by the pursuers.
　　　 The book *was bought* by the student.

(iii) The subject of the corresponding active sentence/clause is represented in the passive sentence/clause by a prepositional phrase consisting of *by + a noun or pronoun.*

e.g. I *saw* the man. (Active)
　　　 The man *was seen* <u>by me</u>. (Passive)

5:46

Transitive/Intransitive (Verb Patterns)

(i) **Transitive** verbs are those which can be complemented (completed) by a direct object (abbreviated *dO**) in the form of a noun phrase, a finite clause, or a non-finite clause which 'suffers' the action of the verb:

e.g. He *denied* <u>the accusation</u> (*dO*). (Complemented by a noun phrase)
　　　 He *denied* <u>that he was guilty</u> (*dO*). (Complemented by a finite clause)
　　　 He *denied* <u>meeting her</u> (*dO*). (Complemented by a non-finite/participial clause)

(ii) Some verbs are always **intransitive**, *i.e.* they never take a direct object or a complement (see **5:46** (iv), page 79):

e.g. *to fall; to arrive; to disappear; to come.*
　　　 The horse *stumbled.*

* A complete list of abbreviations used in this book appears on page vi.

The bus *arrived* at the stop.
The ghost *disappeared* mysteriously.

(iii) Some verbs may be used transitively or intransitively:

e.g. The horse *jumped* the fence (*dO*). (Transitive)
The horse *jumped* well to win the race. (Intransitive)
The boy *rang* the door-bell loudly. (Transitive)
The bell *rang* loudly to announce her arrival. (Intransitive)

(iv) Some verbs in English are neither transitive nor intransitive in their function but are linking verbs between their subjects and their subject **complements**; such verbs are called **copulas** (or linking verbs). Modern grammarians sometimes distinguish them as follows:

(*a*) The verb *to be*;
(*b*) *current copulas* (*i.e.* where the subject and the complement exist currently together or are in a current relationship to each other);
(*c*) *resulting copulas* (*i.e.* where the subject complement results at least partially from the verb itself).

All three kinds of copulas are used with complements that are usually adjective phrases or noun phrases, although some take infinitives or *wh-* or *that* clauses as complements:
Current copulas: *appear, seem, smell, sound, taste, look, remain.*
Resulting copulas: *become, grow, turn, get* (in colloquial forms of the language), *go, make.*

e.g. The woman was *a traindriver.* (Noun phrase)
The truth appeared *that he was guilty.* ('that' clause)
He seemed *to jump.* (Infinitive)
The cake smelt *good.* (Adjective phrase)
The music sounded *difficult.* (Adjective phrase)
The meal tasted *dreadful.* (Adjective phrase)
The Martian looked *grey with fright.* (Adjective phrase)
The Earthman remained *confident.* (Adjective phrase)
The situation became *what he had feared most.* ('wh-' clause)
The boy grew (turned) *angry.* (Adjective phrase)
He got *hot under the collar.* (Adjective phrase, used colloquially)
He went *mad.* (Adjective phrase)
The thought made *him determined.* (Noun phrase)

5:47

Weak (Regular), Strong, and Irregular Verbs

(i) **Weak (Regular)** verbs are distinguished by the fact that in order to form their past tense they add to a base form one of the following:
1 a syllable *-ed* (pronounced *-id*):

e.g. mend/mended; rent/rented

2 a voiced -*d* without an additional syllable:

e.g. resemble/resembled; saw/sawed; row/rowed

3 a voiceless -*t* without an additional syllable (the voiceless -*t* is sometimes written as -*ed*):

e.g. learn/learnt; like/liked; look/looked.

Note that new verbs in English follow this weak or regular pattern:

e.g. computerise/computerised.

(ii) **Strong** verbs originally changed their vowels from the base form to make their past tenses and past participles. They still do and are sometimes classed as 'irregular' verbs:

	Base	Past tense	Past participle
e.g.	*begin*	*began*	*begun*
	sing	*sang*	*sung*
	rise	*rose*	*risen*
	stink	*stank*	*stunk*

NOTE 1 Some verbs which were originally strong have become *weak* or *regular* by analogy with other verbs.

e.g. dive/dived/dived in Modern English still has the form *dove* in American English from an earlier period.

In the seventeenth century the past tense of *climb* was sometimes given as *clomb* (as in Milton's *Paradise Lost*), although in Modern English the simple past tense is invariably *climbed*. (It is worth observing, too, that young children in learning to talk often give strong verbs weak inflexional endings to form past tenses: *e.g. singed* for *sang*.)

NOTE 2 The verb *to hang* is derived from two earlier verbs in Old English, one strong and transitive (*hon, heng*, [ge] *hangen*) and the other weak and intransitive (*hangian, hangode*, [ge]*hangod*). The first gave rise to the Modern English forms *hang/hung/hung* and the second to *hang/hanged/ hanged*. Modern English tends to use the first both transitively and intransitively:

e.g. The artist *hung* <u>her painting</u> (*dO*) on the dining-room wall. (Transitive)
The apple *hung* from the tree. (Intransitive)

The second verb (*hang/hanged/hanged*) is exclusively reserved for judicial hanging but may be used transitively or intransitively:

e.g. The executioner *hanged* <u>the murderer</u> [*dO*] at eight o'clock. (Transitive)
The murderer *hanged* at eight o'clock. (Intransitive)

But native users of the language are failing increasingly to distinguish these usages and, perhaps strangely, the strong form (*hang/hung/hung*) seems to predominate.

NOTE 3 The verbs *to lie* (strong and intransitive) and *to lay* (weak and transitive) are often confused:

Base	Past tense	Past participle
lie	lay	lain
lay	laid	laid

The confusion arises, perhaps because of the identical forms of the past tense of *lie* (*lay*) and the base form of *lay*:

cf. The soldiers *lay* on the ground. (Past tense of *lie*)
The hens *lay* two eggs each day. (Present tense of *lay*)

(iii) The other types of **irregular** verbs are sometimes distinguished, since they do not conform to the way regular verbs form their past tenses and past participles:

(*a*) Verbs which have the same forms in the base, the past tense, and the past participle:

e.g. *cast/cast/cast*
hurt/hurt/hurt
shut/shut/shut
upset/upset/upset

NOTE Some verbs of this kind can also have regular forms but then they may change their meaning or function:

cf. *cost/cost/cost:* *e.g.* The coat *cost* five pounds.
cost/costed/costed: *e.g.* The accountant *costed* the proposal.
sweat/sweat/sweat: *e.g.* The Sales-Director *sweat* blood over the losses.
sweat/sweated/sweated: *e.g.* The plumber *sweated* the ends of the pipes together with his blow-lamp.

(*b*) Verbs where the past tense and the past participle are the same as each other but both are different from the base form:

	Base	Past tense	Past participle
e.g.	beseech	besought	besought
	buy	bought	bought
	catch	caught	caught
	dream	dreamt	dreamt
	fling	flung	flung
	hear	heard	heard
	shine	shone	shone
	tell	told	told

(iv) Some verbs are **defective** in that some parts have fallen out of use and have had to be replaced by new parts from other verbs. Such are

some of the modal verbs (see **5:41**, pages 71–2) which had only one
or two forms of their own:

	Base	Present tense	Past tense	Past participle
e.g.	(to be able)	(*can*)	*could* *	(been able)
	(to have to)	*must*	(had to)	(had to)
	(to be allowed to)	*may*	*might*	(been allowed to)
	(to have to)	*ought*	*ought*	(been obliged to)

(v) The verb *to be* is **irregular**, too; it has an interesting history and is in
fact made up in its forms of at least three originally different verbs:

Base	Present tense	Past tense	Past participle
be	*am/is/are*	*was/were*	*been*

It is, of course, used as a **full** verb (see **5:46** (iv), page 79) and as an **auxiliary**
verb:

e.g. I *am* a teacher. (Full)
I *am* going to school. (Auxiliary: present continuous tense)

5:48

Person, Number, and Gender

The form of a verb depends sometimes on the **Person** (first, second, or third)
and sometimes on the **Number** (Singular/Plural) of the subject. **Gender**
(Masculine/Feminine/Neuter) affects the personal pronouns used with verbs
but does not affect the forms of verbs themselves.

(i) *Person* (see also Pronouns, **5:8–5:20**, pages 48–62)

	Singular	Plural
First	*I*	*We*
Second	*You*	*You*
Third	*He/She/It*	*They*

The form of the verb used with all persons (both singular and plural)
is the same throughout a tense EXCEPT:

(a) in the Simple Present Tense, *third person singular*, where an inflexional
ending (-s, -es) is added to the base:

e.g. I *sing*/he *sings*
You *miss*/she *misses*
They *do*/it *does* (NOTE the change in pronunciation, too.)
I *say*/he *says* (NOTE the change in pronunciation, too.)

---

* The -*l*- in this word has been inserted by analogy with *should* and *would* where the -*l*- is
historically part of the word.

(**b**) in the verb *be*:

Person	Present tense	Past tense
I	*am*	*was*
You	*are*	*were*
He/She/it	*is*	*was*
We	*are*	*were*
You	*are*	*were*
They	*are*	*were*

e.g.

These forms are used whether the verb *to be* is used as a full verb or as an auxiliary.

(**c**) in the verb *have*, third person singular, present tense:
I/You/We/They *have*, but He/She/It *has*

(ii) *Number*

Number affects the forms of most words (*e.g.* see Pronouns, **5:8–5:20**, pages 48–62); it may affect the forms of verbs.

The relation between the number (singular/plural) of the subject and the appropriate form of the verb is known as **agreement** or **concord**.

(**a**) With single nouns or pronouns as subjects the agreement is usually easily established:

e.g. The man *was* ill. (Singular)
The men *were* ill. (Plural)

With some collective nouns the agreement is rather more difficult to establish. (For a full discussion of this problem see **5:3** (ii), page 47.) See, too, the use of the singular form of the pronoun *none* with verbs **5:15** (ii) (*b*), page 54.

(**b**) When the subject is not a single word but a group of words forming a *nominal* (*or noun*) *group*, it is the head word which determines the number of the following verb:

e.g. *He and she were* both present. (*He and she* are a plural subject)
Either *he* or *she was* the thief. (*he/she* are alternative singular subjects)
This *bunch* of flowers *is* too big. (*bunch*, a singular, is the head word in the nominal group functioning as the subject; *of flowers* is a post-modifier of 'bunch')

(**c**) Sometimes the subject of a verb and its complement are different in number:

e.g. Pigs (*S*) *are* one species (*C*) of animal.
The subject (*S*) tonight *is* 'Stars' (*C*).
Potatoes (*S*) *are* a good crop (*C*) to grow.

Nevertheless, it is the number of the subject which determines the number of the verb.

NOTE A commonly quoted exception is 'The *wages* (*S*) of sin *is* death (*C*).'

However, it is usually argued that 'wages' = 'reward', 'salary' and is singular in concept although plural in form. Usage and the authority of the 1611 King James's Bible (Romans 6:23) have entrenched this phrase in the language as it is.

(**d**) Sometimes, however, when the subject offers alternatives, one singular and the other plural, it is hard to resolve the number of the verb. H. W. Fowler in *A Dictionary of Modern English Usage*, second edition, 1965 (page 402), discusses an example of this dilemma:

'Mother or child *is* to die' poses no problem of agreement. (Mother/child are alternative singular subjects.)
But what would happen if the sentence read instead, 'Mother or children is/are to die'?

Fowler argues that the methods of meeting the problem 'in order of merit' are:

1 Evade it by finding a verb of common number:
   'Mother or children *must* die.'
2 Change the order:
   'The mother is to die, or the children.'
3 Give the verb the number of the alternative noun nearest it:
   'Mother or children are to die.'

(**e**) The verb in relative adjectival clauses (introduced by *who/which/that*) can sometimes cause problems of number if the antecedent noun or noun phrase is not immediately established:

e.g. This is one of the best books that *is/are* in the library.
He is one of those people who *arrives/arrive* late at the theatre.

Better sense prevails if the antecedents to 'that' and 'who' are *books* and *people* respectively and so the verbs are more appropriate in the plural. If 'one' is taken as the singular antecedent in the first example, the sense of the whole sentence would be altered to mean 'This is one of the best books (ever written) and it is in the library.' Clearly the sense will not stand such mishandling.

(**f**) Sometimes in speech, and occasionally in writing, a singular verb is used to precede a plural subject because the user of the language has not thought out his sentence before beginning it:

e.g. There *was* gold and silver (*S*) galore for the taking.
At the party there *was* Jack and Mary, Fred and Bill (*S*).

Such lack of agreement is less acceptable in writing than in speech.

(iii) *Gender*

Gender affects the form of some nouns (see **5:7** (iii), page 48), personal, possessive, reflexive and emphatic pronouns (see **5:8–5:12**, pages 48–51), and possessive adjectives (see **5:22**, page 62), but it does not affect the forms of verbs.

5:49

Prepositional verbs

Modern grammarians often distinguish three main kinds of **prepositional verbs** in English:

(i) *The Literal*

This kind occurs where a verb is used + a preposition + a noun phrase (used adverbially):

e.g. The man   looked (*V*)   across (*P*)   the room (*NP*).
He   stayed (*V*)   at (*P*)   work (*NP*).

(ii) *Look and Listen*

Look and *Listen* used transitively, when they require a preposition. Consider the two ways of analysing the sentence John listened to the radio: subject + verb + adverb, and subject + verb + direct object.

John (*S*)   listened (*V*)   to the radio (*A*).
and John (*S*)   listened to (*V*)   the radio (*dO*).

If the second analysis is made, *listened to* is taken as a transitive verb. If the first, *listened* is an intransitive verb.

(iii) *The Idiomatic*

Here the *verb + the preposition* is used idiomatically together as a phrasal verb (see **5:50**, pages 85–6) and together the two parts mean something different from the two parts taken separately. Compare the following:

He   *looked (V)*   into the bag (*A*).
The detective   *looked into (V)*   the problem (*dO*).

He   *stood (V)*   for the National Anthem (*A*).
He   *stood for (V)*   the rudeness (*dO*)   too long before taking action (*A*).

5:50

Phrasal Verbs

Modern grammarians often distinguish four main kinds of **phrasal verbs** in English:

(i) *Verb + preposition*

e.g. get over; go for; jump at; see about; stand by; turn on.

(ii) *Verb + adverb particle* (an adverb particle is distinguished in use from a preposition because it does not govern a noun phrase):

e.g. answer back; back down; break in; break off; break up; clear out (= go away); drop in; fall in/out/through; give in; live in; make up; pull through; ring off; shut up; turn up.

(iii) *Verb + object + adverb particle* (or *verb + adverb particle + object*)

e.g. *Put* (*V*)   your coat (*dO*)   on (*AP*)/
       Put on (*V + AP*)   your coat (*dO*).
       Take work *on*/*take on* work
       Back the boss *up*/*back up* the boss.

(iv) *Verb + adverb particle + preposition*

e.g. *back out of; be up to; face up to; get on with; go through with; look out for; run out of; stand up for/to.*

5:51

Impersonal Verbs

These verbs have as their subject the pronoun *it*; they are all intransitive (*i.e.* they do not have an object):

(i) e.g. It *is raining* hard today.
           It *depends* on what you mean.

In these sentences the pronoun *it* refers to nothing else in the sentence.
(ii) Compare the use of *it* in (i) with the pronoun in the following sentences:

       It seems *that I shall die.*
       It is hoped *that tomorrow will be better.*

In these sentences the word *it* anticipates the *that-* clause which follows. The *that-* clauses are the complement of the verbs *seems/is hoped.*

5:52

The -ing Participle

The grammatical description of the **-ing participle** depends entirely on its function:

(i) As a **participle** to form a continuous (or progressive tense):

e.g. He was *running* along the road. (Past continuous)

(ii) As a **verbal noun** (although the term *gerund* is also applied to this use):
(a) e.g. I like *running.* (Direct object)
           My hobby is *running.* (Complement)
           Running is very relaxing as a hobby. (Subject)

(b) The *-ing* form as a verbal noun may be preceded by a definite or an indefinite article:

e.g. The *singing* of the choir rang through the church.
      I heard a *ringing* in my ears.

(c) e.g. He was fined for *speeding.* (Object of preposition 'for')

(iii) As a **gerund** (G) (*i.e.* a verbal noun + its own direct object):

e.g. I like *running* (G) <u>races</u> (*dO*). (Direct object of 'like')
<u>*Running* (G) races $\overline{(dO)}$</u> is my favourite hobby. (Subject of 'is')

(iv) As an **attributive adjective**:

e.g. I walked beside the *running* stream. (Adjective limiting 'stream')

(v) As a predicative **adjective**:

e.g. I saw the man *sitting* on the bench. (Adjective limiting 'man')
Running, he became dizzy. (Adjective limiting 'he')

NOTE It is important that the adjective is able to limit the noun or pronoun that occurs immediately after the phrase in which the adjective occurs:

e.g. *Running* down the street, he saw the bus leave. (Correct)

Running down the street, a lamppost came in sight. (Incorrect: such participles are called 'mis-related participles')

(vi) When the *-ing* participle is used as **a noun** with a possessive adjective its meaning should be distinguished from the same participle when it is used as a predicative adjective:

e.g. Compare: A I heard George *singing*.
                 B I heard George's *singing*.

    A suggests that 'I heard George *and* George was singing.'
    B suggests that 'I heard the singing of George rather than the singing of someone else.'

5:53

The -ed Participle (the Past Participle)

The grammatical description of the **-ed participle** depends entirely on its function:

(i) As a **participle** to form a perfect tense:

e.g. The boy has *returned* the book to the library. (Present perfect tense)

(ii) As an **attributive adjective**:

e.g. The *broken* glass lay in the road. (Limits 'glass')
The *battered* parcel had fallen off the lorry. (Limits 'parcel')

(iii) As a **predicative adjective:**

(*a*) *e.g.* The boy, *filled* with grief, broke into tears. (Limits 'boy')

(*b*) *e.g.* Shattered, he gave up. (Limits 'he')

NOTE It is important that the adjective is able to limit the noun or pronoun that occurs immediately after the phrase in which it occurs:

e.g. Overwhelmed with grief, the boy collapsed in tears. (Correct)

Overwhelmed by the enemy, a truce was made. (Incorrect: such particles are called 'misrelated participles')

5:54

The Infinitive

There are two forms of the infinitive in English.

(i) **The infinitive without the marker 'to'** (sometimes called 'the bare infinitive'). This is used:

(*a*) after the modal verbs *will, shall, should, would, can, could, may, might, must, dare, need.*

(*b*) after *had better, had best, had rather,* and so on,

e.g. I'd rather *do* this than that.

(*c*) after certain verbs:
let, make, feel, hear, see, watch, notice.

e.g. He let the butterfly *go*.
I heard him *sing*.
She noticed him *pass* by.

(ii) **The infinitive with the marker 'to'.**
This is used:

(*a*) after most verbs:

e.g. The girl began *to sing*.
The boy wanted *to play* football.

(*b*) to express **purpose**:

e.g. He came *to mend* the tap.
He tried *to shut* the door.
He was *to be* here by nine.

(*c*) to express **consequence**:

e.g. He arrived *to find* the train gone.
He tried to sing only *to find* he had lost his voice.

(*d*) to **modify or limit an adjective**:

e.g. This book is easy *to read*.
He was too tired *to sleep*.

(*e*) to **modify or limit a noun adjectivally**:

e.g. He showed a reluctance *to go*.
He found it a pleasure *to meet* her.
She had a room *to let*.

(*f*) as a **noun**:

e.g. *To sing* is quite difficult. (Subject of *sing*)

He liked *to sing*. (Direct object of *liked*)
My sole aim is *to win*. (Complement of *is*)

(iii) **The infinitive may have the following aspects**:

(a) **simple:**

e.g. He tried *to shout*.

(b) **perfective** (with have):

e.g. I was unhappy *to have seen* her so ill.

(c) **continuous** (progressive):

e.g. I expect *to be travelling* all day.

(d) **passive:**

e.g. I am surprised *to be given* this book. (Present)
I was surprised *to have been given* this book. (Perfect)

Adverbs

5:55

An adverb modifies or limits the meaning of all parts of speech *except* nouns and pronouns.

e.g. **(a)** I *never* go there. (Limits verb 'go')

(b) I am *quite* devastated. (Limits adjective 'devastated')

(c) I turned the corner *very* fast. (Limits adverb 'fast')

(d) I moored the boat *rather* near the yacht. (Limits preposition 'near')

(e) I ate it *rather* because I liked it. (Limits adverbial conjunction 'because')

5:56

An adverb may consist of a single word or a group of words:

e.g. **(a)** She arrived *yesterday*. (Adverb of time)
She left *after the ball was over*. (Adverb of time)
(b) She arrived *there*. (Adverb of place)
She caught the bus *at the traffic lights*. (Adverb of place)
(c) She left *hurriedly*. (Adverb of manner)
She left *as if she were worried*. (Adverb of manner)

5:57

The Formation of Adverbs

(i) Many adverbs are formed from adjectives by the addition of **-ly**:

e.g. *bright/brightly; quick/quickly; frequent/frequently.*

(ii) If the adjective ends in **-c**, **-ally** is normally added to form an adverb:

e.g. frantic/frantically; automatic/automatically.

(iii) Some adverbs have a prefix **a-**:
aboard, anew, aside, and so on.

(iv) The adverb corresponding to the adjective *good* is *well*.

(v) Some adverbs have the same form as their equivalent adjectives:

e.g. daily; deep; early; hard; high; kindly; low.

He worked *hard*. (Adverb)/The work was *hard*. (Adjective)
He arrived *early*. (Adverb)/The *early* train was late. (Adjective)

5:58

The Comparison of Adverbs

Most adverbs are gradable and use the following ways of forming their comparatives (with *two* objects, people, groups or sets) and their superlatives (with *three or more than three* objects, people, groups or sets):

(i) By adding *-er, -est*:

e.g. hard/harder/hardest; low, lower, lowest.

(ii) By using *more* (comparative), *most* (superlative) + *adverb* when the adverb has two or more syllables:

e.g. strangely/more strangely/most strangely
frequently/more frequently/most frequently

(iii) Some form their degrees of comparison irregularly:

> *well/better/best*
> *badly/worse/worst*
> *little/less/least*
> *much/more/most*
> *far/farther* or *farthest* or *further/furthest*

5:59

Adverbs of Manner (*quickly, rashly, badly, well,* and so on)

These could answer the following question: *How?*

e.g. He sang *quietly*. (Single adverb)
He ran *with his arms flailing*. (Adverbial phrase)
He stared *as if he had seen a ghost*. (Adverbial clause)

NOTE They are usually placed after the verb or after the direct object (*dO*) if the verb is transitive:

e.g. He sang <u>the song</u> (*dO*) quietly.
He spoke <u>the language</u> (*dO*) fluently.

Sometimes the force of the adverb can be increased if it is moved from its normal position:

e.g. Compare: He sang the song *quietly.* ⎱
He *quietly* sang the song. ⎰

5:60

Adverbs of Time (*then, now, soon, later, still,* and so on)

These could answer the following questions: *When?* (past, present, future) *Since when? For how long?*

e.g. He arrived *yesterday.* (When?)
He has been here *since yesterday.* (Since when?)
He has been here *for two days.* (For how long?)

NOTE:

(i) They are usually placed at the very beginning or at the very end of the sentence or clause. (See the above examples.)

(ii) If there is also an adverb of manner and/or place present, the adverb of time usually follows it (or them):

e.g. He came there [place] *yesterday.*
He came there [place] unexpectedly [manner] *yesterday.*

(iii) (*a*) *Yet* prefers to come at the very end or the very beginning of sentences:

e.g. *Yet* he continues to do it!
He has not understood it *yet.*

(*b*) *Still* is usually placed before the verb:

e.g. He is *still* working.

NOTE Both *still* and *yet* may express anxiety or irritation over and above their 'time' meaning; this is particularly so if the words are stressed in speech:

e.g. You mean to tell me he is *still* there?
He has not left *yet?*

5:61

Adverbs of Place (*here, there,* and so on)

These could answer the following question: *Where?*

He came *here.* (Where?)
He came *to the college.* (Where?)
He came *where he had promised.* (Where?)

These are usually placed after the verb or after the direct object if the verb is transitive (*cf.* Adverbs of manner, **5:59**, pages 90–1).

e.g. He drove the car *here*.
He drove the car *to the college*.
He drove the car *where it was forbidden*.

If there is an adverb of manner present the adverb of place normally follows it:

e.g. He drove the car quickly *here*.

If the speaker (or writer) wishes to emphasise the adverb of manner, however, the positions may be reversed and the stress altered:

e.g. He drove the car here *quíckly*.

5:62

Adverbs of Frequency (relative time) (e.g. *always, ever, frequently, generally, occasionally, often, never, rarely, seldom, sometimes, usually; just, lately, recently, soon, suddenly*)

Except where a special stress or emphasis on the adverb is required, single-word adverbs of this kind:

(i) are placed after simple tenses of the verb *to be*:

e.g. They are *never* at home.

(ii) are placed before the simple tenses of other verbs:

e.g. They *usually* go out.

(iii) are placed after the first auxiliary verb of other tenses:

e.g. They are *often* visiting friends.
They have *hardly* begun to make friends.

(iv) *used to* and *have to* prefer the adverb to precede them:

e.g. They *never* used to do it.
They *always* have to be the centre of attraction.

(v) *Already, lately, recently*, and *soon* normally come at the end of a clause or sentence:

e.g. We have been here *already*.
I haven't seen you *lately*?
You saw me *recently*.
Can you come back *soon*?

5:63

Adverbs of Degree (*almost, hardly, just, nearly, quite, rather, too, very*, and so on)

(i) Adverbs of degree modify or limit adjectives or other adverbs:

e.g. I am *very* happy. (Adjective)
I ran *too* quickly. (Adverb)

(ii) Some adverbs of degree can modify verbs (e.g. *quite, nearly, just*).

e.g. I *quite* liked him in spite of his appearance.
I *nearly* knocked him off his bicycle.
He *just* smiled and drove on.

(iii) Some adverbs of degree (e.g. *absolutely, at all, badly, deeply, extremely, greatly, highly, particularly, really, seriously, utterly*, and so on) act as intensifiers of the meaning of certain adjectives and adverbs:

e.g. I felt *very* tired.
I was *extremely* sad.
I was *not at all* well.
I became *seriously* upset.

5:64

Interrogative Adverbs (*When? Where? Why? How? Whence? Wherefore?*)

These are sometimes called *wh-question words* by modern grammarians (who include the interrogative adjectives and pronouns *Which? What? Who?* within the *wh-question words* category).

(i) Interrogative adverbs (*a*) ask questions, *and* (*b*) modify (or limit) the meaning of adjectives, other adverbs, or verbs:

e.g. *When* did you arrive?
Where did you go?
Why have you come?
How did you get here?

(ii) (*a*) *How* can sometimes be used with adjectives or adverbs to form questions or exclamations:

e.g. *How* good of you to come at once! (Exclamation)
How sincere was he? (Question: how + adjective)
How fast was he driving? (Question: how + adverb)
How often does he go there? (Question: how + adverb)

(*b*) *How* is often used with *much* or *many* to form questions asking for count or mass (quantity):

e.g. *How much* do you earn?
How many books do you have?

5:65

Relative and Conjunctive (connecting) Adverbs

(i) Special 'adjunct' forms for place, time and cause (*where, when, why*) often replace a preposition + pronoun in relative constructions:

e.g. This is the house *where* (=in which) I live.

This is the moment *when* (= at which) I should leave.
This is the reason *why* (= for which) I came.

NOTE Often the antecedent nouns can be omitted altogether:

e.g. This is *where* I live.
This is *when* I should leave.
This is *why* I came.

(ii) Other conjuncts (sometimes called 'sentence adverbs') introduce a new statement and link it with what has already been said or written:

(*a*) *altogether, beside, consequently, however, moreover, nevertheless, therefore;*
(*b*) *as a result, in any case, on the other hand;*
(*c*) *in conclusion, to conclude;*
(*d*) *that is to say, what is more.*

These conjuncts may, however, come at the end of a sentence after a comma or after the opening phrase:

e.g. He could not help his friend, *nevertheless*.
He could, *however*, not help his friend.

5:66

Only; just, merely, simply

(i) *Only* modifies the meaning of a sentence according to where it is placed:

e.g. *Only* I drove the car yesterday.
I *only* drove the car yesterday.
I drove *only* the car yesterday.
I drove the *only* car yesterday.
I drove the car *only* yesterday.

(ii) *Just, merely, simply* also need care in their placing within a sentence:

e.g. Compare: I *just* drove the car yesterday.
I drove *just* the car yesterday.
I drove the car *just* yesterday.
I *simply* told him the truth.
I told him *simply* the truth.
I told him the truth *simply*.

5:67

Prepositions

(i) Prepositions are used with noun phrases (nouns or noun equivalents, *e.g.* pronouns, gerunds) to show the relationship between the noun phrase and some other word(s).

(ii) Prepositions may be **simple** (single words) or **complex** (more than one word):

(**a**) single words: *e.g. between, by, from, to, under, upon, with;*
(**b**) a combination of two prepositions: *e.g. across to, back to, on to, over to;*
(**c**) a phrase: *e.g. by means of, in accordance with, in connection with.*

5:68

Prepositions showing the relationship (often one of time or place) between a *noun + noun* (or *pronoun*):

> *e.g.* The book *on* the table (Noun + noun)
> The cat *near* the fireside (Noun + noun)
> The minute *after* midnight (Noun + noun)
> The work *for* him (Noun + pronoun)
> The problem *on account of* her (Noun + pronoun)

5:69

Prepositions showing the relationship between an *adjective + noun* (or *pronoun*):

> *e.g.* Good *at* games (Adjective + noun)
> Good *for* him (Adjective + pronoun)

5:70

Prepositions showing the relationship between a *verb + noun* (or *pronoun*):

> *e.g.* He sent the letter *to* the girl. (Verb + noun)
> He sent the present *for* her. (Verb + pronoun)

5:71

Prepositions showing the relationship between an *adverb + noun* (or *pronoun*):

> *e.g.* The car ran well *for* its age. (Adverb + noun)
> The girl worked successfully *on account of* her ability. (Adverb + noun)
> The boy worked hard *for* it. (Adverb + pronoun)

5:72

Some adjectives are associated with specific prepositions:

> *e.g.* amazed *at*; averse *to*; different *from*.

5:73

The prepositions *to* and *for* are often omitted after certain verbs before indirect objects:

> *e.g.* He gave (*to*) the boy a book.
> She bought (*for*) him a present.
> The policeman showed (*to*) the motorist a map.

The verbs which can be followed by indirect objects without *to* or *for* include:

> *bring, give, hand, lend, offer, pay, pass, promise, send, show, sing, take, throw, tell;*
> *build, buy, fetch, find, make, order, reserve;*
> *promise, read, show, sing, write.*

5:74

Distinction between a preposition and an adverb

It is the function (use) of a word or phrase which distinguishes whether it is a preposition or an adverb; a preposition is normally followed by a noun (or noun phrase or equivalent) as its complement (object):

> *e.g.* He ran *along* the street. (Preposition)
> He fell *down* the stairs. (Preposition)
> He ran *along* and then fell *over*. (Adverbs)

5:75

Prepositions are followed by nouns or pronouns in the objective case

> *e.g.* Between *you* and *me.*
> Amongst *us.*

5:76

Position (postponed) of prepositions

A number of circumstances allow the preposition to be separated sometimes from its noun (pronoun) equivalent:

(i) Questions beginning with a 'wh-' word:

> *e.g.* Which bus did you go *by*?

(ii) Relative constructions:

> *e.g.* The boy, whom I am talking *about*, is a rogue.
> The story, which I told you *of*, is exciting.

(iii) Exclamations:

> *e.g.* Whatever are you talking about!

It is sometimes preferred not to use a preposition to end a sentence. In many cases, however, it would be stilted to avoid doing so.

Compare: Whatever are you talking about? *and*
          About whatever are you talking?

The second of the two sentences is non-English.

Conjunctions
5:77

Conjunctions join words, phrases or clauses.

> *e.g.* The boy *and* the girl went to school.
> The man sitting at the window *and* reading a book is out of work.
> The man who is out of work *but* is never idle will succeed later in life.

(i) **Co-ordinating conjunctions** join words, phrases, or clauses of equal value (as in the examples given above). Such conjunctions are: *and, but, or, either ... or, neither ... nor.*

NOTE When clauses are linked by co-ordinating conjunctions they form **double** (two clauses) or **compound or multiple sentences** (more than two clauses).

(ii) **Subordinating conjunctions** join phrases, or clauses one of which is subordinate (or of less value) than the other or is dependent on the other. Such conjunctions include: *as, when, that, while, although, if, since, unless, because, before; in that, so that, in order that; provided (that), considering (that), seeing (that).*

NOTE When clauses are joined by subordinating conjunctions they form **complex sentences**.

> *e.g.* They went to the cinema *although* they had little money.
> They wondered *if* he would join them.

5:78

Clauses introduced by subordinating conjunctions may be:

(i) *Adverbial:*

> *e.g.* He left *before* I arrived. (Time)
> He went *where* I could not follow him. (Place)
> He left *although* he was expecting me. (Concession)
> He wanted to leave *if* he could. (Condition)
> He would stay *unless* he was called away. (Negative condition)
> He left *because* he was angry. (Reason)
> He studied hard *so that* he passed. (Result)
> He left *so that* he could avoid me. (Purpose)
> He limped *as though* he had hurt his foot. (Manner)

(ii) *Noun:*

> *e.g.* I was certain *that* he had died.

> (NOTE that the conjunction *that* can sometimes be omitted.)

(iii) *Adjectival:*

> *e.g.* This is the house *where* I was born.
> This is the moment *when* I must leave.

NOTE *How, when, where, why* are sometimes called relative adverbs; *who, which, that* are sometimes called relative pronouns.

Nevertheless, *they can function as conjunctions* to join clauses.

Interjections
5:79

These are single words or whole statements used to express alarm, amusement, annoyance, approval, disgust, joy, pain, sorrow, surprise, warning, and so on.

They are used to express strong emotion or to attract attention and may be accompanied by exclamation marks or question marks:*

e.g. Oh! Oh? Phew! Ugh! My! Well I never! Good gracious!

The sentence

5:80

Consider the following carefully:

(i) Books yesterday him gave Mary two.
(ii) Yesterday Mary gave books two him.
(iii) Yesterday Mary gave him two books.
(iv) Mary gave him two books yesterday.

All four collections of words contain exactly the same items but they are organised differently in each. In (i) there is no organisation which makes sense to a native speaker or writer; it is not a sentence and communicates little. In (ii) there is a greater degree of organisation; it starts well with an adverb (adjunct) + subject noun + verb + object noun; had the word 'two' been spelt 'to', this collection of words would have been an English sentence. In (iii) the words communicate easily a meaning which is complete in itself; it differs little from (iv) except that the placing of the word 'yesterday' at the beginning or at the end alters its emphasis a little; the stress and intonation patterns within (iii) and (iv) would allow a speaker (but not a writer) to emphasise any single word or any words; both (iii) and (iv) are good English sentences.

5:81

A sentence may contain up to five kinds of elements within it:

(i) Subject (*S*)
(ii) Verb (*V*)

---

* The stress and intonation pattern will normally make it clear whether the interjection is being used as an exclamation or as a straight question.
e.g. You did? You did!

(iii) Complement (*C*) (see **5:46** (iv), page 79 for Complements used with copulas)

(iv) Object and/or Indirect Object (*dO*)/(*iO*)

(v) Adverb (*A*)

> *e.g.* Mary (*S*) came (*V*).
> Mary (*S*) came (*V*) yesterday (*A*).
> Mary (*S*) was (*V*) angry (*C*) yesterday (*A*).
> Mary (*S*) gave (*V*) him (*iO*) some books (*dO*) yesterday (*A*).

5:82

Each of the five elements may consist of a few words or a more complex structure within itself:

> *e.g.* *His sister, Mary* (*S*), *had given* (*V*) the boy (*iO*) [whom (*dO*) she (*S*) had met (*V*) the day before (*A*)] *some books* (*dO*) [when (*A*) she (*S*) went (*V*) to the pictures (*A*) with him (*A*)].

It is clear from this example that an element might contain within itself another sub-element or clause with its own subject, verb, adverb, and so on; such sub-elements are termed 'subordinate' and if a subordinate element contains its own finite verb it is termed a **subordinate clause**.

5:83

(i) A **simple sentence** consists of a *subject + a predicate* (*i.e.* what is said or written to add to the sense of the subject). A simple sentence contains only one finite clause:

> *e.g.*   SUBJECT   PREDICATE
>   Mary   came yesterday.

Such simple sentences may be statements, as in the above example, or questions, or commands (imperatives); in commands (imperatives) the subject is not expressly stated but is understood:

> *e.g.*   SUBJECT   PREDICATE
>   Has   Mary   given him the books? (Question)
>
>   (You)   Give him the books. (Command/Imperative)

(ii) If the sentence contains two or more finite clauses each of which may stand independently of the others, the sentence is termed a **double sentence** (for two clauses) or a **multiple sentence** (for three or more clauses):

> *e.g.* Mary gave him the books (1) *and* he was pleased (2). (Double sentence)

NOTE Such double or multiple sentences are joined by co-ordinating conjunctions such as *and, but, or, either ... or, neither ... nor.*

Mary gave him the books (1), (she) helped him to pack them (2), *and* (she) walked with him to the gate (3). (Multiple sentence)

(iii) If the sentence contains two or more clauses, one of which is dependent on (or subordinate to) another word or group of words outside itself, the sentence *is* termed a **complex sentence:**

e.g. Mary gave him the books (1) when she saw him (2).

Here 'Mary (*S*) gave (*V*) him (*iO*) the books (*dO*)' is a clause which can stand independently and make sense on its own, but 'when (*A*) she (*S*) saw (*V*) him (*dO*)' is a clause which is subordinate and depends on the verb it limits in the main clause (*gave*) for its existence. 'When she saw him' is therefore a subordinate clause, and since it contains a subordinate clause the whole sentence is a complex sentence.

It should be remembered that a sentence will make a complete statement on its own, although some of its elements may be omitted or have to be understood from its immediate context:

e.g. 'Mary gave him the books.'
'Good.' (*i.e.* 'It is good that she has given him the books.')
'How many?' (*i.e.* 'How many books has she given him?')

The elements in the sentence

The Subject

5:84

(i) The subject of the verb is usually a **noun phrase** (NP). A noun phrase may consist of any one of the following:

(*a*) a single noun:

e.g. *Mary* (*S*) gave him the books.

(*b*) a noun (or nominal) group:

e.g. *My sister* (*S*) gave him the books.
The girls in my class (*S*) gave him the books.

NOTE In such nominal groups the main noun is termed 'the head' or 'the head word'.

(*c*) a pronoun (see **5:8–5:19**, pages 48–61)

e.g. *She* (*S*) gave John the books yesterday.

(*d*) a pronominal group:

e.g. *None of the girls* (*S*) asked for a present in return.

NOTE   In such pronominal groups the main pronoun is termed 'the head' or 'the head word'.

(ii) A noun clause may also be the subject of a main sentence:

e.g. What caused the accident (*S*) remained a mystery.

A useful test here to determine the function of the noun clause is to replace it temporarily with the pronoun 'it'.

e.g. '*It* (*S*) remained a mystery.'

The Verb

5:85

(For a full discussion of the English verb see above **5:38–5:54**, pages 70–89.)

(i) The finite verb is the central element in a clause; for a clause to be a clause it must contain a finite verb (*i.e.* one with its own subject, or with its own subject clearly understood—as with imperatives: see **5:40** (i) (*a*), page 71).

(ii) The verb may consist of a single word or of auxiliaries or modals + main verb in order to form tenses or moods or passives:

e.g. Mary (*S*) *gave* him the books.
Mary (*S*) *has given* him the books.
Mary (*S*) *may give* him the books.
Mary (*S*) *might have given* him the books.
He (*S*) *might have been given* the books by Mary. (Passive)

(iii) It should be remembered that other elements in a sentence may consist of a subordinate clause; when they do so, the subordinate clause will contain its own finite verb:

| | *Subject* | *Verb* | *Complement* |
e.g. What caused (*V*) the accident was a mystery.

5:86

Complement

Complements of verbs are of two kinds: **subjective** and **objective**.

(i) Subjective complements
These are used to complete (or 'complement') a verb (such as *be*, *become, seem, appear, grow* and *turn* (when they mean (become'), *feel* (see **5:46** (iv), page 79 for a discussion of verbs which take complements); and to refer back to the subject of the verb:

e.g. Mary (*S*) is (*V*) *my sister.* (Subjective complement, s*C*)
She (*S*) became (*V*) *very angry* (s*C*).
When awarded the prize (*A*), she (*S*) felt (*V*) *a princess* (s*C*).

(ii) Objective complements

These are used to complete (or 'complement') a verb (such as *make, elect, appoint*) and to refer back to the object of the verb:

e.g. The Board (*S*) made (*V*) him (*dO*) *chairman*. (Objective complement, *oC*)

The constituency (*S*) has elected (*V*) her (*dO*) *their member of parliament* (*oC*).

The decision (*S*) made (*V*) him (*dO*) *angry* (*oC*).

(iii) From the above examples it will be seen that complements, both *subjective* and *objective* may be adjectives, adjective groups, nouns, or noun phrases (each containing its own 'head' word).

5:87

Objects

Objects of verbs are of two kinds: **direct** and **indirect**.

(i) Direct Objects

These are used with transitive verbs (see **5:46**, pages 78–9) or more accurately, verbs used transitively:

e.g. Mary (*S*) bought (*V*) *the books* (*dO*) yesterday (*A*).

Mary (*S*) saw (*V*) him (*dO*) yesterday (*A*).

(ii) Indirect objects

These are noun phrases or pronominal phrases which could be re-phrased with the propositions 'to' or 'for' in front of them. The indirect object always precedes the direct object:

e.g. Mary (*S*) bought (*V*) *him* (*iO*) the books (*dO*) yesterday (*A*).

NOTE This might have been rephrased: 'Mary bought the books for him yesterday.'

Mary (*S*) sent (*V*) *the boy* (*iO*) a letter (*dO*) yesterday (*A*).

NOTE This might have been rephrased: 'Mary sent a letter to the boy yesterday.'

When the prepositions *to* or *for* are used in such situations the prepositional phrases (*for him, to the boy*) are not indirect objects but are adverbial in their function.

Adverbs

5:88

For a full discussion of adverbs, see **5:55–5:66**, pages 89–94.

(i) Many adverbs (adverbial phrases, adverbial clauses) are adjuncts:

i.e. they add information to a sentence, are part of its structure, but are not essential to it:

e.g. She (*S*) gave (*V*) him (*iO*) the books (*dO*) *yesterday* (*A*).
  She   gave   him   the books   *when she met him* (*A*).
  She   gave   him   the books   *in the street* (*A*).
  She   gave   him   the books   *with a kiss* (*A*).

In all these examples the adverb adds information to indicate the time, the manner, the place, when the giving of the books was carried out. All the adverbs might have been omitted without damage to the structure (but not to the sense) of the rest of the sentence: *e.g.* 'She gave him the books' is structurally a sound English sentence without an adverb in a way that the sentence would not be structurally sound without its subject, verb, or direct object. (NOTE It might be just possible to omit the indirect object, too, without serious structural damage.)

(ii) Adverbs may come at the beginning, in the middle, or at the end of a sentence.

(*a*) An adverb is placed *at the beginning* to emphasise the place, time, manner or frequency of an occurrence:

e.g. *Yesterday* (*A*) she gave him the books.

(*b*) If it is used *in the middle of a sentence* an adverb is not normally placed between a verb and its object:

e.g. She *deliberately* (*A*) gave him the books.
(rather than 'She gave him deliberately the books' or 'She gave deliberately him the books').

NOTE Some single-word adverbs denoting frequency prefer a medial position, however: *e.g. always, never, often, sometimes.*

(*c*) The usual place for an adverb is at the end of a sentence:

e.g. She gave him the books *yesterday* (*A*).

Types of Finite Clause Structure
5:89

There are five basic structures of a finite clause in English:

(i) SUBJECT PREDICATE
  Noun phrase, *NP* + **intransitive verb**, *iV* (+**adverb**, *A*)

e.g. The boy (*NP*) | telephoned (*iV*) (yesterday) (*A*).
  The girl (*NP*) | went (*iV*) there (*A*).
  She (*NP*) | ran (*iV*) (along the street) (*A*).

(ii) SUBJECT PREDICATE
  Noun phrase, *NP* + *to be* (**or copula**) +**complement**, *C*

e.g. The clever woman (*NP*) | was (TO BE) a teacher (*C*).
  They (*NP*) | became ill (*C*).
  He (*NP*) | seemed down in the dumps (*C*).

NOTE The complement, *C*, may be a noun phrase (*a teacher*), or an adjective (*ill*), or an adverb (*down in the dumps*).

(iii)   SUBJECT   PREDICATE
Noun phrase, *NP* + **transitive verb**, *tV* + **direct object**, *dO*
(+ adverb, *A*)

e.g. Mary (*NP*) | saw (*tV*)   him (*dO*)   (yesterday) (*A*).
He (*NP*) | wrote (*tV*) the book (*dO*)   (when he
                                                         could) (*A*).
I (*NP*) | hit (*tV*)   the nail (*dO*)   on the head (*A*).

(iv)   SUBJECT   PREDICATE
Noun phrase, *NP* + **transitive verb**, *tV* + **indirect object**, *iO*
+ direct object, *dO* (+ adverb, *A*)

e.g. Mary (*NP*) | gave (*tV*) him (*iO*)   the books (yesterday) (*A*).
                                                 (*dO*)
The car- | made (*tV*) the custo-   a table   (last week) (*A*).
penter (*NP*)   mer (*iO*)   (*dO*)

(v)   SUBJECT   PREDICATE
Noun phrase, *NP* + **transitive verb**, *tV* + **direct object**, *dO*
+ complement, *oC*

e.g. The headmaster (*NP*) | made (*tV*)   him (*dO*)   a prefect
                                                               (*oC*).
The Board (*NP*) | elected (*tV*) her (*dO*)   managing
                                                               director
                                                               (*oC*).
The meal (*NP*) | made (*tV*)   the guest   ill (*oC*).
                                              (*dO*)

NOTE The objective complement, *oC*, may be either a noun phrase (*a prefect, managing director*) or an adjective (*ill*).

5:90

These five types of finite clause structure may be expanded. Many of the examples given in the section above (**5:89**) used single words as the elements in the clause but quite often the elements might consist of word-groups and even clauses in their own right or noun phrases qualified by clauses.

e.g. Take the following sentence of type (i) above:
(*NP*) + (*iV*) (+*A*):

          SUBJECT   PREDICATE
The boy (who was) in my class (*NP*) telephoned (*iV*) while I was in the bath (*A*).

Here '(who was) in my class' is an adjectival clause limiting the noun *boy* and the adverbial clause 'while I was in the bath' limits the intransitive verb *telephoned* and indicates time.
We have, therefore, clauses within clauses in such **complex sentences**.

5:91

Structures and Punctuation

It is essential that sentences are properly structured if sense is to be communicated easily and readily. The beginnings of sentences must be indicated in written English by capital letters when they open a paragraph or when they follow a preceding full stop, exclamation mark or question mark; the ends of sentences, however simple or complex they may be, must be indicated by full stops, exclamation marks, question marks, or semicolons. If such divisions into sentences are not indicated by the writer, the reader careers wildly on until he discovers he has lost the sense and then he has to return with growing irritation to retrace the sentence-structures for himself in order to understand the meaning.

> *e.g.* Consider the following:

> He was driving along the street walking along the pavement came a mother and child not seeing the bend when a lamppost appeared suddenly in front of him he braked skidded and ran the pedestrians down the shop windows which collapsed in showers of glass burst on impact with so much damage the scene resembled a battlefield.

Then consider the same paragraph with the structures clearly indicated by conventional punctuation:

> He was driving along the street. Walking along the pavement came a mother and child. Not seeing the bend, when a lamppost appeared suddenly in front of him, he braked, skidded, and ran the pedestrians down. The shop windows, which collapsed in showers of glass, burst on impact. With so much damage the scene resembled a battlefield.

Carelessness in structuring sentences and not indicating their structures by accurate, if conventional, punctuation, constitutes the single greatest source of candidates' failure in examinations such as GCE, CSE, and 16 + .

Questions

5:92

(i) Questions are normally marked in English by a rising intonation pattern (indicated by ⟋ in the following examples). Even sentences which appear as statements may become questions if they carry this rising intonation pattern at the end in speech or by the addition of question marks (which indicate a rising intonation pattern) in written English.

e.g. 'How many books were there?' (Direct question)

'There were ten.' (Statement with falling intonation [⟍])

'There were ten?' (Question with rising intonation)

'There were not twelve?' (Question with rising intonation)

A question, therefore, may be formed by giving a rising intonation pattern to an affirmative statement or to a negative statement.

(ii) A marked feature of question-construction in English is the use of 'tags'; questions so-formed are termed **tag-questions**. These are used most frequently in conversation:

e.g. 'He did it, *didn't he?*'

(**a**) an affirmative statement is followed by a negative tag:

(**b**) a negative statement is followed by a positive tag:

e.g. 'He never did it, *did he?*'

The tag normally has a falling intonation pattern and is used to express doubt, incredulity, sarcasm, disbelief, emphasis or even casualness about the inquiry. It is a useful means of indicating the attitude of the speaker or writer.

(iii) Many questions are introduced by words which are termed 'wh-question words': *who, whom, which, where, when, what; how* and *how many* are also included in this category. *Who, whom* are used only as pronouns; *how* is used only as an adverb; the rest may be used either as pronoun or as adjectives modifying or limiting nouns.

(iv) An affirmative statement can often be most simply made into a question by inverting the order of the verb (or its auxiliary or modal part) and the subject.

e.g. 'Mary was pleased with the present.'
'Was Mary pleased with the present?'

'He could do it.'
'Could he do it?'

(v) A negative statement can often be most simply made into a question by inverting the order of the verb + the negative (usually reduced to *n't* in speech) and the subject.

e.g. 'He could not do it.'
'Couldn't he do it?'

Sometimes, for a more emphatic negative question, the negative *not* can be retained where it is and the verb and subject can be inverted.

e.g. Compare: 'Couldn't he do it?'
'Could he not do it?'

(vi) Both negative and affirmative statements can be turned into questions by the addition of an emphatic affirmative word (*e.g. surely, really, positively*).

e.g. 'He could do it.'
'He could do it, surely?'

'He could not do it.'
'He could not do it, surely?'

(vii) the use of *dO + an infinitive* is used in affirmative and negative questions to replace simple tenses in affirmative statements.

e.g. 'He *writes* to me.'
'*Does* he *write* to you?'

'He never *sees* me now.'
'*Does* he never *see* you now?'

Stress and Intonation within English Sentences
5:93

(i) **Stress** is used to indicate the part of a construction which is more prominent than another.

(ii) **Intonation** is used to indicate the way the pitch of a sentence rises or falls in tone.

Both stress and intonation are important in spoken forms of the language where they combine with **rhythm** (a pattern of prominent and less prominent parts of a sentence determined partly by stress and intonation) and **pace** or **tempo** (the speed, slow or fast) with which an utterance is made.

Punctuation marks in written English help to indicate some of these elements corresponding to those in the spoken language. The question mark, for example, often indicates the rise of an intonation pattern (see **5:92** (i), pages 105-6); the exclamation mark may help to indicate the stress needed on particular parts of an emphatic statement: *e.g. Come /here*! (NOTE that the sign [/] indicates that the stress falls on the syllable immediately following it.) But the exclamation mark does nothing to distinguish *How /could you do it!* from */How could you do it!* or *How could /you do it!* or *How could you /do it!*

Punctuation marks are largely inadequate for indicating fully and accurately the intonation, stress, rhythm and tempo of the English sentence. They are, however, sometimes useful in indicating short pauses (commas), longer pauses (colons, semicolons), and stops (full stops, exclamation marks, question marks) and can indicate stress and intonation in questions and exclamations.

EXERCISES

23   Make a list of all the *nouns* in the following sentences and categorize them according to the traditional classification of nouns.

1 Sandra bought sun-lotion, a new bikini, and an air-bed for her holiday on the Costa Brava; her dream was now coming true.
2 Truth in politics is not always an easy path to follow, as many politicians have discovered.
3 A church is made not only of bricks and mortar but of people and ideals.
4 The herd of cows walked straight through the living-room, shattering the furniture and the peace of the afternoon.
5 What did you think of the disco and its flashing lights, beautiful people, sweat, din, and chaos?

24
1 Make a list of ten *collective nouns* not given in Chapter Five as examples. Use them in sentences of your own to show their meaning.
2 Invent a list of possible collective nouns (*e.g.* a *confusion* of generals; an *agony* of doctors, etc.) for groups of the following:

girl- (or boy-) friends; teachers; radio-presenters; pop-groups; anarchists; policemen; Siamese cats; tortoises; fleas; examinations.

25   Form *abstract nouns* (*e.g.* hero: *heroism*) from the following words:

1 war; pacifist; traitor; woman; child.
2 able; light; safe; fierce; true; strong; quiet; vain; anxious; loyal.
3 collide; solve; depart; employ; occur; determine; judge; deliver; refuse; arrange.

26   Write two sentences using each of the following *compound-nouns*; in the first bring out the sense of the word if the first element of the compound is stressed; in the second bring out the sense of the word if the second element is stressed:

1 a gold watch;   **2** mountain roads;   **3** a danger signal;
4 a police station;   **5** a bus driver.

27   Supply an appropriate *personal, possessive,* or *demonstrative pronoun* to re-place each of the dashes in the following sentences:

1 When my husband saw the car —— knew —— was —— by the colour and the registration number.
2 —— may remember seeing —— when —— came to visit —— last year. Your Rover was most impressive and reminded —— of John's. —— was newer, of course, but —— was the same model.

3 Do —— recall that visit? —— were the days! —— were certainly times to remember.
4 What happened to Isabelle? —— was there that day, also paying —— a visit. Her dress was a bright yellow and —— had brown suede shoes. —— were the latest fashion then.
5 —— weren't so bad; —— had very high heels, —— remember. —— was amazing how —— could walk in ——.

28 Supply an appropriate *emphatic, reflexive, reciprocal,* or *interrogative pronoun* to replace each of the dashes in the following sentences.

1 I found —— in a frightening situation. I wasn't worried just for ——; my sister was too young to realise the danger.
2 We gave —— —— anxious glances and they —— spoke volumes.
3 —— was there? There was a car parked outside but —— was it?
4 There was a strange old man sitting in the front seat; we looked at —— —— and in his face there was a flutter of recognition ——.
5 —— were we to do? We considered the situation —— to be very strange.

29 Supply an appropriate *indefinite, distributive, numerical,* or *quantifying pronoun* to replace each of the dashes in the following sentences; (try not to use the same word(s) twice):

1 There was —— to be seen; —— had disappeared as mysteriously as it had come. —— might have thought that ghosts were responsible.
2 Of course, —— do believe in such things. —— is possible at night when noises and lights seem to be magnified a thousandfold. —— —— seem to rise from the skirting boards and —— —— flash and vanish for ever.
3 Such incidents used to be common; —— occur now, although —— are still reported from time to time.
4 Reports flow in but —— has ever been verified. —— of the problem lies in the fact that eerie incidents happen to individuals, never to groups of people.
5 —— can say he or she has seen a ghost; it's another matter proving it to agnostics —— as me.

30 Supply an appropriate *relative pronoun* to replace each of the dashes in the following sentences. (If more than one is possible, give both; if the relative can also be omitted without damaging the sense indicate the fact by using a X at the appropriate point.)

1 This is the book —— I bought in the bookshop on the corner.
2 There are not many science-fiction books —— are worth reading.
3 Is that the book —— you phoned me about the other night?
4 It's the one —— plot I gave you over the phone, do you remember?
5 Those —— write such books don't deserve the success or the money —— they get.
6 It's by the same writer —— produced *Invasion by Aliens,* —— I lent you last year.

7 All I can remember about that was the girl —— make-up never seemed to smudge whatever she did.

8 You're one of those people for —— an author can never do enough.

9 I merely want a story —— I can believe in.

10 That, at least, is something about —— we can both agree.

31 *Relative clauses* function adjectivally; replace each of the relative clauses in the following sentences by an adjectival phrase (which may be a single-word adjective):

1 The boy who succeeded was awarded a scholarship.

2 It should be easy to find the person who is involved.

3 The book which was on the table was very old.

4 The moment which was not convenient was the one, of course, that he chose to call.

5 I found a solution which was far more elegant for the mathematical problem.

6 The car which won was a Lotus.

7 The philosopher, who was very distinguished in his own field, nevertheless glanced about him distractedly.

8 He came out with a remark which was really devastating.

9 The noise that throbbed from the disco annoyed all the neighbours.

10 Even the cat, who was very old, took cover under the table.

32 Form single-word *adjectives* from the following words by adding a suitable suffix; then use the adjective you have formed in a sentence to show that you understand its meaning:

1 attract;   **2** circle;   **3** culture;   **4** danger;
5 dust;   **6** friend;   **7** hero;   **8** read;
9 use;   **10** wool.

33 Add a prefix to the following adjectives to produce *adjectives* of opposite or negative meanings; then use the newly-formed adjectives in sentences to show that you understand their meanings:

1 believing;   **2** disciplined;   **3** lawful;   **4** legible;
5 limitable;   **6** lucky;   **7** moral;   **8** perceptible;
9 plausible;   **10** responsible.

34 Give the comparative and superlative forms of the following adjectives:

1 bad;   **2** clever;   **3** far;   **4** funny;
5 good;   **6** little;   **7** real;   **8** regular;
9 reluctant;   **10** wonderful.

35 Indicate which of the italicised words in the following sentences are *adjectives* and which are *adverbs*; give explanations for your decisions:

1 The potter fashioned the vase *carefully* in his workshop.

2 Snow made conditions very *difficult* last Wednesday.
3 *The carpenter made the table *outside*.
4 The driver drove the car *fast* round the corner.
5 The farmer drove the herd *home* to the farm.
6 *The doctor saw the man *better*.
7 *She left the ward *sad* after her experience.
8 She left the ward *early* which was unusual.
9 He polished the car *hard* until he was exhausted.
10 The polish made the paint *hard*.

(*Establish the possible meanings of these sentences carefully.)

36 Supply an appropriate *adjective* to replace each of the dashes in the following sentences; state the kind of adjective you have used:

1 —— book have you selected from —— library?
2 I thought I could choose —— book ——.
3 There are —— books much more interesting than —— book.
4 Never mind. —— books do you like reading from —— collection?
5 Science fiction. —— stories really grip me with —— fantasy.
6 There are —— romances than science fiction books on —— shelves.
7 —— time I come to the library there are —— new novels.
8 There were —— books alone on romance but a —— number of do-it-yourself books.
9 —— sort of writing have you done yourself? Do you write from —— own experience?
10 Hardly ever. —— own experience is not interesting enough to captivate the average reader.

37 Rephrase the following sentences with the verbs in *progressive (continuous) tenses*:

1 The boy ran along the pavement from the shop.
2 He carried a parcel and limped badly.
3 It was clear that he had stolen the goods from the paper shop.
4 Some police sniffer dogs tracked his course along the pavement.
5 They tried to pick up the thief's trail.
6 Snorting, one dog leapt from one side of the pavement to the other.
7 Minutes later they streaked off in the right direction.
8 The boy turned continually to look over his shoulder.
9 The dogs bounded along, confident of catching their quarry.
10 The boy had paid dearly for his crime ever since—in prison.

38 Rephrase the following sentences with the verbs in the appropriate *perfect tenses*:

1 He listens to the radio every night.
2 He even sang the songs as they came over the air.
3 I cannot understand why he does it.
4 He once offered to explain his strange behaviour to me, but long ago.

5 I never heard of such strange behaviour before.
6 I sleep through most of the programmes he mentioned.
7 It is hard to show any interest.
8 The reception is so poor in that area.
9 I find the right waveband only on the rare occasion.
10 The set slipped off the signal last time I found it.

39 Rephrase the following sentences by putting the verbs into the *passive*:

1 I cooked the dinner today.
2 I burnt the potatoes and the cat ate the meat.
3 My husband came in and turned the gas off.
4 We ate what was left with little enthusiasm.
5 I shall cook the next meal myself without listening to any advice.
6 Too many cooks spoil the broth.
7 He helps me more by reading the newspaper in the armchair.
8 Nevertheless, he is still adorable, although he annoys me.
9 He repairs the car well and saves us some money that way.
10 He painted the car bright mauve the other day, to the amusement of the neighbours.

40 Supply an appropriate *modal verb* to replace each of the dashes in the following sentences; (try not to use the same word twice):

1 I —— do it and nobody is going to stop me.
2 He told me, 'You —— do it whether you like it or not.'
3 I —— do it, but I am not sure how well.
4 I —— change my mind, if it proves too hard.
5 He —— say something like that just to worry you.
6 I —— have known better than to believe him.
7 How —— he suggest such a thing!
8 He —— have told me what he was going to do.
9 He —— be stopped before he does something serious.
10 He certainly —— to be stopped or he will find himself in prison.

41 Indicate whether the main verbs in the following sentences are *transitive* or *intransitive*; state the direct objects in full of the transitive verbs:

1 Did you see the dog on the corner?
2 I could hardly miss him, a dog that size!
3 What was he doing?
4 Oh, he was just bounding about on the pavement.
5 Didn't the passers-by object?
6 Of course, but they quickly got out of his way.
7 Surely, the police should have controlled it.
8 They came at great speed, blue lights flashing, once someone called them.
9 The dog just walked away when they arrived.
10 The police hardly knew what to do.

42 Indicate which verbs are *copulas* and what are their complements in the following sentences:

1 He was green with envy when he saw the new car.
2 She became angry with him when she understood why.
3 The latest stereo in the car seemed far too expensive and they would not be able to afford one.
4 It certainly sounded powerful and shook the whole vehicle when it was switched on.
5 'How can you make such a noise and be so objectionable?' she screamed at him.
6 He remained unconcerned and turned up the volume to drown her protests.
7 'You are impossible!' the girl screamed inaudibly and stormed away.
8 He barely noticed her departure and looked calm.
9 He grew more and more interested and changed the station again and again.
10 Some men are absolute beasts!

43 Give the simple *past tenses* and *past participles* of the following verbs:

1 begin;	2 buy;	3 cast;	4 do;
5 dream;	6 hurt;	7 lay;	8 lie;
9 shut;	10 smell.		

44 Rewrite the following sentences, correcting any mistakes in the forms of the verb as you do so; explain why you have made any alterations:

1 I will be the first to defend Isabelle if she is attacked.
2 The number of students who can tackle advanced academic work are small.
3 Those who were skilled with their hands have been seriously under-rated.
4 Typing up notes, the attention of some secretaries falters.
5 I don't see why they should lay down and take any more insults.
6 Why should they attack me writing up notes because of my handwriting?
7 Isabelle left the examination room as if she was worried.
8 She is one of those people who takes it to heart.
9 I would help her if she lets me.
10 In the list of errors there was a misrelated participle and a faulty use of tenses.

45 Indicate (*a*) the *tense*, (*b*) the *voice*, and (*c*) the *mood* of all the verbs in the following sentences:

1 If I were you, I should not do that.
2 Shut up! There is no danger to it.
3 You'll see. Wait until the thing goes off.
4 First, join this wire to the blue one. And then, let me see.
5 I once knew someone who tried that. They scraped him off the ceiling.
6 And then the blue wire may go into that socket.

7 I've had enough. I'm going to get help.
8 You'll make me really nervous, if you keep on.
9 Try the blue wire in the red socket.
10 Who's doing this? You or me?

46 Indicate the *adverbial clauses* in the following sentences and state whether each expresses (*a*) *reason* or *cause*, or (*b*) *purpose*, or (*c*) *result*:

1 He went there so that he could see her.
2 He was so disappointed to find her out that he left in despair.
3 She had left earlier because she had a date.
4 She left a message, however, so that he would understand.
5 This enraged him so much that he swore vengeance.
6 He immediately phoned Isabelle so that he could make a date, too.
7 There was no answer, since she was in the bath.
8 He was not to know that and he decided to call on her personally so that he could ask her out.
9 She was not pleased because the constant ringing of the door-bell got her out of the bath.
10 She was so annoyed that she slammed the door in his face.

47 Indicate the *adverbial clauses* in the following sentences and state whether each expresses (*a*) *time*, or (*b*) *place*, or (*c*) *condition*, or (*d*) *concession*, or (*e*) *circumstance*, or (*f*) *manner*:

1 He came as soon as he could in response to the call.
2 As he approached the house, the church clock struck ten.
3 He pulled out his watch, although he could not see much in the dark.
4 If he had stopped to think, he would have known there was danger.
5 As he was on his own, he had a set procedure to follow.
6 Unless he was disturbed, he would soon effect an entry.
7 He stumbled where a log lay across his path.
8 As he stumbled, he noticed a light come on in the house.
9 It was strange, as if he were in a dream.
10 He pulled himself together, when he realised his predicament.

48 Give the *adverbs* corresponding to the following adjectival forms:

1 busy;	2 cool;	3 friendly;	4 good;
5 happy;	6 public;	7 quick;	8 scientific;
9 strange;	10 wrong.		

49 Use the adverbs you formed in Exercise 48 in accurate sentences to show that you understand their use.

50
1 Give five *adverbs* formed by the addition of *-ward(s)* to a noun or other adverb; (*e.g.* back/*backwards*).
2 Give five *adverbs* formed by the addition of *-wise* to nouns; (*e.g.* crab/*crabwise*).

3 Use all ten *adverbs* you have found in correct sentences to illustrate their use and meaning.

51   Rephrase the following sentences in order to use an *adverb* or *adverbial phrase* instead of the adjective italicised:

1 The way he talked was very *strange* last night.
2 The evidence suggested that Isabelle was *quicker* at finding the solutions than Jane.
3 The story she told had a *great* effect on me.
4 Isabelle was a *loving* girl in the way she helped everyone.
5 She was *perceptive* in seeing through his lies.
6 The rise of the water was so *gradual* that nobody noticed it until it was too late.
7 Isabelle had a very *clear* understanding of her situation.
8 The pianist showed a very *sensitive* control over the sonata he was playing.
9 He was less *confident* in his approach to the final piece of music in the concert.
10 He was the *best* player in the whole orchestra.

52   Indicate the *adverbs* in the following sentences; describe them and their functions as fully as you can:

1 He drove the car very dangerously.
2 She was already reluctant to admit her guilt.
3 He saw her in the middle of the High Street.
4 'Where can you meet me?' she asked him.
5 The ghost moved uneasily in a swirl of mist.
6 He seemed somewhat tired and was glad to stop working.
7 She had read the same book the week before.
8 He would never admit that he had done it.
9 The spendthrift was hopelessly irresponsible.
10 He had just arrived and seemed flustered.

53   Which are the *prepositions* in the following sentences? State, too, the noun phrase and the other words related to it by the preposition:

1 The man fell down the stairs.
2 There is a green hill far away without a city wall.
3 There was not much love lost between us.
4 What train did you go by?
5 You can have all these but the one you wanted.
6 He paid no attention to her question.
7 She had to answer for her crime.
8 There was nobody there except me.
9 These tomatoes cost fifty pence per pound.
10 From which direction did you come?

54 Write sentences to show that you can distinguish the meanings and uses of the following pairs of phrases. (NOTE that some of these phrases can be used in more than one way.)

   1 to call off / to call on;
   2 to look at / to look for;
   3 to live for / to live on;
   4 to put out / to put off;
   5 to run across / to run along;
   6 to take in / to take to;
   7 to give in / to give out;
   8 to get away with / to get away for;
   9 to walk out on / to walk out with;
10 to break in for / to break in on.

55 Use the following fixed *prepositional phrases* in sentences of your own to show that you understand their meanings and use within contexts:

1 at heart;	**2** by accident;	**3** by rights;
4 in general;	**5** in love;	**6** on business;
7 on sale;	**8** under control;	**9** within sight;
10 out of place.		

56 Use the verbs below with an appropriate *preposition* immediately following them in sentences of your own to show that you know their usage:

1 allow;	**2** borrow;	**3** comment;
4 confess;	**5** criticise;	**6** forgive;
7 lend;	**8** prohibit;	**9** rely;
10 resign.		

57 Use the adjectives below with an appropriate *preposition* immediately following them in sentences of your own to show that you understand their usage:

1 adverse;	**2** conscious;	**3** due;
4 experienced;	**5** guilty;	**6** proud;
7 satisfied;	**8** sensitive;	**9** separate;
10 useful.		

58 Replace the blanks in the following sentences with *conjunctions*; state whether the conjunctions you use are co-ordinating or subordinating (do not use any conjunctions as a substitute more than once):

   1 He could —— read —— write.
   2 I'll join in —— you tell me to.
   3 You'll refuse to paint the house —— I pay you?
   4 I cannot pay you —— you start the work.
   5 —— the room was cheap, the food in the hotel was dear.

6 He came to the top of the cliff —— stopped teetering on the edge.
7 He hesitated so long —— he could not jump.
8 He was later saved —— we were all glad.
9 They asked —— they could write to him.
10 He was pleased —— we had written to him.

59 State whether the subordinate clauses in the following sentences are (*a*) *noun*, or (*b*) *adjectival*, or (*c*) *adverbial* (state the kind) *clauses*:

1 He went where no-one could follow him.
2 He asked how I had done it.
3 This was the moment when we had to act.
4 He wondered where the girl had gone.
5 He demanded to know why anyone had left the scene.
6 He persisted in asking questions because he suspected we were all guilty.
7 He never realised that the stolen goods were hidden behind the sofa.
8 They departed before we gave ourselves away.
9 Their dog finally found the goods where we had put them.
10 After the police returned, we were taken away in the black maria.

60 Rewrite the following short sentences as one continuous complex sentence, using conjunctions to link them in an interesting manner:

1 The door fell in. The windows fell out. Nearby a bomb had dropped. The destruction it caused was stupefying. The person who dropped it must have been without any imagination. He could not have conceived the pain and wounds his act would cause. The deed was barbaric. He was under orders, I suppose. This does not excuse his deed.
2 How could he have done it? I asked myself the question again and again. I needed to find an explanation. I needed to understand him. No explanations were forthcoming. An all-day exploration of the problem would give no answers—at least not answers one could accept. Ultimately such actions cannot be forgiven.

61 Underline all the *objects* in the following sentences and state whether they are *direct* or *indirect*:

1 The postman saw the dog and left immediately.
2 He tried unsuccessfully to give the neighbour the letters.
3 Nobody gave him danger money and his life was precious.
4 He made another attempt but the dog dealt him the same treatment.
5 When he returned he told the Head Postmaster what had happened.
6 'I'll send the owner a telephone message,' he promised the postman.
7 When the call came, the householder could not believe his ears.
8 'Mabel, have you heard this?' he asked his wife. 'Fido never touched him.'
9 'He does bark, dear, and gave the milkman a nasty turn.'
10 'Rubbish! I've something to say to the GPO. Give me my pen.'

62 Which of the *subordinate clauses* in the following sentences function as (*a*) *subjects*, or (*b*) *direct objects*, or (*c*) *complements* to verbs?

1 Looking over the fence, he asked if my apple trees had much fruit on them.
2 'I suppose so,' was my non-committal reply.
3 It seemed he wanted some, if I had understood him properly.
4 He never actually asked what would happen to the fruit.
5 That he had asked me at all was embarrassing enough.
6 Reluctantly, I promised that I would give him some.
7 'Let me help you pick them,' was his immediate eager offer.
8 My heart sank deeper and I said they were not yet ripe.
9 It seemed to him that I had given him an immediate offer.
10 He leapt the fence in one bound and shouted, 'Where shall we start?'

63 Which of the *subordinate clauses* in the following sentences function as (*a*) *adjectives*, or (*b*) *nouns*? Describe their function as fully as you can.

1 The pretty girl asked me if I came to the disco often.
2 The reply I gave her failed to satisfy her curiosity.
3 'Honestly, I'd like to know whether you do come often.'
4 Her insistence, which was both ingenuous and yet sincere, impressed me.
5 'What you suspect is true.'
6 'How do you know what I suspect?'
7 'Your eyes tell me that you suspect something.'
8 'You're talking in riddles, which I can't follow.'
9 'What I do doesn't matter.'
10 'I can't stand here talking. Why don't you ask me if I would like to dance?'

6
Spoken and Written English

Differences between Spoken and Written English
6:1

> Written language has to take on a precision and complexity ... that are not
> demanded in speech. If a reader wishes he can shut himself away with the text,
> giving it his whole attention. The words stand before him on the page, and he
> may vary his speed to match his comprehension, going back to re-read where
> he needs to, or pausing to make sure of a meaning before he reads on, cross-
> referencing for himself backwards and forwards in the text. A listener to speech,
> on the other hand, must catch his message on the wing. Thus it is that
> repetitions, re-phrasing, annotations, and extensions *en route* ... are not only
> permissible in a way they would not be in writing, but may well indeed be
> essential. It is a tendency of the written language to transcend differences in
> time and place, and hence to offer some resistance to change. It is in the nature
> of the spoken language to change in response to changing demands, and for a
> variety of reasons.
>
> (*The Bullock Report*, 1975, p. 144)

The passage outlines some of the major differences between spoken and
written English; it is clear that written English is different in kind from
written-down spoken English. The differences arise mainly from the facts
that written English normally pre-supposes that the person for whom the
writing is intended is not present, that other non-verbal features (gesture,
facial expression) are unavailable, and that stress, rhythm, intonation, and
pace cannot be indicated. The view of Hazlitt (1778–1830) in his essay *On
Familiar Style* is not one that can be supported today: 'To write a genuine
familiar or truly English style, is to write as any one would speak in common
conversation...'

6:2

Some of the main differences between the two aspects of the language are as
follows:
  (i) Spoken English is accompanied by non-verbal features such as move-
       ments of the hands or arms to provide reinforcing or explanatory
       gestures. Spoken forms of some languages (*e.g.* Italian) depend very
       heavily on such movements; it was once said that if the arms were cut

off an Italian he would become dumb. *Facial expression,* too, can convey meaning, mood, or attitude; it frequently indicates to the audience whether they should reply or keep quiet and encourages response. For this reason the language of a telephone conversation often differs from that used in face-to-face conversations. Deprived of both gestures and facial expressions to reinforce and confirm meanings, speakers on the telephone are driven to use and interpret intonation, stress, pauses, inflexion, in order to establish the full surface and deep meanings of the conversation.

(ii) In **5:92** and **5:93** it was shown that punctuation in written English cannot adequately represent *intonation, stress, rhythm,* and *pace,* which are just as much features of communication in written English as they are of spoken English. Word-order and structural arrangements need to be far more carefully planned in written English which is deprived of non-verbal features such as gesture and facial expressions. With written English a reader can adjust his own reading speed to match his comprehension; if a speaker does not understand part of a conversation he must interrupt, ask for a repetition of a statement, seek elucidation, and ask questions.

(iii) Spoken English can afford to re-phrase, repeat, annotate, and extend ideas as it proceeds; written English normally aims to set ideas down economically and precisely so that the words become the idea and encapsulate it.

(iv) Spoken English is readily and immediately adaptable to *conditions, audience,* and *context.* Written English has conventional forms and structures and lacks this direct and immediate flexibility of spoken forms of the language; it needs, therefore, to be more consciously disciplined. It is worth comparing the written recorded version of spoken English and a written speech prepared for public declamation. In both cases a speech of either kind is likely to use more formal aspects of spoken English than that used in colloquial speech. Indeed, the awareness of 'register', or the level on which language is operating, is especially important for using and understanding spoken English; the language of a conversation between friends is different in register from the language of an interview for a post. Compare the following extracts from two speeches by Sir Winston Churchill made during the 1939–45 war; one was delivered spontaneously in the House of Commons and the other was part of a prepared speech delivered also in the House of Commons. Can you decide which was which? What language features led you to your view?

(*a*) We have before us an ordeal of the most grievous kind. We have before us many, many long months of struggle and of suffering. You ask, what is our policy? I will say: It is to wage war, by sea, land, and air, with all our might and with all the strength that God can give us: to wage war against a monstrous tyranny, never surpassed in the dark, lamentable history of human crime. This is our policy. You ask, what is our aim? I can answer in one word: It is victory, victory at all costs, victory in spite of all terror, victory, however long and hard the road may be; for without victory, there is no survival. Let that be realised; no survival for the British Empire; no survival for all that the British Empire has stood for, no survival for the urge and impulse of the ages, that mankind will move forward towards its goal. But I take up my task with buoyancy and hope. I feel sure that our cause will not be suffered to fail among men. At this time I feel entitled to claim the aid of all, and I say, 'Come then, let us go forward together with our united strength.'

(*b*) What a fool and a knave I should have been to say it [Singapore] would fall. I have not made any arrogant, confident, boasting predictions at all. On the contrary I have stuck hard to my 'blood, toil, tears and sweat', to which I have added 'muddle and mismanagement', and that to some extent, I must admit, is what you have got out of it. I do not know what my critics would like me to say now. If I predict success and speak in buoyant terms, and misfortune continues, their pens and tongues will be able to dilate on my words. On the other hand, if I predict failure and paint the picture in darkest hues, I might safeguard myself against one danger, but only at the expense of a struggling army. Also I might be wrong. So I will say nothing about the future except to invite the House and the nation to face with courage whatever it may unfold.

(v) There are some differences in grammar between written and spoken English. Speech, for example, uses features such as contracted forms of negatives (*e.g. n't*) and modals/auxiliaries (*e.g. should've, won't 've, we'll*); the plural *they/their* is often used instead of *one/one's* or *everyone/everyone's*: *e.g.* '*Everyone* sent in *their* forms to the office'; 'misrelated' or 'dangling' participles are often acceptable in spoken English, whereas they are avoided in written English. *e.g.* '*Running* round the track, it's obvious that the leading runner had lost already.' Spoken English is more likely, too, to use simple, double and multiple sentences, whereas written English, with its more formal stylistic awareness, may use complex constructions more often. Tag-questions (see **5:92** (ii), page 106) also are a feature more common in spoken English than in written English. Quite often short responses (with words omitted or understood) are used in speech:

e.g. 'How did you get here?' '*By train*.' (Adverbial)
'What did you bring for me?' '*A book*.' (Direct object)
'Did anyone come with you?' '*Jean*.' (Subject)

(vi) There are differences in *vocabulary* between spoken and written English, but these differences are frequently the result of the distinction between *formal* and *informal* uses of the language. Spoken English uses an informal register more frequently and words such as the following: *get/got, nice, awful, ain't, lovely, great*.

There are cultural and even class distinctions in the way vocabulary changes from what is formal and what is informal or vice-versa. For example, some words have moved from the formal to the informal so that they are used more commonly in colloquial English than in written forms of the language': *e.g. silly* once meant 'happy', 'blessed'; *smug* meant 'neat', 'trim', meanings still given first in *Chambers Twen-*

tieth Century Dictionary; mob now means 'a disorderly rabble' although Swift condemned its increasing use in English as long ago as the start of the eighteenth century. Other words which were once frowned upon in formal language are now acceptable: *e.g. budge, shabby, snob,* and *sturdy*. It is worth considering the words *democracy/democratic* and tracing their use in English through *The Oxford English Dictionary*. Even today the word changes its meaning from speaker to speaker and context to context; at one time it can carry the highest approval of a liberal political attitude and at others almost the exact opposite. Words still continue to fall in and out of favour, are over-used or under-used, adopt formal or informal uses and take on currency in either the spoken or the written forms of the language.

6:3

The distinction between colloquial English and slang, however, is not an easy one to make sharply. In *The Use of English* (1962, pages 89–90) Randolph Quirk acknowledged the difficulty but attempted such a distinction: 'But describing a usage as "colloquial" means only that it tends not to be used on *formal* occasions, though perfectly polite and acceptable in informal conversation. A *slang* usage, on the other hand, is not generally introduced into informal conversation unless the speakers are on very intimate terms ...'

The word 'slang' does not appear in Dr Johnson's *Dictionary* (1755) and *Chambers Twentieth Century Dictionary* says that the word is of doubtful origin. It has been argued that amongst the possible reasons why slang is used are sheer high spirits, the desire to appear novel or to ease social relationships, the attempt to be friendly, and the establishment of one's right to belong to a certain class or set of people. (See M. Alfredo Niceforo, *Le génie de l'argot*, 1912.)

If a slang usage becomes generally accepted, it passes into colloquial English and may eventually pass into standard English. Some of the phrases, which Partridge quotes, have risen from slang to acceptable colloquial speech: *down to bedrock, come up to scratch, a knock-out blow, below the belt*. J. C. Nesfield, the writer of a very popular English textbook in 1916, listed amongst colloquialisms to avoid the following: *peckish* (for 'hungry'), *to be sat upon* (for 'blamed'), *boss* (for 'head man'), *fluke* (for 'lucky stroke'), *jiffy* (for 'instant') – all of which have survived; others, such as *masher* (for 'lady-killer') and *put on the haw-haw* (for 'assume an air of great personal importance') have died. Words like *carouse* (German *gar aus*, quite out: *i.e.* empty the glass), *hoax* (Latin *hocus-pocus*), and *nincompoop* (once thought to be from *non compos mentis*, but now of uncertain origin) were slang words until about 1900, although now they are used in standard English without difficulty.

6:4

Jargon is a term often used with the same sense as the word 'slang'; *Chambers Twentieth Century Dictionary* gives this sense as one of its main meanings. However, the word *jargon* properly refers to a trade dialect. Lawyers, doctors, teachers, carpenters – and the members of any trade or profession – use vocabulary peculiar to themselves. A car workshop manual or a monthly specialist magazine aimed at computer-controllers or wireless mechanics will contain its own special use of language.

Consider the following:

> The primary recuperating valve is now placed in its aperture at the flanged face; it will be necessary to move the pushrod and piston assembly to and fro, to enable the valve to be inserted. Replace the retaining plug, and the spring and circlip on the valve plunger.

This is part of the description of an instruction manual (P. H. Smith, *Ford Cortina 1967–1968 Autobook*, Autopress Ltd, page 127) setting out the procedure for reassembling a brake master-cylinder.

Gray's *Anatomy*, a standard medical textbook, opens its account of the way the jaw moves with the following:

> This is a ginglymo-arthrodial joint, the parts entering into its formation on each side are, above, the anterior part of the glenoid cavity of the temporal bone and the eminentia auticularis; and, below, the condyle of the lower jaw.
>
> (Revised American, 15th, edition, 1977, page 231)

Far from being careless, imprecise, and slovenly language, trade jargon is economical and accurate in its usage; very frequently simple or double sentences are preferred to complex sentences. Jargon is, therefore, distinguishable from other language usages in both vocabulary and grammar. Randolph Quirk in *The Use of English* (1962, page 163) points out that jargon frequently makes use of compound nouns; he quotes as an example 'eight fixed open hearth steel melting furnaces' where some writers might have used 'eight furnaces, of a fixed type with open hearth, for the melting of steel'.

(Eric Partridge in *Slang Today and Yesterday* (third edition 1950, pages 148–272) discusses at length special kinds of slang and jargon.)

6:5

Idiom is a mode of expression peculiar to a language. *Chambers Twentieth Century Dictionary* goes on to define it as 'an expression characteristic of a particular language not logically or grammatically explicable'.

(i) This, if it is true, makes idiom particularly hard to translate from one language to another. Consider, for example, the following:

> He has bats in the belfry.
> Il a une araignée au plafond. (Literally, 'He has a spider on the ceiling.')
> Er hat Raupen im Kopfe. (Literally, 'He has caterpillars in the head.')

(ii) Idiom depends in part, at least, on the dictionary meanings of some words: *e.g.* the word 'fast' as an adverb is defined as: 'firmly, fixedly, steadfastly; quickly, rapidly'. In phrases such as 'To stand fast' and 'To go fast' the word 'fast' carries these two meanings, in the first 'firmly', in the second 'rapidly'.

(iii) Many of the idioms in a language depend on the figurative use of language:

  e.g. He was an odd *fish*.
   This was a pretty kettle of *fish*.
   He drank like a *fish*.
   She was a *fish* out of water.
   He had other *fish* to fry.
   She was a big *fish* in a small pool.
   It was neither *fish*, flesh nor good red herring.

  cf. also, to bury the hatchet', 'strike while the iron is hot', 'unable to see the wood for the trees', 'to feather one's nest', 'a rough diamond', 'a mare's nest', 'a pretty pickle', 'the odd man out', 'a square peg in a round hole', 'a live wire', and many others.

Direct and Indirect (Reported) Speech
6:6

Direct speech quotes the actual words used by a speaker:

  e.g. He said, 'I am ill.'

The words actually used are placed in inverted commas. The introductory words *he said* may precede or follow the words directly used:

  e.g. 'I am ill,' he said.

6:7

Indirect speech (sometimes called *Reported Speech*) reports the words said without actually using the words originally spoken:

  e.g. He said (that) he was ill.

Inverted commas are not used with indirect speech. Notice that the clause following *He said* stands in the relationship of a direct object (*dO*) to the verb 'said':

  e.g. He said *it*. (Direct object)
   He said (*that*) *he was ill*. (Direct object)

  NOTE The relative pronoun may be included or omitted in such indirect statements.

6:8

Indirect speech may report either a statement, or a question, or an exclamation, or a command:

  e.g. He asked, '*Where are you going?*' (Direct question)
   He asked *where he (she, it) was going*. (Indirect question)
   He asked her, '*Can you come with me?*' (Direct question)

He asked her *whether she could come with him.* (Indirect question)
He exclaimed, '*How well you look!*' (Direct exclamation)
He exclaimed how *well he (she, they) looked.* (Indirect exclamation)
He shouted, '*Stop it!*' (Direct command)
He shouted *at him (her, them) to stop it.* (Indirect command)

NOTE Indirect commands, since they contain no finite verb (*i.e.* a verb with its own subject) but use an infinitive, must be used with *either* an indirect object (*iO*) *or* a prepositional phrase:

e.g. He told *him* (*iO*) to stop it.
He shouted *at them* (prepositional phrase) to stop it.

6:9

In changing direct speech to indirect speech a number of changes have to be made (with some minor exceptions). The distancing or *back-shift* needs always to be made carefully with regard to the sense (see **6:9** (iii), (iv), pages 126–7, for example).

(i) *Change of pronouns*

Subject		Object	
I	> he, she	me	> him, her
we	> they	us	> them
you	> he, she, they	you	> him, her, them

e.g. '*I* am ill,' he said. (Direct)
He was ill he said. (Indirect)

He commanded the pupil, 'Give *me* the book!' (Direct)
He commanded the pupil to give *him* the book. (Indirect)

He said, '*We* are keen to attend.' (Direct)
He said *they* were keen to attend. (Indirect)

He said, 'The girl saw *us* get on the bus.' (Direct)
He said (that) the girl had seen *them* get on the bus. (Indirect)

He said, 'You never kept your promise.' (Direct)
He said he (she, they) had never kept his (her, their) promise. (Indirect)

(ii) *Change of verbs*

(*a*) Verbs will all be used in *the third person* (singular or plural) in indirect statements, questions, or exclamations or in the infinitive form in indirect commands:

e.g. He said, 'I *am* ill.' (Direct statement)
He said he *was* ill. (Indirect statement)

He commanded the guards, '*Quick march!*' (Direct command)
He commanded the guards *to quick march.* (Indirect command)

(*b*) The *tenses* of verbs also change.

Direct Speech		Indirect Speech
Present	>	Past

Present perfect ⎱
Past simple   ⎬ > Past perfect
Past perfect   ⎰

e.g. He said, 'I *am* ill.' (Direct: present)
He said he *was* ill (Indirect: past)

He said, 'I *have been* ill.' (Direct: present perfect)
He said he *had been* ill. (Indirect: past perfect)

He said, 'I *came* two days ago.' (Direct: past simple)
He said he *had come* two days before. (Indirect: past perfect)

He said, 'I *had been* ill.' (Direct: past perfect)
He said he *had been* ill. (Indirect: past perfect)

The modal auxiliaries will normally also shift backwards in time:

can	>	could
shall	>	should/would
should	>	should
will	>	would
may	>	might

e.g. He said, 'I can do it.' (Direct)
He said he could do it. (Indirect)

He said, 'I shall do it.' (Direct)
He said he would do it. (Indirect)

NOTE There is a difference in meaning between:

⎰He said he would do it. (Indirect)
⎱He said I should do it. (Indirect: here *I* does not refer back to *He* in *He said*)

⎰He said, 'You shall do it.' (Direct)
or ⎱He said, 'You should do it.' (Direct)

⎰He said, 'The girl will do it.' (Direct)
⎱He said the girl would do it. (Indirect)

⎰He said, 'I may do it.' (Direct)
⎱He said he might do it. (Indirect)

(iii) *Change of this/these to that/those*
Sometimes the back-shift involved in reported speech necessitates the change of *this* > *that* and *these* > *those*. The meaning, however, will determine whether this change is necessary.

e.g. He said, 'I like *this* book.' (Direct)
　　He said that he liked *this* book. (Indirect)
　　He said that he liked *that* book. (Indirect)

Great care is needed to see that ambiguity does not creep into the indirect statement if a change is made. The change should *not* be made automatically.

(iv) *Change of some adverbs*
Again, the back-shift of adverbs needs to be used very cautiously in changing direct to indirect statements. Consider the difference in meanings, for example, in the following:

　　He said, 'I can come *tomorrow*.' (Direct)
　　He said, 'I can come *the next day*.' (Direct)
　　He said he could come *tomorrow*. (Indirect)
　　He said he could come *the next day*. (Indirect)

or He said, 'I can be *here* with her.' (Direct)
　　He said, 'I can be *there* with her.' (Direct)
　　He said he could be *here* with her. (Indirect)
　　He said he could be *there* with her. (Indirect)

or He said, 'I came *two days ago*.' (Direct)
　　He said, 'I came *two days before*.' (Direct)
　　He said he had come *two days ago*. (Indirect)
　　He said he had come *two days before*. (Indirect)

EXERCISES

64   What features of the following passages seem to you characteristic of (*a*) spoken or written English, (*b*) a particular 'register', and (*c*) a formal or informal use of language?

1 The 'appropriate amount of cash' in respect of any stock dividend received from a company is grossed up at the basic rate of 30% in order to arrive at the amount on which higher rate or additional rate tax is chargeable but the basic rate tax is set off against any higher rate tax payable on the gross amount.

2 In the communication which I had the honour to make to you on 1st September, I informed you, on the instructions of His Majesty's Principal Secretary of State for Foreign Affairs, that unless the German Government were prepared to give His Majesty's Government in the United Kingdom satisfactory assurances that the German Government had suspended all aggressive action against Poland and were prepared promptly to withdraw their forces from Polish territory, His Majesty's Government in the United Kingdom would, without hesitation, fulfil their obligations to Poland.

3 It was all very pleasant. Crisp fresh sheets, place to hang my clothes. Even a thing to hang my Gold Hunter on, it made me wish I had a Gold Hunter. I got my head down at 11.30. People tell me the train moved out at midnight, but I didn't know about it.

4 'And where is your party going to be?' asked Angelo.
'In Rome,' said Simon, 'didn't I make that clear?'
'But Rome is still occupied by the Germans!'
'That will add to the interest of it, don't you think? – Why, what's the matter?'
Before Simon could catch him, Angelo fell to the ground in a dead faint.

5 The following is a transcript of a taped conversation. No punctuation marks (other than a capital letter for a name) have been added. The slanting lines (/) indicate breaks or pauses in the conversation.

P.D.	Ian / do you think you should have more help from the state Ian
IAN	yeh
M.D.	what do you mean by help from the state Ian
IAN	well / grants
M.D.	to help them / live at home or have digs or whatever it is they need
IAN	no / to help them get a course done like this / and get em on small holidays / and weeks away / staying at other schools
M.D.	but wouldn't that mean more rates and taxes
IAN	could do / yeh / but that s not really much / they won t be / they wouldn t be putting rates up much more
DAVE	ay oop / tha s tekking it from my wages
IAN	tha don t pay rates

6 A body is thrown vertically downwards with a velocity of 20 ft per sec. When is its velocity 180 ft per sec. if $g = 32$ ft per sec. per sec? How far will it then have travelled?

7 Sea Passages: *S North Sea, Straits of Dover*: Wind N fresh or strong becoming variable light; sea rough becoming slight. *English Channel* (E): Wind variable light becoming S strong; sea smooth becoming moderate or rough. *St George's Channel, Irish Sea*: Wind S light becoming strong to gale, locally severe gale; sea smooth becoming rough.

8 Sieve the flour. Clean and prepare the fruit, and mix with it the spice and one teaspoonful of flour. Cream the butter and sugar; add the flour and the eggs by degrees, beating thoroughly. Add the fruit and the baking-powder mixed with the last spoonful of flour. The mixture should be of a consistency to drop easily from the spoon.

65   What elements of the following passage indicate that this was part of a speech delivered in an impromptu manner?

I think you all know —er— what service John has given the company over the last thirty-five years — or is it thirty-five years, two months, and three days, John? Day in and day out he's been behind his desk sorting out other people's problems ... troubles. I remember the first day he came here, a young man just back from the war and just married—what a help Mary has been to him all these years. He learnt quickly and was quick to move through the ranks, so to speak, if I can call them that, to become chief clerk; not an easy position, far from it. After all, he's the one who really runs the whole show. Never late for work and never a day off for illness, all that time! Now he's looking forward to his well-earnt retirement. A little cottage in North Devon, isn't it, John? Where he can see and draw the wild flowers he loves so much and knows so much about. We shall miss him, that's for sure. I shall miss him. His humour when paper's flying in all directions; his knowledge of where every memo is filed; his liking of people. I hope he'll miss us, too, and as he looks at his gold watch on the long, leisurely days of retirement, he can think of us all here, slogging away over hot desks. A happy retirement, John, from all of us.

66   What elements of the following passage indicate that this was part of a prepared speech?

Fourscore and seven years ago our fathers brought forth on this continent a new nation, conceived in liberty and dedicated to the proposition that all men are created equal.

Now we are engaged in a great Civil War, testing whether that nation, or any nation so conceived and so dedicated, can long endure. We are met on a great battle-field of that war. We have come to dedicate a portion of that field as a final resting-place for those who here gave their lives that that nation might live. It is altogether fitting and proper that we should do this.

But, in a larger sense, we cannot dedicate—we cannot consecrate—we cannot hallow—this ground. The brave men, living and dead, who struggled here have consecrated it far above our own poor power to add or detract. The world will little note nor long remember what we say here, but it can never forget what they did here. It is for us, the living, rather to be dedicated here to the unfinished work which they who fought here have thus far so nobly advanced. It is rather for us to be here dedicated to the great task remaining before us—that from these honoured dead we take increased devotion to that cause for which they gave the last full measure of devotion—that we here highly resolve that these dead shall not have died in vain—that this nation, under God, shall have a new birth of freedom—and that government of the people, by the people, for the people, shall not perish from the earth.

(Abraham Lincoln, 19 November 1863)

67 What elements of the following passage indicate that this was part of a written letter?

It is impossible not to feel for the unhappiness of the young lady which you have so well described; but it is not so easy as you imagine to apply the remedy. It appears that I should be guilty of a breach of discretion if I were to send for the fortunate object of this young lady's affections, and to apprise him of the pressing necessity for his early return to England; the application for permission to go ought to come from himself, and, at all events, the offer ought not to be made by me, and particularly not founded on the secret of this interesting young lady. But this fortunate Major now commands his battalion, and I am very apprehensive that he could not with propriety quit it at present, even though the life of this female should depend on it; and, therefore, I think that he will not ask for leave.

We read occasionally, of desperate cases of this description but I cannot say that I have ever yet known of a young lady dying of love. They continue, in some manner, to live, and look tolerably well, notwithstanding their despair and the continued absence of their lover; and some have even been known to recover so far as to be inclined to take another's lover, if the absence of the first has lasted too long. I don't suppose that your protegée can ever recover so far, but I do hope that she will survive the continued necessary absence of the Major, and enjoy with him hereafter many happy days.

(Arthur Wellesley, Duke of Wellington, 1769–1852)

68 The following is one half of a telephone conversation; give what you think might have been the whole conversation. (The words of Speaker **A** will suggest what Speaker **B** might be saying and suggest the relationship that exists between them.) *Use an appropriate 'register'.*

(*The phone rings at least ten times before Speaker **A** picks up the receiver.*)

A Westbury 87964.
B —
A Oh, hello; long time, no see. Sorry I didn't answer straight away. I was upstairs.
B —
A Yes, how did you get on?
B —
A They always say that.
B —
A Did she mention Janet?
B —
A However did she know? It must've been Gary!
B —
A I saw him at the bus station on Wednesday. He never said anything but he's still out of work.
B —
A Well, you've done what you can.

B	—
A	You're not going to try again?
B	—
A	Yes.
B	—
A	Em.
B	—
A	Oh well, nobody can say you haven't tried.
B	—
A	O.K. Let me know, won't you?
B	—
A	Yes.
B	—
A	You can say I'll help if I'm needed.
B	—
A	Of course I mean it.
B	—
A	Thanks. Keep in touch.
B	—
A	Bye.

(*Speaker **A** puts down the receiver thoughtfully.*)

69 The following represents the middle part of a conversation between two friends both aged about 18. They are sitting in a well-worn living room of a semi-detached house on the outskirts of a large industrial city. Write the dialogue which might have preceded it and the dialogue which might have followed. *Use an appropriate register.* The total conversation should be about 400 words in length.

LINDA	You never give me a chance.
JOHN	What do you mean?
LINDA	You know what I mean. What about the time Fred and Jackie asked us to Mary's party?
JOHN	You know I had to work late that night.
LINDA	Work, work, work! That's all you do!

70 (Before you begin this exercise listen to several radio and television commentaries on sporting events. How do they differ from each other? How can you account for the major differences?)

1 Imagine that you are watching a sporting event on television. Write part of the commentary accompanying it; try to give it your own distinctive stamp.

2 Imagine that you are listening to a radio commentary on the same sporting event as that being televised in (**1**) above and that you are taping it for your own use. Make a transcript of this radio commentary as you play it back.

71

1 Write two paragraphs, both of which have been prepared as contributions to a formal debate on the motion 'That this house considers nuclear arms should be banned'; one of the contributions supports the motion and the other opposes it. (Be conscious, as you write, of an audience listening intently to a formal debate at school, in college, or in a TV studio and of the speakers passionately (or coolly) presenting their arguments.)

2 Write a conversation between two young people who have met on a street corner. One is trying to persuade the other that nuclear weapons should be banned but the other is resisting the arguments. (Suppose that the two speakers are friends, are in their late teens, are thoughtful and intelligent, and enjoy discussing political, religious, and moral issues together.)

72 Use each of the following *idiomatic expressions* in a sentence of your own to show that you understand its full meaning and implications for the context. (You may adapt the grammatical form of the idiom if you wish.)

1 Going for a song.
3 Run rings round.
5 Ride rough-shod over.
7 Hitting a brick wall.
9 To be left high and dry.

2 As easy as falling off a log.
4 Sell someone short.
6 To be under the weather.
8 Laughing in one's face.
10 To be over the moon.

73 Use each of the following phrases in two different ways in sentences of your own; in the first use the phrase *literally*, and in the second *figuratively*:

1 break through;
4 send up;
7 blow over;
10 shrink from.

2 climb down;
5 come to;
8 sink under;

3 pack in;
6 string along;
9 rise above;

74 Rewrite the following passage in *indirect (reported) speech*:

'Who are you talking to?' said the King, coming up to Alice, and looking at the Cat's head with great curiosity.

'It's a friend of mine—a Cheshire Cat,' said Alice; 'allow me to introduce it.'

'I don't like the look of it at all,' said the King; 'however, it may kiss my hand if it likes.'

'I'd rather not,' the Cat remarked.

'Don't be impertinent,' said the King, 'and don't look at me like that!' He got behind Alice as he spoke.

'A cat may look at a king,' said Alice. 'I've read that in some book, but I don't remember where.'

'Well, it must be removed,' said the King very decidedly, and he called to the Queen, who was passing at that moment, 'My dear! I wish you would have this cat removed!'

The Queen had only one way of settling all difficulties, great or small.

'Off with his head!' she said, without looking around.

75 In Shakespeare's play *Julius Caesar*, after the murder of Caesar by the conspirators, the Roman crowd are stunned and confused; they hardly know how to act, as the security of the state is in jeopardy. BRUTUS, a leading conspirator, addresses them partly to reassure them, partly to justify his own actions. MARK ANTONY, a close friend of Caesar, with Brutus's permission, also addresses them, but he is forbidden to blame the conspirators' actions and must restrict his comments to praise Caesar's achievements. Here are the speeches as Shakespeare wrote them:

(a)   BRUTUS Romans, countrymen, and lovers! hear me for my cause; and be silent, that you may hear: believe me for mine honour, and have respect to mine honour, that you may believe: censure me in your wisdom, and awake your senses, that you may the better judge. If there be any in this assembly, any dear friend of Caesar's, to him I say, that Brutus' love to Caesar was no less than his. If then that friend demand why Brutus rose against Caesar, this is my answer: Not that I loved Caesar less, but that I loved Rome more. Had you rather Caesar were living, and die all slaves, than that Caesar were dead, to live all free men? As Caesar loved me, I weep for him; as he was fortunate, I rejoice at it; as he was valiant, I honour him; but, as he was ambitious, I slew him. There is tears for his love; joy for his fortune; honour for his valour; and death for his ambition. Who is here so base that would be a bondman? If any, speak; for him have I offended. Who is here so rude that would not be a Roman? If any, speak; for him have I offended. Who is here so vile that will not love his country? If any, speak; for him have I offended. I pause for a reply.

CITIZENS None, Brutus, none.

BRUTUS Then none have I offended. I have done no more to Caesar, than you shall do to Brutus. The question of his death is enrolled in the Capitol; his glory not extenuated, wherein he was worthy, nor his offences enforced, for which he suffered death.

Enter ANTONY *and Others, with* CAESAR'S *body.*

Here comes his body, mourned by Mark Antony: who, though he had no hand in his death, shall receive the benefit of his dying, a place in the commonwealth; as which of you shall not? With this I depart: that, as I slew my best lover for the good of Rome, I have the same dagger for myself, when it shall please my country to need my death.

(b)   MARK ANTONY Friends, Romans, countrymen, lend me your ears;
I come to bury Caesar, not to praise him.
The evil that men do lives after them,
The good is oft interred with their bones;
So let it be with Caesar. The noble Brutus
Hath told you Caesar was ambitious;
If it were so, it was a grievous fault,
And grievously hath Caesar answer'd it.
Here, under leave of Brutus and the rest,—
For Brutus is an honourable man;
So are they all, all honourable men,—
Come I to speak in Caesar's funeral.
He was my friend, faithful and just to me:

But Brutus says he was ambitious;
And Brutus is an honourable man.
He hath brought many captives home to Rome,
Whose ransoms did the general coffers fill:
Did this in Caesar seem ambitious?
When that the poor have cried, Caesar hath wept;
Ambition should be made of sterner stuff:
Yet Brutus says he was ambitious;
And Brutus is an honourable man.
You all did see that on the Lupercal
I thrice presented him a kingly crown,
Which he did thrice refuse: was this ambition?
Yet Brutus says he was ambitious;
And, sure, he is an honourable man.
I speak not to disprove what Brutus spoke,
But here I am to speak what I do know.
You all did love him once, not without cause:
What cause withholds you then to mourn for him?
O judgment! thou art fled to brutish beasts,
And men have lost their reason. Bear with me;
My heart is in the coffin there with Caesar,
And I must pause till it come back to me.

1 Using the arguments contained in these speeches and observing the audience, situation, and constraints on the speakers, write *two* speeches, one by Brutus and the other by Mark Antony, as they might have been given in a modern play had Shakespeare been a twentieth-century playwright working for the modern theatre.

2 Imagine two members of the crowd in a Roman street who have just listened to Brutus and Mark Antony's speeches; they are shocked and confused. Try to write a conversation between them, expressing this shock and confusion, in the language of everyday, twentieth-century English, of the kind that might be used by two middle-aged people with the safety of their families to consider, afraid yet angry, worried yet determined to take some kind of action. (This conversation should not be written as part of a play but should be as true a representation of an actual conversation as you can make it.)

76 Rewrite in *reported speech* the following exchange in the House of Commons as an article for publication in an educational column of a serious national newspaper. Do not add material or change ideas but report what was said fully and accurately:

MR HASELHURST Does the Department have no view on how careers education might be improved? If there is to be a meaningful improvement in careers education, should not the responsibility be vested in the careers service, with perhaps a careers officer seconded to each school, with sole responsibility for the guidance of secondary school children therein?

MR OAKES The careers service has an important role to play, but it is different from that of careers teachers. The role of my Department is purely to advise, guide and encourage. As long

ago as 1973, in survey No. 18 'Careers Education in Secondary Schools', we reported to local authorities on the deficien-
cies in the provision of careers education. But the local authorities have to determine the amount of careers education that
they provide.

MR STOKES Will the Minister encourage industrialists and others to visit
schools and colleges and point out the attraction of careers in
industry and commerce, which is vital for the country's
future?

MR OAKES We encourage visits to schools by industrialists and trade
unions, and there is a strong link between individual schools
and firms. The more links there are, the better it will be for
the entire community and education.

MR ASHTON Is my hon. Friend aware that many children do not go into
industry because their fathers have had a long experience of
bad conditions and low wages? Will he tell the career advisers
to talk more to parents to stop the situation where they advise
bright children to choose the safety of the town hall, building
society or bank?

MR OAKES I agree that industry must do a lot to improve its image. In
the past there has been a tendency on the part of schools to
underrate commerce and industry, as distinct from other
more glamorous professions. However, there has been a mas-
sive increase in the number of people now taking science,
applied science and engineering courses.

(*Hansard*, 13 March 1979)

77 Rewrite the following passage of reported speech in *direct speech*. Do not
add material or change the ideas. You may add some brief 'stage directions'
if you need to indicate the action:

The tumult died down. Napoleon now called upon the four pigs to confess their
crimes. Without further prompting they confessed that they had been secretly
in touch with Snowball since his expulsion, that they had collaborated with
him in destroying the windmill, and that they had entered into an agreement
with him to hand over Animal Farm to Mr Frederick. They added that
Snowball had privately admitted to them that he had been Jones's secret agent
for years past. When they had finished their confession, the dogs promptly tore
their throats out and in a terrible voice Napoleon demanded whether any
other animal had anything to confess.

The three hens now came forward and stated that Snowball had appeared
to them in a dream and incited them to disobey Napoleon's orders. They, too,
were slaughtered. Then a goose came forward and confessed to having secreted
six ears of corn during the last year's harvest and eaten them in the night. Then
a sheep confessed to having urinated in the drinking pool—urged to do this, so
she said, by Snowball—and two other sheep confessed to having murdered an
old ram by chasing him round and round a bonfire when he was suffering from
a cough. They were all slain on the spot.

Later Boxer said he did not understand it and would not have believed that
such things could have happened on their farm. It had to be due to some fault
in themselves. The solution, as he saw it, was to work harder. From then
onwards he would get up a full hour earlier in the mornings.

(Adapted from George Orwell, *Animal Farm*)

78

(*a*) Rewrite the following sentences in *direct speech*:

1 The girl argued that it was not her fault if the old lady had left her front door open. It had simply asked her to go in.
2 The policeman could not accept that and told her he would arrest her for the theft of five pounds and a china dog.
3 The girl protested her innocence and alleged that the old lady had given her the money and the dog as presents.
4 The old lady, of course, denied that she had done any such thing and said that the dog was precious to her as it had been given to her by her now dead husband as a birthday present.
5 The policeman declared he had heard enough and that he would take the girl to the police station to charge her. He reminded the pensioner that she might be required to give evidence later and the old lady agreed.

(*b*) Rewrite the following sentences in *reported speech*:

6 'I tell you, I didn't do it,' the girl protested. 'Why is it that nobody will believe me?'
7 PC Jones merely replied, 'I have heard enough. Anything you now say will be taken down and may be used in evidence later against you.'
8 At the police station WPC Atkinson asked, ' Where do you live? You know that your parents will need to be informed?'
9 'Why bring them into this? In any case, they won't care. They never care about me.' The girl broke down in tears.
10 'Make a note of her details and find out where she lives,' said Jones. 'Then I'll call round to see the parents.'

7
Vocabulary

7:1

The form of a word presented in a dictionary is known as its **lexical** form.

7:2

Most dictionaries present words alphabetically and indicate for each entry the part of speech a word can be:

> *e.g.* **level** *n.*   an instrument for testing horizontality: a horizontal position: a horizontal plane or line: height: the thing aimed at;
> *adj.*   horizontal: even; smooth: uniform: well-balanced;
> *adv.*   in a level manner: point-blank;
> *v.t.*   to make horizontal: to make flat or smooth: to raze: to aim;
> *v.i.*   to make things level: to aim: to make one word, form, the same as another.
>
> (See *Chambers Twentieth Century Dictionary*, p. 756)

7:3

The entry in an etymological dictionary also gives the origin of a word, usually at the end of the definition and within brackets:

> *e.g.* **level** [O.Fr. *livel, liveau* (Fr. *niveau*)—L. *libella*, a plummet, dim. of *libra*, a balance.]

7:4

Words which have the same, or very similar, meanings are termed **synonyms.** A living language will not tolerate exact synonyms, words with exactly the same meanings, for long. Usually one of three developments will take place:

(i) One of the words will slightly change its meaning:

> *e.g. n.*   *work: labour;*
> *v.i.*   *toil: travail;*
> *adj.*   *nice: foolish.* (NOTE Both Chaucer and Shakespeare use the word 'nice' in the sense of 'foolish'.)

(ii) Both words will change their meaning and the original sense will be conveyed by a newly introduced third word:

e.g. Old English   *scyrte*   *shirt*
        Old Norse   *skyrte*   *skirt*
        New Word (Latin)   —   *tunic*

(iii) One of the words will fall from the language leaving the other alive:

e.g. Old English   *niman;*   Mod. English *take*   (from Old Norse)
        Old English   *torn;*   Mod. English *anger* (from Old Norse)
        Old English   *wolcen;*   Mod. English *sky*   (from Old Norse)

Strict synonyms do not remain in the language long as synonyms, therefore. A glance at a book which sets out lists of synonyms and antonyms (words with opposite meanings) will show just how refined meanings of synonymous words have become.

e.g. **love, v.:** *love, like, fancy, care for, favour, become enamoured, fall or be in love with; revere, take to, make much of, hold dear, prize, hug, cling to, cherish, pet; adore, idolize, love to distraction, dote on, desire; throw oneself at, lose or give one's heart.* Slang: *go for, fall for, be sweet on, be nuts about, go steady, spoon;*

A book which lists words in this fashion is usually known as a *Thesaurus*; the most famous of such collections is Roget's *Thesaurus*, first published in 1852 by an English doctor, but revised several times since.

7:5

Words of opposite meaning are termed **antonyms,** but strict antonyms, like strict synonyms, are rare. For example, the antonyms of *increase* may be *contract, lessen, shorten, diminish, shrivel,* as well as *decrease.* In a similar way the antonyms of *silent* may be *loud, noisy, deafening, ear-splitting, sonorous.*

7:6

Words with the same spelling and sound but with different meanings or use are termed **homonyms:**

e.g. *bear*   = animal
                 = to carry
        lie   = to tell an untruth
                 = to assume a horizontal position.
        fair   = light-coloured
                 = an entertainment

7:7

Words written in the same form but with different meanings and possibly pronunciations are termed **homographs:**

e.g. *lead*   = to show the way
                 = a metal

tear	=	to split apart
	=	water from the eye
wound	=	a hurt
	=	past tense of 'to wind'

7:8

Words with the same pronunciation but with different spellings and meanings
are termed **homophones:**

e.g.	*read*	=	past tense of the verb 'to read'
	red	=	a colour
	read	=	present tense of the verb 'to read'
	reed	=	a marsh grass
	bear	=	to carry; an animal
	bare	=	naked

(*cf. to/too/two; write, right, rite; their, there; quay, key; heir, air*) It is worth noting
that some words have become confused in their usage because of their
similarity in pronunciation:

> *e.g. practice* (a noun) / *practise* (a verb)
> *licence* (a noun) / *license* (a verb)
> *principal* (= main; head) / *principle* (= a fundamental quality)

The Size of an Individual's Vocabulary and Language Control
7:9

It is sometimes asserted that Shakespeare used only about 20,000 words and
Milton 8,000 (not including the various and numerous inflected forms of
words already counted). Ordinary people have a much larger vocabulary
than the few hundred words they are sometimes alleged to control. Leonard
Bloomfield (in *Language*, 1934, p. 277) puts the estimates much higher: 'Every
adult speaker uses at least somewhere round 20,000–30,000 words; if he is
educated ... he uses many more. Everyone, moreover, understands more
words than he uses.'

The control over a language does not simply depend on the size of an
individual's vocabulary, the lexical units (*morphemes*) which he has. It depends, too, on his or her control over sentence-types, constructions and the
ability to substitute one construction for another (*tagmemes*).

Levels of Vocabulary Usage
(*The 'registers' of vocabulary*)
7:10

(i) The lexical meaning of a word is merely one guide to its use; native
users of the language are conscious of the level(s) at which a word

may be used within its own context. This is why one word is said to be 'better' or 'worse' than another for a specific use.

(ii) Fowler's *A Dictionary of Modern English Usage*, 1965 (revised by Sir Ernest Gowers), recognises this fact in the section on 'Working and Stylish Words' (page 717). It rejects the notion that one can improve one's style merely by using 'stylish' words: 'The writer who prefers the stylish words for no better reason than that he thinks it is stylish, so far from improving his style, makes it stuffy, or pretentious, or incongruous.' Amongst the examples it gives of such words are the following:

'STYLISH'	*'WORKING'*
angle, vb.	fish
beverage	drink
deem	think
description	kind, sort
implement, vb.	carry out
initiate	begin
partake	share
reside	live
terminate	end

It implicitly makes the point that the context will determine the appropriateness or inappropriateness of the use of a particular word within it.

(iii) There is often a choice of 'synonym' in English for use within a given situation. For example, *stench, smell, pong, scent, aroma, perfume, fragrance, odour* and *stink* are not readily interchangeable from one context to another: *scent, perfume, fragrance* are used to denote 'pleasant' smells; *stench, stink, pong* denote 'unpleasant' smells. The word *aroma* usually conveys a peculiar or a particular smell. *Odour* may be used to denote either pleasantness or unpleasantness according to its context.

Malapropisms

7:11

This term is used to describe a confusion in use between words that superficially seem similar. It is taken from Mrs Malaprop, a character in Sheridan's play *The Rivals* (1775), who frequently confuses and misuses words:

e.g. 'I would by no means wish a daughter of mine to be a *progeny* of learning.' (*prodigy*)
'As she grew up, I would have her instructed in *geometry*, that she might know something of the *contagious* countries.' (*geography, contiguous*)

Mrs Malaprop, however, was not the first character to misuse words for humour in a play. Shakespeare's Dogberry in *Much Ado about Nothing* had a similar affliction nearly two hundred years before:

e.g. 'Is our whole *dissembly* appeared?' (*assembly*)
'Flat *burglary* as ever was committed.' (*perjury*)

Malapropisms occur because of the *unintentional* misuse of a word by a writer or speaker; the effect is sometimes humorous. A GCE candidate wrote in a recent examination: 'The beggar without any legs sat at the side of the road begging for arms.'

EXERCISES

79 Consult an etymological dictionary and describe the connection between the current meaning(s) in present-day English of each of the following words and its origins:

1	biro;	**2**	gerrymander;	**3**	mesmeric;
4	pamphlet;	**5**	pander;	**6**	pasteurise;
7	quixotic;	**8**	sandwich;	**9**	tawdry;
10	wellington.				

80 Consult an etymological dictionary and describe the connection between the current meaning(s) in present-day English of each of the following words and its origin:

1	autograph;	**2**	blitz;	**3**	marmalade;
4	pandemonium;	**5**	parable;	**6**	phosphorus;
7	proletarian;	**8**	renaissance;	**9**	robot;
10	thesaurus.				

81 Write sentences to show how the following *synonyms* might be distinguished in use. (The contexts you create in your sentences will be vital for bringing out distinctions.)

1	love;	favour;	idolize.
2	hate;	despise;	abhor.
3	deception;	lie;	fraud.
4	time;	season;	epoch.
5	crowd;	assembly;	mob.
6	bulky;	gigantic;	vast.
7	skill;	competence;	accomplishment.
8	slave;	drudge;	addict.
9	road;	path;	track.
10	true;	loyal;	sincere.

82 Write sentences to show the essential differences in meaning between the words in the following pairs of *antonyms*:

1	permission; restraint.		**2**	handy; useless.
3	handsome; hideous.		**4**	elegant; vulgar.
5	crucial; unimportant.		**6**	change; stability.
7	bravery; cowardice.		**8**	true; counterfeit.
9	borrow; lend.		**10**	seize; release.

83 Find an *antonym* for each of the following words and then write a sentence which uses both the word and its antonym in such a way that their contrasted meanings are brought out clearly:

1	achieve;	**2**	credulous;	**3**	dear;
4	hinder;	**5**	loss;	**6**	loud;

7 obstacle;   **8** permanent;   **9** pleasure;
10 reluctance.

84 Write sentences to show the difference in meaning between each of the words in the following pairs. (You may wish to write one sentence for the pair of words or one sentence for each of the words.)

1	accept;	except.	**2**	allusion;	illusion.
3	emigrant;	immigrant.	**4**	explicit;	implicit.
5	forceful;	forcible.	**6**	imaginary;	imaginative.
7	lose;	loose.	**8**	momentary;	momentous.
9	practicable;	practical.	**10**	precede;	proceed.

85 Define, as for a dictionary, *one* meaning of each of the following words. Then use the word in a completely different sense, but without changing its form:

1	bear;	**2**	bill;	**3**	fair;
4	fine;	**5**	mean;	**6**	row;
7	sole;	**8**	toast;	**9**	tramp;
10	ward.				

86 The following words and phrases have been taken into English as part of its living development. Explain, by a definition, what each of them means and then use the word or phrase in a sentence to show that you know its current use:

1	au fait;	**2**	bona fides;	**3**	caveat emptor;
4	debacle;	**5**	esprit de corps;	**6**	ex officio;
7	fait accompli;	**8**	modus operandi;	**9**	post mortem;
10	sauna.				

87

(*a*) With the help of an etymological dictionary, divide the following words into the parts which historically make them up and explain the meaning of the parts and of the word. (*e.g. Philosopher*: Greek *philos*: 'a friend'; Greek *sophia*: 'wisdom'; therefore 'a lover of wisdom'.)

1	agnostic;	**2**	astrology;	**3**	automobile;
4	benefactor;	**5**	biennial;	**6**	computer;
7	gramophone;	**8**	Mediterranean;	**9**	sympathy;
10	unilateral.				

(*b*) Now use each of the words in a sentence to show that you know its full current meaning in present-day English. Bear in mind that the current meaning may not correspond exactly with the sum total of the parts which historically make up the word.

88 The following are current words or phrases used in present-day English. (*a*) Explain the meaning of each clearly but briefly. (*b*) Use each in a sentence of your own to show that you know its use.

1 To take French leave. (The French equivalent, interestingly, is *filer à l'anglaise.*)
2 An old chestnut.
3 To go off the rails.
4 Double-Dutch.
5 To play fast and loose.
6 Swings and roundabouts.
7 To go Dutch.
8 Beyond the pale.
9 To be under the weather.
10 One over the eight.

89 Define each of the words in the following pairs of *homophones* in order to bring out the differences between them in meaning and then use each in a sentence of your own to show that you know the current usage in present-day English.

1	assent; ascent.	2	boarder; border.
3	cord; chord.	4	councillor; counsellor.
5	desert; dessert.	6	freeze; frieze.
7	hoard; horde.	8	pair; pare.
9	sight; site.	10	vein; vain.

90 Each of the following sentences contains a *malapropism*. Rewrite them substituting for the malapropism the correct word:

1 I found it impossible to believe his indelible statements.
2 Although he repeated his controversial statements, they remained irre-prehensible.
3 He managed to impound his felony by stealing another car immediately.
4 At the age of eight the infant progeny played the violin concerto with remarkable confidence.
5 However much she tried, she could not illicit the information she sought.
6 He deprived great satisfaction from his elevation to the bishopric.
7 He poured the contents of the pressure-cooker through the calendar in order to drain them.
8 He was able to dissolve the deliberations by showing that both arguments were suspicious.
9 He asked the pharmacist to make up his proscription according to his requirements.
10 Because of the averse weather conditions, they could not ascend the precipitous slopes.

8
Composition

8:1

Most writing bears three things in mind:

(i) the point of view of the writer;

(ii) the content or subject-matter;

(iii) the reader for whom it is intended.

The structure of *composition* (Latin *compositus*, put together) is of considerable importance, therefore. In most 'writing' situations in life these three elements feature strongly; letters to tax inspectors, boy- or girl-friends, prospective employers, businesses, and diaries, reports, personal notes, memoranda all take account of them.

To write for oneself, to express ideas and feelings, is valuable and personal writing does play a part in life, but such 'composition' also bears in mind the three elements: the writer's viewpoint, the subject-matter, and the person for whom the writing is intended.

It will be convenient to consider composition or the art of structuring writing under the headings of *the essay*, *letters*, and *reports*.

The Essay
8:2

The word 'essay' comes from an Old French word (*essai*) meaning 'an attempt'; it is usually applied to a formal, and well-structured piece of writing and is often used as a synonym for composition. The formal literary essay has now, perhaps, been superseded by the magazine article, the periodical paper, or the newspaper column.

8:3

The **essay,** as the term is frequently used in schools and colleges, text-books and examinations, may be defined as it is set out in the University of London's *GCE Regulations and Syllabuses, 1983–4*:

> The composition 'will give candidates the opportunity to respond to one of a range of topics in an *ordered* and *appropriate* way'. The topics set are 'designed to stimulate *ideas* and *reactions*, and candidates will have opportunities to write *narratively*, *descriptively*, *discursively*, or in *dramatic* form ... Candidates will be able to demonstrate their *sense of audience* and their awareness of, and control

over, forms of *transactional* and *expressive* writing...' (The italics are not in the original text.)

The emphasis therefore, is on *order, appropriateness, ideas, reactions, narrative, description, discussion, drama, a sense of audience* and *transactional* and *expressive writing*.

An essay is usually assessed under 'Content', 'Expression' and 'Accuracy'.

8:4

The ordering and selection (planning) of appropriate ideas and reactions

The planning and the arrangement of the content of an essay are vital to its success. About a sixth of the time available for an essay is usually well-spent in such planning.

(i) *The ideas and reactions to a topic first need to be gathered* and, since they are unlikely to come in an ordered sequence, it is probably best to range as widely as possible over possible responses and to jot them down just as they come. Again and again it is necessary to go back to the topic to keep on course and to come at it from as many different angles as possible. For example, the topic 'A Leap in the Dark' might suggest the following:

Narrative treatment?
literal meaning followed
use of title as start or finish?
why 'dark'?
why 'a leap'?
build up a sense of climax
who are the characters?
what can be the central situation?
creation of suspense
go straight into the narrative

Figurative treatment?
man's uncertainty
conflict of reason and faith
complex problems
making a decision
courage to jump;
what is the darkness? ignorance?
pressures of life
essentially a personal problem/decision
relationships with others
historical characters who did this theologically (St Augustine, Luther, Niemuller, Mother Teresa)
scientists need imaginative leaps to find truth (Newton, Brunel, Alexander Fleming)
poets, too (Shelley, Keats, Hopkins, T. S. Eliot)

The ideas and responses come bubbling in any order; often one triggers off another. If all else fails, the questions *Who? What? Where?*

Why? How? When? applied to the topic can help to produce ideas and responses and to change direction. It is important to be lively, flexible, and open to whatever the topic suggests.

(ii) Once the list of ideas and responses has come, a decision needs to be made about *the direction from which the writing will be angled.* For example, with the topic 'A Leap in the Dark' the fundamental choice between a narrative or a figurative approach needs to be made. Description may be considered but it is not very productive, possibly, in this instance with this topic. A narrative treatment often seems the easy way out, but in fact it is very hard to write a good, well-composed short story in an instant; too often weak candidates choose a narrative style because they think it is an 'easy' approach and as a result they often spend two or three pages working themselves towards the topic only to fail to make it central to the story. Quite frequently a thoughtful, discursive approach is more productive.

(iii) Once the direction has been decided upon, *the list of ideas and responses needs to be arranged* into an effective order. If the 'figurative' treatment of the topic 'A Leap in the Dark' were being followed, a possible re-arrangement of the list would be:

man's uncertainty: doubt v. the need to know
conflict of reason/faith
decisions not easy/courage needed

examples of those faced with such problems
religious men and women/scientists/poets

essentially personal decision but relationships with others important
pressures on choice
darkness/ignorance

Within this bare arrangement the paragraphs begin to suggest themselves. The paragraphing should follow consistently a clear line of development and jumps between paragraphs should be avoided.

8:5

The paragraph is the fundamental unit of good writing in the essay; it is essentially concerned with the development of a single idea or response or a group of ideas and responses. Its length will depend on both the nature and the number of ideas and responses. A paragraph should be a unity with the development of a central theme at its heart.

Some early textbooks on the writing of paragraphs suggest that every paragraph should have a sentence which embodies its main theme ('the topic sentence') and that this sentence should come at the beginning or the end of the paragraph. Such a construction indicates to the reader what the theme is going to be or what it has been. Consider the following paragraphs:

The one thing certain about man is his uncertainty; he goes through life insecure and searching for assurance that always eludes him. The need to know dominates his thinking and activities from the cradle to the grave. His early education at school encourages him to experiment with experiences but the challenges of adult life perplex and frustrate him; as he nears death the biggest uncertainty of all remains—what lies on the other side of the grave?

To resolve this uncertainty man needs faith, although this faith often comes into conflict with reason. Some areas of experience can never be fully explained but an explanation is demanded . . .

'The topic sentences' are those in italics; they clearly indicate the theme to be developed in the rest of the paragraphs. It is well, too, to create links within the essay between one paragraph and another—as in the example given above. This continuity creates a fluency and ease and helps to establish a sense of progession within the essay. The art of effective paragraphing is not an easy one to learn and too many careless writers break up their work capriciously as if they were merely sawing logs from a branch. Certainly, there is nothing to suggest that paragraphs should be of equal length; on the contrary, variation in the length can be an effective way to control the pace of a piece of writing and a useful way to indicate a dramatic change of direction in the development of ideas and responses.

8:6

The narrative treatment/approach

(i) Again, the order in which the narrative is presented is of considerable importance; *the composition needs to start relevantly and engage the reader's interest at once.* Too often long accounts of getting-up in the morning, idyllic descriptions of the sun-rise or potted histories of the writer's family are thought necessary before the heart of the matter is reached. It is much better to go quickly and centrally into the topic.

In the course of writing *a surprise or two*, points where the narrative renews its strength or where it changes direction or where it develops dramatically, sometimes enliven it, but do not introduce wild or bizarre elements merely for their own sake. The ending must resolve the narrative by completing the story or even, perhaps, by pointing to the questions which have not yet been resolved; ghost stories frequently make use of the unresolved ending since part of their appeal lies in their mystery and inconclusiveness. Consider the following brilliant story by L. P. Hartley entitled *A High Dive*.

A High Dive

THE circus-manager was worried. Attendances had been falling off and such people as did come—children they were, mostly—sat about listlessly, munching sweets or sucking ices, sometimes talking to each other without so much as glancing at the show. Only the young or little girls, who came to see the ponies, betrayed any real interest. The clowns' jokes fell flat, for they were the kind of jokes that used to raise a laugh before 1939, after which critical date people's sense of humour seemed to have changed, along with many other things about them. The circus-manager had heard the word 'corny' flung about and didn't like it.

'What shall we do?' he asked his wife. They were standing under the Big Top, which had just been put up, and wondering how many of the empty seats would still be empty when they gave their first performance. 'We shall have to do something, or it's a bad look-out.'

'I don't see what we can do about the comic side,' she said. 'It may come right by itself. Fashions change, all sorts of old things have returned to favour, like old-time dances. But there's something we could do.'

'What's that?'

'Put on an act that's dangerous, really dangerous. Audiences are never bored by that. I know you don't like it, and no more do I, but when we had the Wall of Death——'

Her husband's big chest-muscles twitched under his thin shirt.

'You know what happened then.'

'Yes, but it wasn't our fault, we were in the clear.'

He shook his head.

'Those things upset everyone. I know the public came after it happened— they came in shoals, they came to see the place where someone had been killed. Then what do you suggest?'

Before she had time to answer a man came up to them.

'I hope I don't butt in,' he said, 'but there's a man outside who wants to speak to you.'

'What about?'

'I think he's looking for a job.'

'Bring him in,' said the manager.

The man appeared, led by his escort, who then went away. He was a tall, sandy-haired fellow with tawny leonine eyes and a straggling moustache. It wasn't easy to tell his age—he might have been about thirty-five. He pulled off his old brown corduroy cap and waited.

'I hear you want to take a job with us,' the manager said, while his wife tried to size up the newcomer. 'We're pretty full up, you know. We don't take on strangers as a rule. Have you any references?'

'No, sir.'

'Then I'm afraid we can't help you. But just for form's sake, what can you do?'

As if measuring its height the man cast up his eyes to the point where one of the two poles of the Big Top was embedded in the canvas.

'I can dive sixty feet into a tank eight foot long by four foot wide by four foot deep.'

The manager stared at him.

'Can you now?' he said. 'If so, you're the very man we want. Are you prepared to let us see you do it?'

'Yes,' the man said.

'And would you do it with petrol burning on the water?'

'Yes.'

'But have we got a tank?' the manager's wife asked.

'There's the old Mermaid's tank. It's just the thing. Get somebody to fetch it.'

While the tank was being brought the stranger looked about him.

'Thinking better of it?' said the manager.

'No, sir,' the man replied. 'I was thinking I should want some bathing-trunks.'

'We can soon fix you up with those,' the manager said. 'I'll show you where to change.'

Leaving the stranger somewhere out of sight, he came back to his wife.

'Do you think we ought to let him do it?' she asked.

'Well, it's his funeral. You wanted us to have a dangerous act, and now we've got it.'

'Yes, I know, but——' The rest was drowned by the rattle of the trolley bringing in the tank—a hollow, double cube like a sarcophagus. Mermaids in low relief sported on its leaden flanks. Grunting and muttering to each other the men slid it into position, a few feet from the pole. Then a length of hosepipe was fastened to a faucet, and soon they heard the sound of water swishing and gurgling in the tank.

'He's a long time changing,' said the manager's wife.

'Perhaps he's looking for a place to hide his money,' laughed her husband, and added, 'I think we'll give the petrol a miss.'

At length the man emerged from behind a screen, and slowly walked towards them. How tall he was, lanky and muscular. The hair on his body stuck out as if it had been combed. Hands on hips he stood beside them, his skin pimpled by goose-flesh. A fit of yawning overtook him.

'How do I get up?' he asked.

The manager was surprised, and pointed to the ladder. 'Unless you'd rather climb up, or be hauled up! You'll find a platform just below the top, to give you a foot-hold.'

He had started to go up the chromium-plated ladder when the manager's wife called after him: 'Are you still sure you want to do it?'

'Quite sure, madam.'

He was too tall to stand upright on the platform, the awning brushed his head. Crouching and swaying forty feet above them he swung his arms as though to test the air's resistance. Then he pitched forward into space, unseen by the manager's wife who looked the other way until she heard a splash and saw a thin sheet of bright water shooting up.

The man was standing breast-high in the tank. He swung himself over the edge and crossed the ring towards them, his body dripping, his wet feet caked with sawdust, his tawny eyes a little bloodshot.

'Bravo!' said the manager, taking his shiny hand. 'It's a first-rate act, that, and will put money in our pockets. What do you want for it, fifteen quid a week?'

The man shook his head.

'Well, twenty then.'

Still the man shook his head.

'Let's make it twenty-five. That's the most we give anyone.'

Except for the slow shaking of his head the man might not have heard. The circus-manager and his wife exchanged a rapid glance.

'Look here,' he said. 'Taking into account the draw your act is likely to be, we're going to make you a special offer—thirty pounds a week. All right?'

Had the man understood? He put his finger in his mouth and went on shaking his head slowly, more to himself than at them, and seemingly unconscious of the bargain that was being held out to him. When he still didn't answer, the knot of tension broke, and the manager said, in his ordinary, brisk voice,

'Then I'm afraid we can't do business. But just as a matter of interest tell us why you turned down our excellent offer.'

The man drew a long breath and breaking his long silence said, 'It's the first time I done it and I didn't like it.'

With that he turned on his heel and straddling his long legs walked off unsteadily in the direction of the dressing-room.

The circus-manager and his wife stared at each other.

'It was the first time he'd done it,' she muttered. 'The first time.' Not knowing what to say to him, whether to praise, blame, scold or sympathize, they waited for him to come back, but he didn't come.

'I'll go and see if he's all right,' the circus-manager said. But in two minutes he was back again. 'He's not there,' he said. 'He must have slipped out the other way, the crack-brained fellow!'

This story begins with a problem: 'What shall we do?' The rest of the story explores the apparent stroke of luck which seems for a time to provide the answers but, as in many successful short stories, the ending carries its surprises—the stranger refuses the job, he reveals that this is the first time he has jumped, and then he disappears as mysteriously as he has arrived. The characters are sharply drawn by what they saw, what they do, and by what they say about each other. The narrative has a number of points of heightened interest: does the man mean what he says? Will he jump? Will he survive? Will he take the job? Why does he refuse? The irony is, of course, that the problem with which the story opened remains unsolved—the manager and his wife still have no solution to it. The reader almost certainly did not expect the man's comment: 'It's the first time I done it and I didn't like it.'

An interesting feature of the story is the manner in which the writer advances his story by dialogue interspersed with passages of plain narrative. This technique is a difficult one to master but it allows an author to change the point of view from which the story is being told.

(ii) The point of view of the narrator is of considerable importance to a story. In *A High Dive* the narrative begins with a comment by the 'omniscient author', as he is sometimes called, the author who knows everything, even knowing what people are thinking secretly; this is a device which most readers are prepared to accept without question. The point of view is changed to that of the circus-manager and his wife—and here a tension is introduced, since their anxieties reveal a disagreement between them about the best thing to do. The point of view changes again when the man butting in introduces the stranger and from now on L. P. Hartley moves the story along first from one angle and then from another. The switch from the 'omniscient author' to dialogue lifts the narrative from the third person into the

I/we and *you* of the first and second persons easily and naturally. The reader acts as an eavesdropper. In writing any narrative the author must determine very early on the viewpoint(s) from which the story will be told.

A High Dive has a clear shape with an interesting beginning which sets the scene, introduces the main topic, and brings in two of the main characters. It has a good middle full of surprises. It ends effectively, albeit on a note of mystery and a return to the opening problem.

(iii) It is a useful exercise to practise writing openings to compositions using a narrative approach in order to establish ways of moving fast into the topic and the main point of view to be used. Look at *Wuthering Heights* by Emily Brontë, where you will find that the narrative is told initially by Lockwood who arrives on the scene to witness the events as a stranger, partly by Ellen Dean, an old housekeeper, and partly by the characters themselves in dialogue. The change of viewpoint is often one of the ways in which the reader can be surprised.

8:7

The descriptive approach

This approach to the essay demands control—control of pace, mood, and the patterning of language—and a clear point of view. The use of adjectival phrases is of considerable importance here, together with observation, good detail, and the ability to stimulate the reader's own visual imagination.

(i) Examine the ways in which Daniel Defoe described Man Friday in *Robinson Crusoe*:

Friday was a comely, handsome fellow, perfectly well-made, with straight strong limbs, not too large, tall and well-shaped, and, as I reckon, about twenty-six years of age. He had a good countenance, not a fierce and surly aspect; but seemed to have something very manly in his face; and yet he had all the sweetness and softness of a European in his countenance, too, especially when he smiled. His hair was long and black, not curled like wool; his forehead very high and large, and a great vivacity and sparkling sharpness in his eyes. ... His face was round and plump; his nose small.

Another vivid description well worth studying, this time sharpened by dialogue, is that of Fagin in Charles Dickens's *Oliver Twist*.

(ii) Description of natural scenes often plays a major role in composition work. The following paragraph is deceptively simple but in it Robert Louis Stevenson superbly orders his details of Treasure Island at its first appearance until specific features became identifiable. The point of view from which the description is made is established in the very first sentence: it is the deck of a boat gradually drifting off the coast; those who look for topic sentences can find one here:

The appearance of the island when I came on deck next morning was altogether changed. Although the breeze had now utterly failed, we had made a great deal of way during the night, and were now lying becalmed about half a mile to the south-east of the low eastern coast. Grey-coloured woods covered a large part of the surface. This even tint was indeed broken up by streaks of yellow sandbreak in the lower lands, and by many tall trees of the pine family, out-topping the others—some singly, some in clumps; but the general colouring was uniform and sad. The hills ran up clear above the vegetation in spires of naked rock. All were strangely shaped, and the Spy-glass, which was by three or four hundred feet the tallest on the island, was likewise the strangest in configuration, running up sheer from almost every side, and then suddenly cut off at the top like a pedestal to put a statue on.

(iii) The description may also be of a process; in such accounts order, detail, and clarity are essential. Consider Hilaire Belloc's description or explanation of how to sharpen a scythe—without losing a finger or a hand:

There is an art also in the sharpening of a scythe, and it is worth describing carefully. Your blade must be dry, and that is why you will see men rubbing the scythe-blade with grass before they whet it...

Then also your rubber must be quite dry, and on this account it is a good thing to lay it on your coat and keep it there during all your day's mowing. The scythe you stand upright, with the blade pointing away from you, and you put your left hand firmly on the back of the blade, grasping it: then you pass the rubber first down one side of the blade-edge and then down the other, beginning near the handle and going on to the point and working quickly and hard. When you first do this you will, perhaps, cut your hand... To tell when the scythe is sharp enough this is the rule. First the stone clangs and grinds against the iron harshly; then it rings musically to one note; then, at last, it purrs as though the iron and stone were exactly suited. When you hear this, your scythe is sharp enough.

(From Hilaire Belloc, *The Mowing of a Field*)

8:8

The discursive approach (discussion)

This is perhaps the most difficult of the approaches to master and yet, curiously, it is the one which is more commonly of practical use.

A good leading article in *The Times* or *The Guardian* will give an everyday demonstration of the art of discursive writing. Sometimes the author wishes to remain objective and not appear to take sides, but at other times he may wish to make clear his position and therefore his 'bias'. Consider this opening to an article, for example, from *The Times*, directed presumably at the educated reader who is interested in establishing the facts and wanting to hear the arguments presented on both sides:

The failure of the European summit arrests the development of the Community at a moment when it badly needs to move forward. It will undermine public confidence, and is a sad way of bringing to a close Britain's initially hopeful period in the chair. This should have been the summit at which the political leaders of the member nations lifted their eyes above narrow interpretations of national interest and broke through bureaucratic obstacles into a new era of reform.

There is, after all, a lot at stake. Public opinion is not particularly enthusiastic about the Community. Unemployment is growing. Industrial re-structuring is not only Britain's problem. The Common Agricultural Policy will be made even more impossible by the admission of Portugal and Spain. Foreign affairs increasingly demand a European voice—there is, for instance, no reason why so much of the burden of bringing the super powers together should fall on Herr Schmidt personally. Europe is also going to need more unity and coherence if problems continue to mount in eastern Europe. Fortunately, political cooperation has made progress in spite of differences in other fields but it needs a better foundation of general agreement if it is to prosper.

In many ways the task should have been easier now than it was in the past. The mood is calmer than when Mrs Thatcher was dominating the scene with her demands for rectification of Britain's contributions to the budget. Although further agreements are still necessary, Britain has done better than expected because of developments in world trade. Too much of the burden has now fallen on West Germany, but it should not be beyond the Community to cope with this problem. Moreover the day when the community's budget resources run out has become more remote. In addition France has generally become slightly more accommodating on the budget and even towards the principle of reforming the common agricultural policy, though she still has her special interests to protect.

Yet failure came anyway, and there now seems only a slim chance of reaching agreement by the end of this year, which was the aim set in May of last year. But work will go on, and perhaps some of the ground has been cleared in London. It is not the end of the world, or of the Community. It is, however, an indication of just how powerful and intractable are the conflicts of national interest, and how difficult it is to overcome these even in an atmosphere considerably friendlier and more rational than it has sometimes been in recent years. When agreement is eventually patched up there will remain a feeling that momentum has been lost at a moment when it was particularly needed.

The Times, 28 November 1981

There is an impressive list of facts here and an attempt to present them in a balanced way. The clumsiness of the 'First ..., Secondly ..., Thirdly ...' approach and of the 'On the one hand ... whilst on the other hand' approach is totally avoided. An editor who wished to slant the ideas more politically might have done so by selecting different facts, omitting details, or using a style deliberately designed to lead the reader to agree with or to reject the stance and the views put forward.

8:9

Dramatic writing

Compositions sometimes take the form of extended dialogue or may even, more formally, assume the structure and lay-out of a scene from a play. When such compositions are set in examinations, an opening is given, which sets the scene, introduces the main characters, establishes a situation of dramatic tension, and begins the dialogue. For example:

Write a short play by continuing the dialogue below in a manner which develops the dramatic situation.

(Do not copy out the extract before you begin your work, but you are advised to continue its method of setting out the dialogue. If you wish, you may introduce one or two more characters or add a further scene.)

> *A living-room. Mrs Baxley and Elsie are sitting at a small card table; Mrs Baxley is a woman in her forties and Elsie is a pretty but rather petulant and discontented girl of twenty or so. Elsie shuffles a pack of cards and passes them to Mrs Baxley who studies them with the air of a clairvoyant.*

MRS BAXLEY	Um ... Um ... Well, the first thing I see, Elsie, is a great surprise. Yes, you're going to have a great surprise.
ELSIE	A surprise? When?
MRS BAXLEY	Very soon.
ELSIE	How soon? Next week?
MRS BAXLEY	Perhaps sooner.
ELSIE	Well, it can't be much sooner. It's Sunday night and nearly next week now.
MRS BAXLEY	Well, it's coming very soon. And it isn't a nice surprise. I don't think you'll like it.

It is not easy to write dialogue for a play without considerable practice since the level of the language (the 'register') is not necessarily the same as that of everyday speech. Consider the language, for example, in the following opening scene:

Write a short play by continuing the dialogue below in a manner which develops the dramatic situation.

(Do not copy out the extract before you begin your work, but you are advised to continue its method of setting out the dialogue. If you wish, you may introduce one or two more characters or add a further scene.)

> *As the curtain rises, Sally Brooks and her father, Derek Brooks, are sitting in the front row of desks in a school classroom. Derek is in his late forties and Sally is sixteen years old; both are sitting tense and motionless.*
>
> *Derek gets up quickly and awkwardly as Helen Davis, an attractive young teacher of about twenty-five, comes into the room.*

HELEN	Oh, is this your father, Sally?
SALLY	Yes, Miss Davis.
HELEN	How are you, Mr Brooks? Please sit down. I'm Sally's class teacher. (*She and Mr Brooks shake hands and sit down.*) It was kind of you to come straight away. I'll tell you why I had to write to you as I did.
DEREK	My wife and I are both quite worried.

The language of some plays, for example passages in works by Arnold Wesker, Shelagh Delaney, and John Osborne, comes closer, perhaps, to the language of everyday talk, but the selection of material and the use of imagery often gives them a quality which allows for interpretation on more than one level.

In compositions of this kind it is best to aim at some of the following: fluency in dialogue and the development of an idea from one speaker to the next; the establishment of clear characters and some kind of dramatic tension between them; the posing of a problem or problematical situation and its resolution; surprise; supportive stage-directions; a level of language which can be maintained easily—if you need to depart from the level it will become significant for your audience. A common error is to allow the dramatic dialogue to deteriorate into passages of extended narrative.

8:10

A sense of audience

Increasingly, public examinations are taking into account the fact that most writing is produced for a specific readership or 'audience'. Advertisers and broadcasters spend huge sums of money in researching the customers for whom a product is intended so that they can slant it accurately and effectively, present it at the most opportune time and include in it qualities with the greatest appeal.

Consider the following extracts to see if you can decide on the 'audience' for whom they were intended:

(i) 'Remember, it costs only a few pence to dial a call to find out if the person you want is there. This may be cheaper than paying for a 'personal' call via the operator because the 'personal fee' is payable whether or not the call is successful.'

(ii) Are you being served? Find out what happened when Noel, Keith and Maggie, took on a part-time job halfway down the motorway. Keith sings! Or does he? He and twin brother Jeff have got together and recorded a song—can we prevent them from performing it today?

(iii) A silk shirt should be a delight to wear, a versatile asset to any wardrobe, and a quality buy which will last you for years. Sadly, some silk shirts are not. They're thin, easily-crumpled, skimpily seamed, and quickly look very tired indeed. Our superb heavy Pongee silk shirt lives up to everything a silk shirt should be...

(iv) COURSAC Enveaux, a comfortable old cottage in a very peaceful spot amidst lush green countryside. Fishing and hunting locally at 1 Km. Lounge, kitchen, 3 bedrooms (2 double and 4 single beds), shower-room, carport, grounds. Shopping in the village (2 Km) or at Perigueux (10 Km). Farm produce.

(v) Mumps is very infectious, and the danger of infection is not over for a fortnight to three weeks after the symptoms appear; then the incubation period is also up to three weeks, so no household that has had a case of mumps is safe from it until nearly six weeks have elapsed.
Symptoms. Fever. The swelling of the glands of the neck under the ear and perhaps under the chin. These are the parotid glands and the submaxillary glands.

(vi) If you do not agree with the amount of the assessment, you or your professional adviser may appeal against it. The grounds of your appeal should be stated and the appeal must be made within 30 days from the date of issue shown on the notice. This will enable the assessment to be altered if necessary when the appeal has been determined. If the Inspector cannot agree the amount of the assessment with you, the appeal will be heard and determined by an independent body of Commissioners.

(vii) Use the table below to help you decide how much to invest each month; then just complete the simple application form opposite and return it to us. There is no obligation. Send no money now. We will give you a personal quotation together with details of how to make your monthly investment. You will have two weeks to review our offer and be satisfied that it meets your needs.

(viii) We shall fight on the beaches, we shall fight on the landing-grounds, we shall fight in the fields and in the streets, we shall fight in the hills; we shall never surrender; and even if, which I do not for a moment believe, this Island or a large part of it were subjugated and starving, then our Empire, beyond the seas, armed and guarded by the British Fleet would carry on the struggle.

(ix) Take a piece of copper foil in a pair of tongs and hold it in a bunsen flame. The metal becomes red hot and, on cooling, is covered with a black layer. This is black copper oxide. If the metal is scraped, the surface layer is obtained as a powder and the fresh copper exposed can be similarly treated.

(x) Truss the fowl, inserting some pieces of vegetables in the body. Rub the breast of the bird with lemon, wrap in buttered paper and put in pan with sufficient stock or water to cover. Add remainder of vegetables, salt and bouquet garni and cook gently until fowl is tender.

All of the extracts imply a context; there is an audience for whom, and a set of circumstances in which, each of the passages was written. Some of the circumstances can be established from the vocabulary and the attitude of the writer. What characteristics of the language reveal the purpose of each passage and its 'audience'?

8:11

Letters

Letters are often divided into two categories: **personal** letters and **business/formal** letters, the division being made both because of content and because of style and form.

8:12

The personal letter

This form of writing is one which most people will continue to use throughout the rest of their lives long after the writing of English for examination purposes has vanished into the past. The art of writing an interesting personal letter is hard to acquire but one well worth pursuing.

(i) There are few 'rules' about the content or the style of the personal letter; but both content and style will be determined by:

(**a**) the specific set of circumstances in which the letter is being written: *e.g.* the exchange of information about experiences, families, jobs; to ask for help or advice; to express thanks for a present or an invitation to a meal; to keep in touch and to maintain friendship over time and distance; to express feelings and responses.

(**b**) the closeness of the relationship between the writer and his correspondent: *e.g.* family ties; close friendship; 'pen-friendship' with someone abroad; boy/girl-friend; fiancé(e), husband, wife; casual acquaintance.

(ii) Personal letters need not be full of inaccuracies and slang expressions. Indeed, the closer the correspondent the more careful one should be, it might be thought; there seems little excuse for a slipshod and slovenly letter to a close friend or relative.

Consider the following extracts taken from personal letters; you will see that most of them are sensitively and very carefully 'composed':

(**a**) *Sir Walter Raleigh, to his wife, the night before he expected to be put to death at Winchester, 1603*

You shall now receive, my dear wife, my last words in these my last lines. My love I send you, that you may keep it, when I am dead, and my counsel that you may remember it, when I am no more. I would not by my will present you with sorrows, Dear Bess. Let them go into the grave with me ... and seeing it is not the will of God, that I shall see you any more in this life, bear it patiently, and with a heart like thy self. First I send you all my thanks ... for your many travails and care taken for me...

Secondly I beseech you, for the love you bare me living, do not hide yourself many days after my death ... Thirdly you shall understand, that my land was conveyed bona fide to my child; the writings were drawn up at midsummer twelve months; my honest cousin Brett can testify so much, and Dalberni too, can remember somewhat therein. And I trust my blood will quench their malice that have thus cruelly murdered me...

Love God and begin betimes to repose yourself on him ... Teach your son also to love and fear God whilst he is yet young, that the fear of God may grow up with him; and the same God will be a husband to you, and a father to him; a husband, and a father, which cannot be taken from you. Baylie oweth me £200 and Adrian Gilbert £600. In Jersey, I have also much money owing me ... And howsoever you do, for my soul's sake, pay all poor men...

As for me, I am no more yours, nor you mine. Death hath cut us asunder; and God hath divided me from the world, and you from me ... I can say no more; time and death call me away...

My dear wife, farewell. Bless my poor boy. Pray for me and let my good God hold you both in his arms.

Written with the dying hand of sometime thy husband but now, alas, overthrown.

Wa: Raleigh

Yours that was, but now not my own.

The poignancy of this last letter depends as much on the pace and the control of the writing as on its contents. It is ordered and balanced, with ideas set out in a warm, understanding, and even business-like manner. It says much for Raleigh's dignity and comments implicitly on the relationship between himself and his wife.

(**b**) A letter from one friend to another, following the celebration of a wedding anniversary:

18 Franklin Rd.,
Reigate,
Surrey.

19 December, 1983

Dear Chris and Jane,

Many thanks indeed for that splendid bottle of champagne you gave us on Saturday. We're going out to dinner this evening but we shall open the bottle on our return and certainly think of you then.

Thanks, too, for the flowers and for thoughtfully sending them on the day before the party. I don't know whether I explained or not, but as well as those white spiky chrysanthemums downstairs the white and mauve ones were part of the bouquet. What a surprise they were when they came! They looked really beautiful—and still do.

And thank you both for coming. I didn't have much opportunity to talk to either of you at length but the celebrations wouldn't have been complete without you.

A happy Christmas and best wishes for the New Year—especially for the new job, Jane.

With love,
Maureen

Again, the letter is warm and filled with references to personal details which give the writing an immediacy; it is well-structured and to the point, without being at all brusque. The tone is appropriate and the writing well directed.

(**c**) A letter from a soldier in the front line in France to his family back home in London.

Somewhere in France.
July, 1944

Dear Mum, Dad, and Rachel,

Somewhere in France; I can't say where partly because I don't know and partly because I wouldn't be allowed to say so if I knew. One thing that is sure: I'm sharing this dug-out with twenty-others who also don't know where they are. Somewhere out there beyond the next clump of trees or over the hill or in the next village there must be some Germans who also don't know where they are—except that they are not where they want to be. They're all trying to get home as fast as possible.

It's a funny thing but the countryside doesn't know there's a war on. The birds are still singing in the trees and the weeds are growing as usual. Even the clouds pay no attention to what we are doing down in this field. It makes me wonder what it's all about. Will anyone care one hundred years on?

How's Tibby? That night he turned up on our doorstep in the middle of an air-raid was a stroke of luck for him. Do you remember how you gave him some fish heads to eat the next day, Mum? He barely stopped eating for a week! How's Gran these days? Give her my love when you see her; this is the second war for her and she must be heartily sick of it all. To spend one's whole life with rationing, bombs, soldiers marching off to fight on foreign shores is not the best way to spend one's days. Perhaps this time it will be the war to end all wars. If it isn't it will be our fault—mine and the rest of these young blokes huddled round their rifles in the dug-out...

A special big kiss for Rachel. Look after her. You're what I'm fighting this war for!

Lots of love,
Michael

This letter is thoughtful and expresses personal reactions to the soldier's situation; its style is appropriately colloquial and yet the warmth of the relationship is implicit in the details and attitude of the writer.

(*d*) This is the last letter written by Wilfred Owen, the poet, on Thursday, 31 October 1918, at 6.15 p.m. He was killed in the attack at 5.45 a.m. on 4 November 1918; one week later the war was over.

[2nd Manchester Regiment]

Dearest Mother,

I will call the place from which I'm now writing 'The Smoky Cellar of the Forester's House'. I write on the first sheet of the writing pad which came in the parcel yesterday. Luckily the parcel was small, as it reached me just before we moved off to the line ... My servant and I ate the chocolate in the cold middle of last night, crouched under a draughty Tamboo, roofed with planks. I husband the Malted Milk for tonight, & tomorrow night. The handkerchief & socks are most opportune, as the ground is marshy, & I have a slight cold! So thick is the smoke in this cellar that I can hardly see by a candle 12 ins. away, and so thick are the inmates that I can hardly write for pokes, nudges, & jotts. On my left the Company Commander snores on a bench: other officers repose on wire beds behind me. At my right hand Kellett, a delightful servant of A Company ... radiates joy & contentment from pink cheeks and baby eyes. He laughs with a signaller, to whose left ear is glued the Receiver; but whose rolling with the gaiety shows that he is listening with his right ear to a merry corporal who appears, at this distance away, nothing [but] a gleam of white teeth and a wheeze of jokes.

Splashing my hand, an old soldier with a walrus moustache peels & chops potatoes into the pot. By him, Keyes, my cook, chops wood; another feeds the smoke with damp wood.

It is a great life. I am more oblivious than alas! yourself, dear Mother, of the ghastly glimmering of the guns, outside, & the hollow crashing of the shells.

There is no danger down here, or if any, it will be well over before you read these lines.

I hope you are as warm as I am; as serene in your room as I am here; and that you think of me never in bed as resignedly as I think of you always in bed. Of this I am certain you could not be visited by a band of friends half so fine as surround me here.

Ever,
Wilfred

X

This letter is poignant because of the imminent death of its writer. Nevertheless, it is full of home details and moves from the general description of the soldier's immediate situation to the more private descriptions of his fellow-soldiers and friends and his mother in bed.

8:13

The form of the personal letter often follows a conventional pattern.

(i) *The address* is put at the top right-hand corner of the sheet. The name of the person writing the letter is *not* included. This address should be consistently punctuated with commas at the end of every line or with no punctuation marks (other than capital letters) used:

e.g.   *Either*   'St. Cross',
     25(,) Beaulieu Rd.,
     Dorchester,
     Dorset.

(Sometimes a comma is also placed after the number of the house.)

     or   St Cross
     25 Beaulieu Road
     Dorchester
     Dorset

(ii) *The date* is placed directly beneath this address, usually on the next line but one. It may take a number of forms with a variety of punctuation styles:

     24th December 1982
     24 December 1982
     24th December, 1982.
     24 December, 1982.
     December 24th 1982
     December 24th, 1982.
     December 24 1982
     December 24, 1982.

(iii) The introductory '*salutation*', as it is sometimes called, can also be varied according to the degree of intimacy aimed at, but this salutation must be placed conventionally *either* on the line immediately after the date *or* on the next line but one, towards the left side of the sheet of paper:

e.g.   Dear Isabelle,
     My dear Isabelle,
     Isabelle, my dear,
     Darling Isabelle,
     My darling,
     Isabelle, darling,

The salutation may be as formal or as informal as the body of the letter requires; the reader will certainly see some significance in the way he or she is addressed.

(iv) Following the body of the letter the '*subscription*' or the 'conclusion' may take a number of forms in order to reflect the degree of intimacy between the correspondents.

e.g.   Yours sincerely, (NOTE: there is no apostrophe in *Yours*)
     Sincerely yours,

Yours affectionately,
Affectionately yours,
Your sincere friend,
Yours,
As ever,
With love,
Love,
Best wishes, *and so on*

Once again, the recipient will place some significance in this subscription and it needs to be chosen with care so that the right 'register' is chosen. Whichever form is used, it is followed by a comma, and the name of the writer (usually only the first name) is placed on the next line. Only the first letter of the subscription is in capitals.

(v) A typical layout of an informal or personal letter would look like this:

25 Beaulieu Rd.,
Dorchester,
Dorset.

24 December, 1982.

my dear Isabelle,

[Body of the Letter]

As ever,
Lou

25 Beaulieu Road
Dorchester
Dorset

24 December 1982

Isabelle, darling,

[Body of the Letter]

with love,
Lou

8:14

Business/formal letters

(i) Letters of this kind are expected to follow a conventional lay-out and their contents are usually presented in an appropriate register, which is usually marked by *clarity, relevance, courtesy, accuracy,* and *brevity.* Such letters need to come quickly and clearly to the main topic without any preamble, other than a reference to any previous correspondence. The main topic is sometimes presented between the formal salutation and the body of the letter and any reference numbers or letters are included there.

> 25 Beaulieu Road,
> Dorchester,
> Dorset.
> 24 December, 1982.
>
> J. Cooper and Co., Ltd.,
> Solicitors,
> 32 Hay Lane,
> Dorchester,
> Dorset.
>
> Dear Sir,
> House purchase: 9, Hope Street, Dorchester.
> (Your reference: AB/ns 15/901)
>
> [Body of the Letter]
>
> Yours faithfully,
>
> [Signature]
>
> (Mr) R. Smith

(ii) *The selection and arrangement of the content* of a formal letter are important. Often the recipient of such a letter is busy, has little time he is willing to spend on irrelevance, and is anxious to move on to the next matter. It is helpful, therefore, if the content is as clear, 'relevant, courteous, accurate, and as brief as is consistent with the subject.

Again, there are no 'rules' about this selection and arrangement of the content but it is usually best to begin with a short paragraph outlining the main topic:

e.g. 'Thank you for your letter of 24 March, 1983. We are sorry to learn that the washing-machine you bought from us is not working satisfactorily.' The remaining paragraphs should set out the main points of the reply:

e.g. acceptance of responsibility; offer to send a serviceman to repair the machine; suggestion of how to arrange a mutually convenient date and time; assurance of concern and sound servicing under the guarantee.

25, Beaulieu Rd.,
Dorchester,
Dorset.

24 December, 1982.

Dorchester Domestic Appliances Ltd.,
23 Honey pot Lane,
Dorchester,
Dorset.

Dear Sir,

'Spindry' Washing Machine: no. HZ 32472

[Body of the Letter]

Yours faithfully,

[Signature]

(Dr) J. S. King

(iii) *The formal letter should be free from stilted language,* now sometimes referred to as 'commercialese': *e.g.* 'we are in receipt of'; 'we beg to acknowledge'; *ult., inst.*; 'Your communication of'; 'with reference to the same'; 'your esteemed favour', and so on. Such words and phrases are old-fashioned and contrary to the style of formal letter-writing today.

(iv) *The layout of formal letters is conventional* but minor variations in the layout are possible according to the nature of the letter itself. The remarks given above about the punctuation of addresses and dates in personal letters apply also to addresses in formal letters (see **8:13**, pages 161–2).

```
                        Dorchester Domestic Appliances Ltd.,
                        23 Honeypot Lane,
                        Dorchester,
                        Dorset.

                                29 December, 1982

        Dr. J. S. King,
        25 Beaulieu Rd.,
        Dorchester,
        Dorset.

        Dear Sir,

                'Spindry' Washing Machine: no. HZ 32472


                        [Body of the Letter]


                        Yours faithfully,

                        [Signature]

                        M. P. Hendrick
                        (Sales Director)
```

Some points are worth noting.

Letters *to* a company include its name and address above the formal salutation, 'Dear Sir'.

The salutation 'Dear Sir/Madam' is usual, unless the writer were deliberately seeking to 'personalise' and make less formal the letter, when the salutation 'Dear Dr King', or 'Dear Mr Hendrick,' might have been used. If, however, the name of the person to whom the formal letter is addressed has already appeared in the address above the salutation, it is more usual *not* to repeat the personal name in the salutation itself but to use the 'Dear Sir/Madam' formula.

The subscription to formal letters is either 'Yours faithfully' or 'Yours truly'. It is followed by a comma. The word 'faithfully' or 'truly' is spelt with a small letter and 'Yours' takes a capital letter but no apostrophe.

8:15

Formal invitations

A formal invitation normally is made in the third person; it sets out the name(s) of the person(s) making the invitation, the name of the person being invited, the place, time, and nature of the event to which the person is being invited and an address to which a reply should be addressed, often under the heading of *R.S.V.P.* (*Répondez s'il vous plaît*).

The Principal and Staff
of Stranraer College
request the pleasure of the company of

Mr and Mrs A. Smith

at

the Annual Speech Day
on Wednesday, 9th May, 1984,
at 7.30 p.m.

R.S.V.P.

The reply is usually made in the present tense and in the person appropriate to the invitation itself:

Mr and Mrs A. Smith have great pleasure in accepting the invitation of the Principal and Staff to the annual speech Day to be held on Wednesday, 9th May, 1984, at 7.30 p.m.

Had the invitation been in the more direct form of:

You are invited
by the Principal and the Staff
of Stranraer College
to the annual Speech Day
to be held
on Wednesday, 9th May, 1984,
at 7.30 p.m.

R.S.V.P.

then the reply would have been made in the first person:

We are very pleased to accept the invitation of the Principal and Staff of Stranraer College to the annual Speech Day to be held on Wednesday, 9th May, 1984, at 7.30 p.m.

Mr and Mrs A. Smith

Reports
8:16

Reports are formal and factual, although the presentation of facts in one form rather than another will provide its own gloss and commentary on them. The very act of selection and arrangement puts a level of meaning on a series of 'facts'.

Reports may be presented in the layout of a formal/business letter or in a manner which sets out the *subject of the report, its source, its destination* and *the date*. One such layout (and there are several others) which allows for these details might be this:

```
              'Spindry' Washing Machines Ltd

    From:   A. K. Jones, Sales Director

    To:     Sir James Woolcroft, Managing Director


    Date:   4 May, 1984



       Survey on the reliability of the X.14 range of
       'Spindry.' washing machines: Scunthorpe,
       March - April, 1984.


                      [Body of the Report]

                                         [Signature]
                       Signed:  ..............
                                      (Sales Director)
```

Reports on an investigation, for example, normally set out:
  (i)   the details of what was to be investigated; the manner of the investigation (including the names and structure of the investigating team);
  (ii) the details of the investigation itself;
  (iii) an attempt to summarise the effectiveness and/or limitations of the investigation;
  (iv) conclusions;
  (v)   recommendations.

Statistical tables and supporting material are best presented as appendices in order not to clutter up the report itself and so reduce its impact.

8:17

Formal reports, for example from one committee to another, may also follow a more stereotyped pattern. Headings, under which the substance of such reports falls, often include:

(**a**) *Terms of reference*: an introductory statement which sets out as precisely as possible the scope of the work undertaken, *e.g.* 'To investigate ways in which the company's market share of tinned food sales can be increased'.

(**b**) *Procedure*: an outline of the ways in which the individual or the committee set about the work that was undertaken. This might refer, for example, to the setting-up of working parties, the reception of papers relating to the work, statistical surveys undertaken, and questionnaires drawn up and issued. This section should refer to the personnel undertaking the work (together with their status), the Chairmanship of the committee, and the dates on which meetings were held. (If the meetings have been too frequent to list, it is common practice to include a general statement such as, 'The Committee met thirty-nine times between 1 June 1982 and 31 May 1983.')

(**c**) *Findings*: this section is best kept short and very factual. Those reading the report will need to master the things discovered as quickly as possible.

(**d**) *Conclusions*: again, the statements here should be concise and factual. If qualifications to a conclusion are given, they should be as precise as possible.

> *e.g.* The company's market share can be increased by twenty per cent provided (i) the warehouse at Stavely Road is extended by 50,000 square feet; (ii) television advertising time is bought (estimated cost £15,000 in the current financial year); (iii) the sales force is restructured according to the suggestions below (see *Recommendations*, section x, subsection y).

(**e**) *Recommendations*: this section should be specific, factual, and concise.

(**f**) *Signature, with status, and date*:

> *e.g.* R. J. Croft (Chairman)   25 June 1983

8:18

In order to present facts objectively and in order to suggest impartiality, reports are often best written in the *third person*. Statements which are impersonal (e.g. 'It was clear that ...' rather than 'We thought ...'; 'The Committee considered that ...' rather than 'Mr Crayshaw and I believed that ...') best maintain this detached, objective register. Be careful to avoid, however, too many passive constructions (*e.g.* 'Sales can be undertaken'); such 'lifeless passives', if used too frequently, rob a report of thrust and impact.

EXERCISES

Section A: The essay

In tackling the work in this section remember particularly the following:

(i)   Essays must be relevant to the topic.

(ii)   Their content should be arranged in an appropriate manner.

(iii)   The opening must engage the reader's attention at once; the ending must resolve or conclude the narrative, description, discussion, or dramatic piece in a manner consistent with the rest of the writing.

(iv)   Careful paragraphing which allows the appropriate development of the subject matter is essential; order the material within the paragraphs and make links between paragraphs firm and relevant.

(v)   Write accurately; grammar, punctuation, and spelling should be given the greatest attention.

Part One: Narrative

91   Write compositions, using a *narrative* approach, on the following topics. Your work on each should be at least 450 words in length:

1 The Hunt.

2 A Strange Encounter.

3 Lost in the Fog.

4 The Break-through.

5 A Shock to the System.

6 Lightning never strikes twice in the same place.

7 Truth is stranger than Fiction.

8 'A funny thing happened to me on the way to the examination . . .'

9 The Castle.

10 Caught in the Act.

11 Hooked.

12 A Lost Cause.

13 Never say Die.

14 Daylight Robbery.

15 An Incident at a Railway Station.

16 'The Ground opened up beneath my feet.'

17 Down but not Out.

18 The most moving experience in my life so far.

19 A friend in need . . .

20 'I turned the corner but the house was no longer there.'

Part Two: Descriptive

92   Write short descriptions of the following articles for advertising copy. Mention particularly the use, appearance, and special features of the objects which might attract customers. The copy is intended for a special 'Advertising Feature' in a local newspaper; each description should be between 150 and 200 words in length.

1 A record-player of new, attractive design.
2 A four-slice electric toaster.
3 A simulated-log gas fire.
4 A coffee-filter machine.
5 A new TV electronic game.
6 A video-recorder.
7 An ornamental garden pool.
8 A shower-unit for the home.
9 A sewing-machine with several new stitching features.
10 Equipment for an amateur's photographic dark room.

93

1 Read the following short descriptive passages carefully and then try to
  formulate detailed answers to the questions which follow them:

(*a*) I went on tiptoe through the darkness to his bedroom door, brushing
against the furniture and upsetting a candlestick with a thump. When I saw
there was a light in the room I felt frightened, and as I opened the door I
heard grandpa shout, 'Gee-up!' as loudly as a bull with a megaphone. He
was sitting straight up in bed and rocking from side to side as though the bed
were on a rough road; the knotted edges of the counterpane were his reins;
his invisible horse stood in a shadow beyond the bedside candle. Over a white
flannel nightshirt he was wearing a red waistcoat with walnut sized brass
buttons. The overfilled bowl of his pipe smouldered among his whiskers like
a little, burning hayrick on a stick. At the sight of me his hands dropped from
the reins and lay blue and quiet, the bed stopped still on a level road, he
muffled his tongue into silence, and the horses drew softly up.
  'Is there anything the matter, grandpa?' I asked.

  (i) How do the introduction and the conclusion of this passage contri-
       bute to the 'strangeness'?
  (ii) Explain how this description is both frightening and funny.
  (iii) Dylan Thomas uses comparisons, contrasts, and surprising details to
       build up this picture of grandpa. Give some examples of these
       features.

(*b*) 'Now what did you gather from that woman's appearance? Describe it.'
  'Well, she had a slate-coloured, broad brimmed straw hat, with a feather
of brickish red. Her jacket was black, with black beads sewn upon it, and a
fringe of little black jet ornaments. Her dress was brown, rather darker than
coffee colour, with a little purple plush at the neck and sleeves. Her gloves
were greyish, and were worn through at the right forefinger. Her boots I
didn't observe. She had small, round, hanging gold ear-rings, and a general
air of being fairly well-to-do, in a vulgar, comfortable, easygoing way.'
  Sherlock Holmes clapped his hands softly together and chuckled.
  ''Pon my word, Watson, you are coming along wonderfully. You have
really done very well indeed.'

  (i) How does Holmes's attitude to Watson contribute to the air of
       strangeness?

    (ii) Although the detective applauds Watson for his careful description only the woman's dress is described. No account is given of her face, figure, hands, or size. Why does the writer omit these details?

   (iii) How does the use of colour in this passage differ from that in (*a*) above?

(*c*) Jem Rodney, the mole-catcher, averred that, one evening as he was returning homeward, he saw Silas Marner leaning against a stile with a heavy bag on his back, instead of resting the bag on the stile as a man in his senses would have done; and that, on coming up to him, he saw that Marner's eyes were set like a dead man's, and he spoke to him, and shook him, and his limbs were stiff, and his hands clutched the boy as if they'd been made of iron; but just as he had made up his mind that the weaver was dead, he came all right again, like, as you might say in the winking of an eye, and said 'Good-night' and walked off.

    (i) Silas Marner's strangeness seems all the more startling because of Jem Rodney's contrasting normality. Give some examples of this contrast.

   (ii) Jem Rodney was not afraid of Silas Marner. What is there in this description that makes Marner, nevertheless, a frightening figure?

   (iii) What is strange about the use of the phrase 'in the winking of an eye' at the end of the passage?

From your study of these three extracts you will have seen that writers use many devices to produce vivid descriptions of people. Amongst those used here were:

    A setting appropriate to the mood of the character;
    a selection of colourful details;
    the careful selection of details to be included;
    comparisons and contrasts;
    the balancing of one character with another;
    the arrangement of the details chosen.

2 Write an account, in not more than 450 words, of: 'A person I hope never to meet again'.

94 Write compositions, using a mainly *descriptive* approach, on the following topics. Your work on each should be at least 450 words in length:

1 Beauty is only skin-deep.
2 The Snow came at Midnight.
3 A Tree across the Road.
4 A Strange Cove.
5 Life through the eyes of the old paper-seller on the corner.
6 The Mongrel.
7 A Seventeenth-century Cemetery.
8 The Village in the Valley.
9 One of the Gang.
10 The Prisoner's Release.

11 A Ship of Fools.
12 The New Cathedral.
13 The Chance of a Lifetime.
14 The Hitch-hiker.
15 My Grandparents.
16 The House on the Corner.
17 'You should have seen them! What a sight!'
18 Sounds of High Summer.
19 Sounds Strange.
20 A Question of Taste.

Part Three: Discursive

95   Write compositions, using a *discursive* (*discussion*) approach, on the following topics. Your work on each should be at least 450 words in length:

1 'Life is a comedy to those who feel, a tragedy to those who think.'
2 Giving and accepting advice.
3 Youth is wasted on the young.
4 What arguments can you find for *either* being a pacifist *or* rejecting pacifism?
5 If you were a member of the present government, what would be your priorities? How would you introduce them?
6 'Liberty means Responsibility' (G. B. Shaw). How far is this true?
7 What do you consider are the essentials for you to lead a happy life?
8 How valuable are traditions in life today?
9 What would justify a strong Men's Lib. movement today?
10 'Do not do unto others as you would they should do unto you; their tastes may not be the same.' (G. B. Shaw) How far is this sound advice?
11 How justified are some young people today in attributing their acts of vandalism to 'being bored'?
12 What *major* improvements would you like to see in your or your children's school *or* college *or* office *or* workshop? Justify your suggestions.
13 What advantages and disadvantages would there be in paying everybody the same basic weekly wage?
14 What do you understand *either* by the term 'democracy' *or* by the term 'social justice'?
15 What features in your own formal education have you most regretted? How might they have been altered and improved?
16 How far could you justify the introduction of a period of compulsory social service for all young people between the ages of eighteen and twenty?
17 What do you understand by the term 'class-distinction'?
18 Can physical violence ever be justified?
19 What arguments can you find in favour of *and/or* against world government?
20 How would you justify *either* the belief in *or* the rejection of a belief in *one* of the following?

(*a*) Life after death;
(*b*) Life on other planets;
(*c*) Reincarnation.

Part Four: Dramatic

96   Write some short plays by continuing the dialogues below in ways which develop the dramatic situations. You may introduce further characters if necessary or add further scenes. Set out the dialogue and stage directions consistently; you may, if you wish, follow the way in which the extracts are set out.

1   *The action takes place in what was once a country railway station.*

SALLY   Ben must have been out of his mind to buy this place.
RAYMOND   Well, it was cheap, right in the country, and lots of room for people.
SALLY   I wish the trains *did* still come through. I could throw ham rolls at the passengers.
RAYMOND   There's still one a week.

2   *It is ten o'clock on a winter's night. The wind can be heard blowing through the dried elms outside the curtained window and its gusts occasionally buffet down the chimney in hollow moans.*

Mr Phillips, a man in his late forties and wearing a suit like an unmade bed, is listening to Stephen, his seventeen-year-old-son. Isabel, a pretty girl with long, blonde hair, is a little younger and she is clearly afraid.

STEPHEN   I saw it as I came down the stairs, I tell you.
MR PHILLIPS   Well, I'm going to take a look for myself. We can't have the whole household upset.
              (*He moves towards the door, a little hesitantly, perhaps.*)
ISABEL   Don't. Please, don't go out there. Stop him, Stephen.
STEPHEN   Isabel's right. We'd better stay in here. There's nothing we can do.

3   *All the cage doors are open and the place is in a state of terrible disorder. We hear the wailing sirens of police cars. Timothy and Sarah are sitting on a bench crying. The Director of the zoo comes in followed by a police constable. The Director is a big, ruddy, irritable man.*

DIRECTOR   Is that all you can do? Sit and blubber?
TIMOTHY   Well since we let them out, it'd be inconsistent to help to catch them again.
DIRECTOR   All I want to know is why! Why? (*Looking at the constable*) Constable, give these two maniacs the latest————
              (*The constable pulls out a notebook and reads.*)
CONSTABLE   One wombat in Tunbridge Wells; a cheetah at Headcorn; two tigers and an elephant on the A20; three wolves sighted near Ashford; gorilla heading for Canterbury. (*He looks unbelievingly from Timothy to Sarah.*) In fact. sir, (*to the Director*) the country's swarming with all sorts of ferocious animals.
              (*Pause.*)
DIRECTOR   Well?

4 *A bright Saturday morning.*
Stanley and Louise, a middle-aged couple, are seated at a table finishing their breakfast.

                      (*Stanley looks at his watch.*)

STANLEY Is Clive coming down at all today?

LOUISE I've let him sleep on. He was very late last night.

STANLEY What time did he get in?

LOUISE I haven't the faintest idea. I didn't wait up for him.

STANLEY That's a wonder.

                      (*She looks at him with irritation. Upstairs, Clive appears on the landing. He is a boy of nineteen, quick, nervous, and likable.*)

CLIVE Pam! Pam! (*There is no answer. He goes on downstairs, hesitantly, conscious of being very late.*)
            Good morning.

STANLEY Good afternoon! What do you think this place is—a hotel?

5 *The living room of a surburban house. Furniture clutters the room; there is little space to move. Gary, a gangling youth of seventeen, is worried and stands facing the fireplace with his back towards Maureen and Sean, who are about the same age as Gary, and look equally concerned.*

GARY (*after a few moments*) I wish you hadn't told me. What will Mum and Dad do now?

MAUREEN We had to tell you; surely you see that!

SEAN It would have been worse if we hadn't. At least we've got a chance now to do something about it.

MAUREEN Nobody else knows. (*She hesitates a little.*)
            Except for Mary, of course.

GARY What do you mean? How can she know?
            (*At that moment Gary's mother enters the room; she is an open, warm, and kind person but with a hint of steel in her face.*)

MOTHER Are you and your friends ready for tea now, Gary?

Section B: Letters

Part One: Personal (Informal) Letters

97 Write letters, accurately set out and punctuated and using the right 'register', as follows:

1 To a person of the opposite sex whom you met on holiday and would like to see again. Recall some of the happy times you had together and suggest, without insisting, some ways in which the friendship can be resumed and continued.

2 To a close friend from childhood days, telling him or her that you are going to live abroad. Mention some of the things you will remember and some of the things you will miss. Finally offer your friend a sincere invitation to come to stay with you for a holiday once you have settled in.

3 To your parents after you have been away from home for two months at a new college, in a new job far from them, or in a new country. Reassure them that you are well, missing the family, but enjoying your new experiences. Give some details of your new life.

4 To an acquaintance who has recently written to you after a silence of several years to ask a special favour of you (*e.g.* lending him/her £500; putting him/her up for six months; joining in some dubious business venture). Your letter should decline the invitation firmly but tactfully.

5 To a close relative at whose home you have spent a month's happy holiday in order to thank him or her for the enjoyable time you spent together.

6 To a former schoolfriend whom you met recently whilst out shopping. The purpose of the letter is to invite him or her to dinner. Recall some of your experiences at school together.

7 To a colleague or close friend who has recently suffered a major setback (*e.g.* death of a relative, loss of a job, serious disappointment) and for whom you feel a deep sympathy.

8 To a friend who has written to you to say that he or she is thinking of taking up a hobby in which you have been interested for some years. Imagine that his or her letter asked for some advice on how to begin. Your reply should set out what information or equipment is necessary, pitfalls to avoid, and some short-cuts learnt by experience. Above all make sure that your letter reflects your own enthusiasm and encourages your friend.

9 To an old relative who lives alone and is feeling particularly lonely but who has remembered your birthday and sent you a card. Try to make your letter cheerful and comforting.

10 To the child of a neighbour. Imagine that the child is a young teenager who has had to enter hospital for an emergency operation but is now recovering. Clearly he or she will be feeling anxious about family and friends and is looking forward to being discharged. Make your letter reassuring and full of information.

Part Two: Formal Letters

98 Write letters with appropriate names, addresses, superscriptions, and subscriptions, accurately set out and punctuated and using an appropriate 'register' as follows:

1 To the Managing Director of a chain of supermarkets; imagine that you have bought a suite of furniture from a store within the chain, that the furniture is split, and that you get no satisfaction from the local manager. The purpose of your letter is to set out the facts, remind the Managing Director politely of his legal responsibilities, and seek his help in having the goods replaced urgently.

2 To the Tutor for Admissions in a college to ask for information about courses available to someone of your interests and qualifications and to seek for an advisory interview.

3 To the editor of a national newspaper to comment on a topic of major national interest and importance. Order your arguments appropriately to make your points powerful and persuasive.

4 To a customer from the Sales Director of a large firm of car distributors, in response to a letter of complaint which had listed five serious defects in a vehicle that had been supplied: rust under the wings, a juddering clutch, loose steering, an engine oil-leak, and an ill-fitting windscreen. The customer was, understandably, very annoyed in his letter to the firm. (Before you compose the reply, consider carefully many of the important factors—legal requirements, the company's loss of reputation, bad publicity, financial consequences, etc.—which make up the context in which your letter will be written.)

COLLEGE LEAVER

c. £5000

This exciting post as an assistant to a literary agent is an ideal introduction to the world of publishing for an energetic, hard-working young man or woman of skill and initiative. Good typing and shorthand necessary. The work will include meeting authors and making contacts with journalists, publishers, and editors, and becoming part of a lively and successful team.

---

5 To Miss McKenzie of the Executive Recruitment Consultancy of 27 Beaulieu Place, Wimbledon, SW19 7OS, in response to the following advertisement placed in *The Sunday Review*:

6 To the Personnel Director of a nationalised company who has written to you to ask for a reference for one of your friends who has applied for a position as a trainee computer operator with them. The post particularly requires someone who is able to adapt to new situations, is quick and willing to learn, and who can work as part of a young and enthusiastic team. (You should make it clear how long you have known the applicant and refer in detail, perhaps with examples, to his professional experience and his personal qualities.)

7 To British Telecom to question the size of the telephone bill you have recently received. The total amount has increased enormously over your last quarterly account; the number of metered units and calls connected via the operator seems excessive.)

8 To your member of parliament to ask for his/her help in securing improved facilities for handicapped children and disabled people in public buildings. Give some specific examples of the improvements you are looking for and some detailed suggestions how he or she might help.

9 To the mayor of your local council inviting him to open the village fête. Give some examples of the day's programme and indicate clearly what rôle you expect the mayor to play in the day's events.

10 To the manager of a package-tour company to complain that the holiday

you received in Spain fell far short of what you had been led to expect in terms of food, accommodation, facilities, and travel arrangements when you paid your fee. The purpose of your letter is to ask for a substantial refund.

Section C: Reports

99 Write a report for the director of a course you have recently followed on its content, approach, assessment methods, and professional value to students. Your report should include reference to areas where you have been particularly pleased or displeased. Present your ideas in an orderly way.

100 Write the annual report for the committee meeting of elected representatives of a sports and social club of which you are secretary. The report should deal with membership, activities, achievements, past and future plans, and significant developments (*e.g.* the extension of the club's social amenities, contributions to local good causes, newly-developed links with similar clubs in neighbouring areas, etc.).

101 Imagine that you have completed the first year of work in your chosen career and that the director of your section has asked you for a report of your own experiences and reactions during that year. The report is intended to test your own powers of self-evaluation as well as to indicate ways in which the director can improve the work-experience of newly recruited employees.

102 Imagine that you are seeking £50,000 to exploit and develop a totally new product which you have invented and which you believe has considerable marketing potential. Write a report on the invention and its sales possibilities for the manager of the local branch of a major bank to persuade him to finance the production of your idea in its early stages of development.

103 Write a report for an official police inquiry into a serious road accident which you witnessed. The report should be as factual as possible and any speculations should be kept to a minimum and indicated as being what they are; your statement should be balanced and objective. It will be used in the preparation of papers for a coroner's inquest on a person killed in the accident and may contribute to the prosecution of anyone guilty of an offence.

9
Summary; Summary and Directed Writing; Précis

9:1

The ability to summarise a passage depends on the art of reading closely, understanding meaning and significance within a context, recognising what is relevant, and arranging and setting down ideas coherently.

The purpose of a summary may be to re-present facts objectively, present a balanced argument, amuse or interest, explain, inform, or instruct. The shape of the final draft of a summary will depend on its purpose. The form a summary takes may be that of an informal or a formal letter, a newspaper article, a report, a speech, a contribution to a college or school magazine, the 'copy' for the blurb on a record sleeve, or any other kind of writing where a summary of facts has to be presented. It is essential that the conventions of the form required are respected and, above all, the register of the language must be appropriate.

9:2

There are two main kinds of summary most often set in public examinations.

(i) The first consists of reading a passage closely and selecting from it only those facts which are required to meet a prescription; the remaining facts may be disregarded. The selected details are then written-up into a final draft; the original wording of the passage is best avoided, but where a word or a phrase cannot be economically replaced it is permissible to retain it.

For this kind of summary it is important that the facts are selected accurately and an approach that is systematic and thorough is recommended. Too many candidates in final examinations fail to produce good summaries because their selection of basic material is initially skimped and deficient.

(a) The sense of the whole text and the viewpoint of the writer should be established by a careful *first* reading; these impressions should be confirmed or modified by a careful *second* reading.

(*b*) During a *third*, slower, reading of the passage the relevant facts should be extracted and detailed notes made; these notes should not be in the words of the original text if possible. Quite often at this stage repetitions and unnecessary examples may be spotted; central and fundamental meanings are those to extract.

(*c*) Once the material has been selected it should be arranged according to the purpose and form of the summary; this arrangement should bear in mind matters such as progression of ideas, fluency, and coherence.

(*d*) The notes that have been made should be checked against the original passage during a thorough *fourth and final* reading. The purpose of this reading is to check that no important facts have been omitted and any notes which retain the words of the passage are best re-examined to see if they can be re-expressed economically but accurately. The notes should be made in full sentences wherever possible.

(*e*) Summaries normally have to fall within a given *word limit* and it is at this stage that the number of words used in the preparatory notes should be checked. If they exceed the total allowed for the final draft they will need to be amended. The 'slanting' or 'directing' of the writing will normally take up some word space and allowances must be made for this.

(*f*) Some writers of summary believe that individual facts and details should be generalised; this is not so. *Accuracy* and the *ability to discriminate* between what is central to the passage and what is merely an example are central to this exercise; the ability is usually acquired only after much practice.

(*g*) Decisions now have to be made about the 'register' of the language to be used and the form the final draft should take. The form (*e.g.* letter, dialogue, report, article) is the easier to decide since it is usually specified in the rubric to a summary exercise. Decisions about the register will depend on recognising what is appropriate and what is not and on being able to use vocabulary and sentence-construction sensitively. The final version should be on the right level and should be accurate in matters of grammar, syntax, and punctuation. However, it is often advisable to make *a preliminary draft* at this stage from the notes without reference to the passage which might lead to the infiltration of words from the original text into the summary. Again, the number of words used needs to be checked.

(*h*) *The final version* can then be written up from the preliminary draft and afterwards checked to make sure that the writing is clear, accurate, and appropriate. Amendments should be made if they are necessary.

(*i*) *The exact number of words used* should be indicated at the end of the summary. Examiners are instructed to check to see that the final total falls within the limit allowed and usually any writing which exceeds the limit is disallowed.

The preparation of the preliminary notes and first draft may seem laborious but it is at these stages that the success or failure of the summary is established. Those that rush into draft after draft usually produce garbled and irrelevant writing. Paradoxically, perhaps, the final draft of a summary is quickly done; the thorough preparation of it takes the time.

(ii) The second kind of summary set in public examinations retains much of the form of an exercise which was formerly referred to as *précis*. This kind of summary must be clearly distinguished from the first. Fortunately, the distinction is sharp since this second type consists of the reduction in accurate and continuous prose of a whole passage to about a third of its original length. The passage will often contain a logical sequence of details, most of which will need to be included in the final summary.

(*a*) The 'argument' or 'sequence' of the facts will usually be set out in a number of *stages* which must be identified.

(*b*) Often a number of examples illustrating a central idea will be included; it is essential to *synthesise* these examples and extract from them the central point being made.

(*c*) *The words of the original text should not be used* in the final précis unless it would be cumbersome and uneconomical to replace them. Summarising should not garble or falsify meaning but should aim to re-present it accurately.

(*d*) The making of *preliminary notes* is essential to précis; these should be made on the third detailed reading of the passage after two earlier readings have been made to establish the main tenour of the passage and the point of view of the writer.

(*e*) This kind of summary (précis) aims to re-present what is in the passage without any new or revised slanting or directing of the writing. It is, therefore, best to retain the tone of the original text as far as possible. It is also advisable to retain its tense, too; there is no need at all to feel that only the past tense should be used.

(*f*) The final précis should read fluently and accurately reflect the whole sense of the original passage. State at the end the exact number of words that have been used.

9:3

This second kind of summary (précis) has been dropped as an exercise in some public examinations, since it has at its heart the implicit assumption that a passage can submit to drastic cutting without the loss of sense or essential meaning. Such passages would either be of inferior literary quality or lose layers of meaning during such major surgery. Moreover, the summarising of a passage for no specific purpose or for no specific reader seems to some an artificial exercise which encourages a scissors-and-paste approach, dependent on verbal dexterity rather than comprehension skills.

The first kind of summary admits that not all the details in a passage may lend themselves to a particular single line of development. For example, at the simplest level, a passage may present the case both for and against an argument and the summary may wish to set one side of the case only; such an exercise calls for both understanding and discrimination.

9:4

Examples of each kind will illustrate the differences between them.

(i) First consider an exercise in *summary* which asked the candidate to extract relevant information from a long passage; many of the facts it contained were not relevant to the prescription contained in the rubric. The candidate was then required to write a summary but no audience was specified to receive it.

Passage One

The following passage is taken from an article on homework. *Using only the information in the passage*, make a summary consisting of *two* paragraphs as follows:

(a) the present situation, and criticisms that are made, regarding homework; *and*

(b) arguments in favour of homework and ways of improving the present situation.

Select the material you need and arrange it in a sensible order within the appropriate paragraph. *Write in clear and correct English.* Some words and expressions cannot be accurately and economically replaced, but do not copy out long expressions or whole sentences; *use your own words as far as possible.*
Your whole summary should not exceed 150 words altogether; at the end of your work you must state the exact number of words you have used.

Homework, once associated almost exclusively with the grammar schools, now plays an important role in the lives of children attending comprehensive schools. It is usual for an eleven-year-old to bring home in September a homework timetable, with some notional indication of how much time is to be spent every night on homework, the type and quantity varying from subject to subject. The mathematics teacher sets what might be called traditional homework—so many examples worked to be handed in the day after the homework is set—closely related to classwork. The geography teacher tells the pupils to follow up their own interests and 'get on with their projects', which he will expect to see after half-term. The zealous new teacher sets homework too difficult for the lower half of a mixed-ability group, who react with frustration and non-compliance; the teacher responds by starting to set vague homework tasks: 'Do as much as you can of . . .'

The pupils soon learn that homework, unpredictable in what form it will take and when it will be required of them, is not always central to the work in class. Research would probably reveal large proportions of children who rarely do it. Does this matter? It is arguable that a school controls its children for six hours a day and that should be sufficient at least to impart the basic skills. After four o'clock children should be free to live their own lives and make their own choices. Against this argument several important factors must be weighed. The first is that many parents expect homework to be set, often rating schools by the amount that is given. A second consideration is that homework extends the time available for formal learning. The importance of this will vary, according to the pupil's age and the subject being studied. Physical education is normally conducted without any formal homework (though individual pupils may spend a great deal of their time on it), whereas preparation for external examinations requires a great deal of homework. It is clearly important for schools to encourage children to work on their own, with the support of the teacher withdrawn. This seems a vital preparation for both work and leisure in adult life which will not be learnt if all serious work is done only in the classroom, or if homework is handed in punctually merely under the impulse of fear, or if so much homework is set that the pupil works every night from six o'clock until bedtime. Nevertheless, some learning is better done at home on one's own: for example, the revision of French verbs or the first reading of a novel. Much writing may be economically tackled by starting it off in class and completing it for homework. To spend a whole class period writing is to waste a teacher's talents and presence.

To argue for homework, however, is not to argue for the present practice. Many of the difficulties which teachers experience flow from the framework set up by the school. An effective homework policy needs to be thought through by a whole staff, preferably in co-operation with the parents. Ideally, an eleven-year-old would receive clear and structured tasks to do at home. Gradually more open-ended homework would become more usual, and, by the time the pupil was sixteen, he or she would be capable of self-directed work. Many of the problems associated with homework arise from the fact that it occurs too frequently. A pupil may be doing two pieces of homework a week in, for example, mathematics, English, general science, and French, and one each in history, geography and religious education. It would be much more helpful to spread these seven subjects not over one week but three. Each subject would be expected to carry one substantial homework in that period. Teachers would then be able to plan and prepare homework in advance and integrate it into their teaching. Pupils would be faced regularly with a solid piece of real work to plan for in their own time, and the problem of two different homework tasks competing for time on the evening of a football match would be reduced when the work was known well in advance. An indirect result might be that pupils began to think for themselves, read more than merely the set books, and tried to express individual opinions.

Points which might be extracted according to the prescription in the rubric would include the following:

(a) *The present situation, and criticisms that are made, regarding homework*
 1 Homework is important in the lives of children in comprehensives which issue homework timetables.
 2 Its *type* and *quantity* vary according to subject.
 3 It is sometimes related to classwork or allows individual interests.
 4 It may be demanded the following day or later in the term.
 5 The work set is sometimes too difficult (for some of the lower ability pupils), and vague (or not central to classwork).
 6 Many do not do it and fear regulates its punctual presentation.
 7 It restricts a child's freedom and ability to choose.
 8 Too much is set too frequently and clashes with other interests occur.

(b) *Arguments in favour of homework and ways of improving the present situation*
 9 Parents expect it and judge schools by the amount set.
10 It extends time for (formal) learning and is important for preparing for external examinations.

11 It encourages children to work independently, a useful skill for later adult life and leisure.
12 Some work is better done on one's own, classtime is saved, and teacher skills are conserved.
13 A school needs a homework policy, devised preferably with parents' help.
14 The nature of homework should suit pupils' ages and development or abilities.
15 Fewer but more substantial pieces done over a longer period should be set.
16 Teachers should pre-plan homework and integrate it with classwork.
17 Pupils would *regularly* have to *organise* their homework programmes,
18 and so might learn to think independently, extend their reading, and express their own opinions.

(ii) A similar *summary* exercise but with *directed writing* included might take a form such as the following:

Passage Two

(*Read the instructions very carefully before beginning your work.*)

The following passage sets out some of the advantages and disadvantages of taking up sport as a career.

Imagine that you have a sixteen-year-old friend who is seriously thinking of becoming a professional sportsman or sportswoman. You know that other friends have been emphasizing the attractions of such a career.

Using only the information given in the passage, write a letter to your friend presenting the other side of the argument by putting *persuasively but accurately* the disadvantages of taking up sport as a career.

Your letter should be short, between 150 and 170 words. State the exact number of words you have used, but do not count the words in the address, the date, Dear——, and your ending.

You should not attempt to summarise everything there is in the passage, but select from it only the material you need for your argument. *Use your own words as far as possible*, although you may retain words and expressions which cannot be accurately or economically replaced.

Use an appropriate form for a letter sent from one friend to another and write in clear, accurate English.

Sport has rapidly become an established part of the entertainments industry and the smallest detail of sportsmen's private lives is exposed by the media to public scrutiny. Top professionals are often described as 'stars' and large business interests exploit their skills. Considerable profits are made out of selling sports gear which is a replica of that used by the professionals; newspapers sell more copies if their sports coverage is good, and substantial gains can be made out of the spectators' willingness to gamble on results. The increasing demand for new talented sportsmen serves to strengthen the popular image of professional sport as a highly glamorous occupation, the jealousy shown to players who succeed and the failure-rate of young entrants are ignored by the press. Even those who reach the heights maintain their supremacy for only a relatively short period and then desperately need help to establish themselves in a new career.

It is always attractive to do something interesting and to do it as well as possible, but serious injury or an unaccountable loss of form quickly halts the progress of many a young sportsman. A handful of top professionals can afford a house in London, another in the country, and a third on the French Riviera, as well as a Rolls-Royce and a yacht in the Bahamas, but most professional players just manage to gain a bare living from their sport. Outdoor life can be delightful except when the prevalent weather conditions are rain, wind, snow, fog or ice. It is flattering to hear one's name chanted with acclaim by thousands on the terraces but crowds are fickle and soon forget, once time takes its toll of muscle and mind. Tommy Lawton, the football hero of the forties, spent his later years in poverty, forgotten by all but a small band of his closest friends.

Sportsmen at the height of their profession travel the world and visit exotic places. The English cricket team may spend its winters in Australian summers and the Wimbledon women champions may spend the year bathed in sunshine, but their own social lives are disrupted and leisure hours have to be sacrificed to hard, exhausting practice. All professional sportsmen must adhere to strict training schedules to maintain their physical fitness; their lives are devoted to keeping the body in peak condition by exhausting exercise combined with a strict regime of self-discipline and moderation in food and drink.

At an early age comes retirement. The financial rewards gained will probably not provide enough to live on for the rest of life and the early-retired sportsman has to seek a new career. He enters this fifteen years later than his contemporaries and often with not enough reputation in his sport to persuade an employer to pay him a high salary.

Perhaps, after all, it is better to remain a keen amateur.

Points which might be extracted according to the prescription and used as a basis for the *directed writing* exercise would include the following:

The disadvantages of taking up Sport as a Career
1 Sportsmen's private lives are minutely exposed to public examination.
2 Big business interests exploit top professionals (or stars)
3 by selling sports gear copying theirs.
4 The successful are envied
5 but young failures are ignored by the press.
6 The best (or those at the top) are at their peak for only a short time
7 and need help to begin new careers.
8 Serious injury or loss of form affects players.
9 Most merely gain a meagre living.
10 Players face bad weather conditions and crowds are fickle.
11 Time takes its toll of players' bodies and minds.
12 Players' social lives are disrupted
13 and leisure has to be given up to hard and tiring practice.
14 Strict training schedules have to be followed to keep fit
15 and exhausting exercise, self-discipline and moderation in food and drink are essential.
16 Retirement comes early and often not enough money has been earned.
17 Sportsmen take up careers later than their contemporaries,
18 with not enough reputation to command high salaries.

(iii) Next, consider an exercise which asks candidates to summarise a
passage in about a third of its original length, an exercise sometimes
called *précis*:

Passage Three

The following passage contains about 500 words. Summarise it in 160–70
words, *avoiding as far as possible the original language of the passage.* Give at the
end the exact number of words in the summary.

Almost from the moment of its creation a volcanic island is foredoomed to
destruction. It has in itself the seeds of its own dissolution, for new explosions,
or landslides of the soft soil, may violently accelerate its disintegration. Whether
the destruction of an island comes quickly or only after long ages of geologic
time may also depend on external forces: the rains that wear away the loftiest
of land mountains, the sea, and even man himself.

Sometimes the disintegration takes abrupt and violent form. The greatest
explosion of historic time was the destruction of the island of Krakatoa. In 1680
there had been a premonitory eruption on this small island in Sunda Strait,
between Java and Sumatra in the Netherlands Indies. Two hundred years
later there had been a series of earthquakes. In the spring of 1883, smoke and
steam began to ascend from fissures in the volcanic cone. The ground became
noticeably warm, and warning rumblings and hissings came from the volcano.
Then, on August 27th, Krakatoa literally exploded. In an appalling series of
eruptions, that lasted two days, the whole northern half of the cone was carried
away. The sudden inrush of ocean water added the fury of superheated steam
to the cauldron. When the inferno of white-hot lava, molten rock, steam, and
smoke had finally subsided, the island that had stood 1,400 feet above the sea
had become a cavity a thousand feet below sea level. Only along one edge of
the former crater did a remnant of the island remain.

Krakatoa, in its destruction, became known to the entire world. The eruption caused a hundred-foot wave that wiped out villages along the Strait and
killed people by tens of thousands. The wave was felt on the shores of the
Indian Ocean and at Cape Horn; rounding the Cape into the Atlantic, it sped
northward and retained its identity even as far as the English Channel. The
sound of the explosions was heard in the Philippine Islands, in Australia, and
on the island of Madagascar, nearly 3,000 miles away. And the clouds of
volcanic dust, the pulverised rock that had been torn from the heart of Krakatoa, ascended into the stratosphere and were carried around the globe to give
rise to a series of spectacular sunsets in every country of the world for nearly a
year.

Although Krakatoa's dramatic passing was the most violent eruption that
modern man has witnessed, Krakatoa itself seems to have been the product of
an even greater one. There is evidence that an immense volcano once stood
where the waters of Sunda Strait now lie. In some remote period a titanic
explosion blew it away, leaving only its base represented by a broken chain of
islands. The largest of these was Krakatoa, which, in its own demise, carried
away what was left of the original crater ring. But in 1929 a new volcanic island
arose in this place—Anak Krakatoa, Child of Krakatoa.

The points that would need to be made in reducing this passage to about a
third of its length might be:

1 Volcanic islands may be destroyed by new explosions or landslides,
2 by erosion, or even by man.
3 The most violent explosion known to history
4 was that of Krakatoa, an island in the Netherlands Indies.
5 After an explosion in 1680, it was quiescent for two centuries,
6 but in 1883, after some warning signs,
7 a series of explosions, lasting for two days,
8 blew away half the island and let in the sea.
9 Save for a fragment, the 1400 foot island became a cavity 1000 feet beneath the sea.
10 The resulting wave killed thousands of people on neighbouring islands,
11 and could still be identified as far as the English Channel.
12 The sound was heard up to 3000 miles away,
13 and the dust-clouds caused extraordinary sunsets all over the world for nearly a year.
14 An even greater explosion of a prehistoric volcano seems to have created Krakatoa,
15 and in 1929 a new explosion in the same place produced another island called Anak Krakatoa.

For a further detailed discussion of summary and directed writing skills see R. A. Banks and F. D. A. Burns, *Summary and Directed Writing* (Hodder and Stoughton, 1980).

EXERCISES

104   Summarise, *in your own words as far as possible*, the following passage for an item in a feature programme on clever animals being put out by a local broadcasting station at peak-listening time. Your summary should not add ideas of your own but should aim at reducing the passage to between 180 and 200 words. (At the end show the exact number of words you have used.)

The most famous case of an animal said to be capable of counting is that of a horse in Germany called Clever Hans. The episode occurred at the beginning of the present century. The horse's owner believed that animals can think and reason as we can and that this faculty can be brought out by training the animals. He trained Clever Hans to give the answers to problems of arithmetic; the horse gave the correct answer by tapping the right number of times with its forefoot. Clever Hans was taught to tap units with one forefoot and tens with the other. The animal gave the correct answers not only to additions but to other processes of arithmetic, including converting fractions to decimals. It gave the right answers too when the questions were not spoken but shown to it written on a card.

This case was so much talked about in the newspapers that a committee of scientists was formed to investigate the astonishing powers of the horse. The committee, after a careful investigation, found that the owner and trainer of Hans was an honest man, that he had not purposely trained his horse to stop tapping, and so to give a correct answer, by giving it a slight cue as is done with performing circus animals. The absence of any such trickery was proved by the fact that members of the committee themselves got the right answers from Hans even when the owner was not present.

It looked as if the horse really could think and count. But soon after this another scientist discovered what really was the truth of the matter. He found that if the horse was asked questions to which none of the people present knew the answers, then the animal never gave a correct answer. It could not even answer the simplest question. The questions were asked by showing the horse a card which the questioner himself had not read. The biologist soon discovered that, when the horse gave the correct answers, what really occurred was this: the horse responded to almost imperceptible movements of head or body made by a questioner who knew the answer. These movements were quite unconscious, and the questioner did not know that he made them. But the questioner was aware, of course, of the number of taps that the horse should make. He counted the taps to himself, and when the horse arrived at the right number, the questioner's tension would be relieved by a very slight unconscious head or body movement. It was to this movement that the horse responded by stopping the tapping of its foot. Questioners who did not know the answer made no such movements; so the horse was confused. The horse had really taught itself to answer these very small movements during its training; it was always induced to try its best by rewards of corn or sugar.

105   Summarise the following passage in not more than 200 words as a brief article in a nature magazine aimed at teenage readers. Do not add ideas of your own but use your own words as far as possible. Adopt an appropriate 'register' for your writing.

The Monarch butterfly, one of our rare visitors, presents rather exceptional problems. It was first captured in Britain in 1876 and, in all, one hundred and fifty-seven specimens have been reported as seen here, sixty-two of which have been captured. Most of the records of those which were not caught are probably correct, since this is such a large and unmistakable insect. It is an inhabitant of America, and the milk weeds upon which it feeds are not found in this country, so that it could not possibly maintain itself in Britain.

As the species is a noted migrant, it has often been maintained that the specimens which are caught here have flown the Atlantic. This view involves great difficulties. To perform such a feat the butterfly must obviously fly all night as well as all day, or be capable of resting on the sea in mid-ocean. Even so, it may be asked why it should reach Britain at all, for it should be immensely commoner in the Iberian Peninsula and along the west coast of France than here. Now the Monarch has been recorded only six times from Continental Europe, twice from France and four times from Spain and Portugal (we may neglect the specimen found in a greenhouse in The Hague). Considering the conspicuousness of the butterfly, these records seem too few from countries where, if it really migrates, it should be far commoner than in Britain; such records are indeed few, even allowing for the scarcity of observers abroad. Again, if it really migrates, it should mainly be found on the west coast of Ireland when it does reach these islands, but only three of the records are from that region. Is it not remarkable, moreover, that such a striking insect was never reported until 1876 if it has really always been making its way here? And we must bear in mind the extensive knowledge of British butterflies already possessed by the end of the eighteenth century.

We may, in fact, be confident that the Monarch usually crosses the Atlantic on ships. The purser of one vessel, himself a collector, has stated that on the American side of the Atlantic numbers were generally to be seen flying round the potato-locker on his boat. Some of these would survive the voyage, and he had seen them fly away when the locker was opened on reaching England. Few, if any, specimens would reach us until the Atlantic service became frequent in the latter part of last century, and before fruit-boats, with which the species is particularly associated, were introduced.

Yet there seems some slight indication that this notable migrant may occasionally travel from America by its own powers of flight. Perhaps a great migratory swarm left that country in 1933, a minute proportion of which survived to swell the exceptional total of thirty-eight seen in Britain that year. Two pieces of evidence tend to support such a view. It is said that several specimens were captured on a steamer outward bound from Glasgow about 1880 when 200 or 300 miles from British shores, though none of these appear to have been preserved. Also one settled on the rail of H.M.S. *Abelia* in mid-June 1941, when the ship was 800 miles due west of Queenstown. Unfortunately it was not captured.

106 The following passage is based on an article about leaving school. Using only the information given in the passage write an article for publication in a careers information pamphlet issued to help young people seeking their first job. Your article should consist of two paragraphs as follows:
 (*i*) the things which influence young people in choosing a job; *and*
 (*ii*) the difficulties faced by young people as they go to work for the first time.
Do not try to summarise everything there is in this passage, but select from it

only the material you need for the two paragraphs. Write in clear, concise English and *use your own words as far as possible*, although you may retain words and brief expressions which cannot be accurately or economically replaced. Your article should not exceed 200 words altogether; at the end state accurately the number of words you have used.

As young people approach the time to leave school, they spend more and more time thinking and talking about what they will choose as a job or a career. Their choice switches rapidly from one occupation to another when they are still in their early years but as they grow older they look at the situation more realistically and examine critically the opportunities for employment—particularly within the area where they already live.

After studying more than sixteen hundred school-leavers, one research worker found that roughly three-quarters of the children settled down in a job only after having changed their ideas very often about what they wanted to do. Many began with fanciful notions about work but in the end their decisions about employment were based on a realisation of what their physical and mental abilities would allow them to do. Once at work the dreams have to cease. Young people find the din of clattering machines, the dirt of lathes, and the frenzy of the typing-pool or workshop quite different from the atmosphere they knew at school; moreover, foremen are usually less tolerant about errors and much more impatient than the strictest teacher.

Very often school-leavers follow in the steps of parents or other respected relatives; if nursing or train-driving runs in the family, the young person may well have hopes of becoming a nurse or train-driver. What the adolescent often misses, as he condescendingly watches his tired parents slumped in armchairs in front of the television set in the evening, is the fact that earning a living requires considerable physical or mental effort, but he soon finds that the first job—nursing, train-driving, or some other longed-for career—is exhausting.

It is useful for young people to watch a craftsman at work or to see the conditions in an office before making up their minds about a career to follow. A few schools arrange visits to help young people reach a decision and an interest or ability in certain subjects can be matched sometimes against the demands of a particular job. The immediate rewards of work, in the form of a weekly pay-packet or monthly salary, need to be weighed up against long-term opportunities for promotion and work-satisfaction.

The first day at work is often marked by a strong feeling of isolation; old friends are no longer there to lend their support and all the occasions to use one's initiative, so carefully nurtured at school, are replaced by the demand to conform and become part of a team whose aims are decided by others who may be very remote. Experiments are often discouraged lest the plant or office grinds to a halt; mistakes at work are seen not as part of a natural process of learning but as carelessness which jeopardises the whole factory or business. Most young people seem prepared to accept the idea of a lifetime of such hardships, provided they can feel sure that their jobs will not be threatened by redundancy and offer security. Because retirement seems so distant a prospect, pension rights play a less prominent part in choosing a career but some far-seeing young people take them into account. Facilities for sport, recreation, dancing, outings, and cheap purchases through the firm's social club are additional attractions to balance against the burdens of further study in order to gain qualifications and the lack of status a young newcomer to work often finds. It is not at all easy to exchange the position of prefect, first-eleven captain, or leading actor in the drama society at school for that of junior clerk, apprentice, or student-nurse.

107   Use the following passage, taken from an article dealing with changes in village life, to produce a short feature article in *Radio Times* setting out in *two* paragraphs

(*a*) the social structure of village life in the past; *and*
(*b*) the pattern of village life today.

Select the material you need and arrange it in a sensible order within the appropriate paragraph. *Write in clear and correct English.* Some words and expressions cannot be accurately and economically replaced, but do not copy out long expressions or whole sentences; *use your own words as far as possible.*

Your whole summary should not exceed 190 words altogether; at the end of your work you must state the exact number of words you have used.

Perhaps one of the reasons underlying the success of 'The Archers' as a popular radio serial is that the everyday picture of country life which it presents takes some account of the fact that the world of the village evolves gradually; its changes are rarely sudden or dramatic but they are relentless and irresistible.

The social structure of the English village, even half a century or so ago, was clearly defined and established according to an easily understood hierarchy based on position or occupation. At the head was the squire or the aristocratic inhabitant of the 'great house'. Then there came a miscellaneous group of gentry, often retired and sometimes relatives of landed families in the county; in this group the village parson must be included. There followed in the scheme of things the large farmers and below them the school teacher, the farm bailiff, the shop-keepers, and certain skilled craftsmen. Finally there were the small-holders and then the workers who had their own occupational prestige scale according to their jobs: shepherd, ploughman, cowman, pig-keeper, and farm-hand.

The 'great house' and its family was no doubt an object of respect and a source of bounty. Deference was demanded—and received—from tenants and cottagers whose livelihood was partly dependent on the goodwill of the owner. Many of the working-class laboured on the estate or in the house itself and this dependence inculcated attitudes of respect. The aristocrat and his family were often completely ignorant of local affairs and surrounded by hangers-on. Today, however, the squire is more likely to be sitting on the magistrates' bench and aware of the social problems that help to cause delinquency or, as a member of the local council, taking an active interest in housing the poor, providing better social amenities, or offering services to the aged. His own social position, nevertheless, is being challenged in today's changing world.

The parson is still there but his position, too, has altered. He has to look after many parishes and his former lucrative living is no longer comfortable as inflation grows and his benefice remains constant. He cannot rely on his former status or income as rector or vicar and finds it impossible to maintain much of an appearance in the community, as he crouches in an enormous rectory, helps his wife with the washing-up, and worries about the cost of heating and cleaning such a vast mansion.

The changing life of the village is perhaps best reflected in the life of the farm-worker. His improved general education, his higher wages negotiated by a powerful trade union, his working hours that are permanently fixed, and his more humane conditions of service reveal a different attitude towards the lot of the labourer. Not so long ago he was expected to live in sub-standard housing, accept depressed wages as his lot, and, without thought of changing employment, devote the whole of his life and energies to the needs of one farm, where he counted himself fortunate to be employed. Hours of work were not reckoned, holidays were neither offered nor expected, and machines were not available to relieve him of drudgery. Cows had to be milked; sheep were not clock-watchers in the lambing season; and a fine light evening could not be idly spent when there was a harvest to be brought in. Today the farm-worker has a standard working-week beyond which he calculates his overtime as readily and easily as the factory-worker on a car-production line.

108 The following passage is taken from an article dealing with the life of children and attitudes towards them in the seventeenth and eighteenth centuries. *Using only the information in the passage,* make a summary consisting of *two* paragraphs for inclusion in a chapter in a school history text-book, as follows:

(a) the life of children and the attitude of adults towards them in the seventeenth century; *and*

(b) the life of children and the attitude of adults towards them in the eighteenth century.

Select the material you need and arrange it in a sensible order within the appropriate paragraph. *Write in clear and correct English.* Some words and expressions cannot be accurately and economically replaced, but do not copy out long expressions or whole sentences; *use your own words as far as possible. Your whole summary should not exceed 180 words altogether.*

There were some parents in the seventeenth century who were so ignorant about their children that they did not even know how many children they had; it surprises us to learn that many could bury their children without feeling very much emotion at all. For the majority of families there was a coldness, almost a callousness, in the relationship between parents and children. Almost as soon as they were born, babies were stretched out on a board and bound tightly in swaddling clothes so that they could not move and become a nuisance to those around them. They were changed very infrequently and often they were sent out to a wet-nurse, who might have as many as five or six babies to look after. She was likely to live in a home alive with dirt and disease. It is not surprising, therefore, that one in four children died before the age of one and at least fifty per cent of children died before they reached their teens.

With the turn of the century child mortality, though still high, began to decrease, partly because of a steadily increasing food supply and partly because the scourge of smallpox was gradually being eliminated. Parents began to devote more of their time to their children and they had more money to spend on them. Public opinion about the upbringing and punishment of children also began to change. For instance, following Locke's work on education, by 1700 opinion began to move gradually against the merciless flogging and beating of children. Everybody had believed that human nature was basically wicked and sinful and that the best way to keep evil down was to whip the child regularly to instil in him subservience and the willingness to obey; very few escaped the rod for long.

All these developments helped to create a new world for children. In the seventeenth century you expected your children to follow the trade you had grown up in. In the eighteenth century there were all sorts of new and exciting economic opportunities for the child of skilled workers who managed to get just a little education.

Naturally when such parents began to spend their money on their offspring they spent it first of all to give them a better start in life. They tended to use an increasing part of their resources on books, on schools, and on things which would improve their child's chance of getting on in life; so we see the change first taking effect in the contents of what a child read in school. In the seventeenth century there had been very few books designed especially for children; there were school books, but they were very difficult to comprehend without learning by rote. They were not made to attract the eye of a child. This began to change about 1740 when a publisher called Newbury began to produce books with attractive drawings especially for small children. Books of this kind rapidly proliferated and by the end of the eighteenth century there were hundreds of titles every year of new children's books, often beautifully illustrated and teaching almost everything that there was to be taught. It was not only the children of the middle classes who could enjoy this literature, because publishers realised that those of less affluent parents formed just as promising a market. So they began to issue books in parts, children's encyclopaedias published part by part at a penny a week—a practice which has its modern counterparts and imitators.

There was also a development in toys. In the seventeenth century the children had very few toys indeed and these were made without any sophistication. But from 1730 onwards the shrewd shopkeepers began to realise that parents were willing to spend money on well-made toys, particularly those which would help educate a child, such as toy looms which could be dismantled and reconstructed, model farmyards, playing cards designed to teach the alphabet, and the jig-saw puzzle, a British invention, which was devised to teach children geography.

10
Comprehension

General Comments

10:1

Skill in summary (see Chapter Nine) depends essentially on the ability to read a passage closely and accurately. Careful reading should help to establish meaning and it is with the concept of *meaning* that many of the most pressing problems arise for students of English.

Some forms of English (*e.g.* those used to draft laws, to set out conditions of sale, to give precise instructions) do aim to convey one clear meaning without ambiguity; other forms of English (*e.g.* a love-letter, a lyric poem, a politician's reply to a TV interview) deliberately explore ambiguities in language in order to convey different shades or levels of meaning or to express emotions and ideas which cannot (or ought not to) be defined and set within limits.

The art of 'comprehension', therefore, is complex. Even to understand 'legal' English is complex enough since it presupposes knowledge and attitudes on the part of the reader and frequently needs to be interpreted in terms of centuries of case-histories. There are critics who maintain that only what is on the page as a text constitutes meaning; others argue that a poem may mean different things to different readers, since all of us bring to bear our own experiences in interpreting what we see and hear; others have attempted to recreate what they think the author intended in the light of what they know of his life, times, and writings; others talk of 'text' and 'subtext', 'surface' and 'deep structure'. The use of figurative language (see pages 199–200) introduces levels of interpretation which contribute to the complexity of the comprehension exercise.

10:2

Humpty Dumpty, in Lewis Carroll's *Through the Looking Glass*, made an interesting remark about the meaning of words:

> 'When *I* use a word,' Humpty Dumpty said, in rather a scornful tone, 'it means just what I choose it to mean—neither more nor less.'

The moment, of course, that words are placed within a context their meanings clearly change, and yet words on their own convey some meaning. A glance at any *Thesaurus* (*e.g.* Roget's) will show that close synonyms attempt to differentiate meaning:

e.g. **bright,** *adj.* brilliant, shining, glistening; luminous; clever, intelligent; flashing, sparkling; etc.

The ability to establish the context in which a word is used will help to determine its meaning:

e.g. The *brilliant* girl entered Oxford at the age of eleven.
The *brilliant* lights dazzled the oncoming driver.

10:3

Those who deliberately use language for propaganda purposes are very aware of its richness; often they bring words together within a context which presents or interprets the ideas they wish to emphasise. Joseph Goebbels, the Nazi Minister of Propaganda during the Second World War, managed at one party rally to urge the audience to call for 'Total War'. He persuaded the Germans that their position was bad but not hopeless and he exaggerated stories of allied atrocities to make his compatriots fight to the end. Words in particular contexts carry feelings of approval or disapproval, convey suggestions that because we recognise a word we understand what it represents, and produce emotions which can lead to non-logical and irrational responses. The word *democracy*, for example, means 'mob-rule' to one speaker, 'freedom and liberty' to another, and 'political dishonesty' to a third. It was the philosopher Jeremy Bentham (1748–1832) who said: 'When we have words in our ears, we imagine that we have ideas in our minds.'

Tackling Comprehension Exercises

10:4

The careful and close reading of the passage is fundamental to success. Such a reading will help to establish such things as mood, the author's point of view, pace, tone, coherence, slanting, the use of figurative language, the part played by examples, implications, inferences, and the effect of repetition. (*cf.* The Bellman in Lewis Carroll's *The Hunting of the Snark*: 'What I tell you three times is true.')

10:5

Exercises which test these very complex responses to a passage are often complex in themselves. Some of the areas they specifically set out to test are: (*i*) summary; (*ii*) vocabulary; (*iii*) inference; (*iv*) implication; (*v*) figurative writing; (*vi*) the influence of punctuation on meaning; (*vii*) idiom; (*viii*) comparisons and distinctions; (*ix*) ambiguities; (*x*) content.

10:6

Most answers can, and should be, established from what the text actually says and means. Occasionally some questions invite personal responses and extended writing based on ideas found in the passage, but it is usually very unwise to stray far from the text even in such questions; even here there must be direct links between the text and the response.

Kinds of Comprehension Exercises

10:7

There are essentially two basic kinds of comprehension tests:
  (i) those which use questions which test understanding and the candidate's ability to re-express what he has understood in a single operation, and (ii) those which test understanding only and use multiple-choice or objective test items.
Both are considered below in detail.

10:8

The Testing of Comprehension and the re-expression of the ideas understood

Read carefully the following passage (which has for your convenience been divided into three sections) and then answer the questions following it.

A
Behind the shop was a room where my eyes were tested in the rough and ready way customary in those days. The chemist hung an open framework that felt like the Forth Bridge around my ears and on my nose. Lenses were slotted into this, and twisted about, while I was instructed to read the card of letters beginning with a large 'E'. 5

I remember still the astonishment with which I saw the smaller letters change from a dark blur into separate items of the alphabet. I thought about it all the following week, and found that by screwing up my eyes when I was out of doors I could get to some faint approximation of that clarity, for a few seconds at a time. 10

This made me surmise that the universe which hitherto I had seen as a vague mass of colour and blurred shapes might in actuality be much more concise and defined. I was therefore half-prepared for the surprise which shook me a week later when, on the Saturday evening, we went again to the shop on Lavender Hill, and the chemist produced my pair of steel-rimmed 15 spectacles, through which I was invited to read the card. I read it, from top to bottom! I turned, and looked in triumph at Mother, but what I saw was Mother intensified. I saw the pupils of her eyes, the tiny feathers in her necklet; I saw the hairs in Father's moustache, and on the back of his hand. Jack's cap might have been made of metal, so hard and clear did it shine on 20 his close-cropped head, above his bony face and huge nose. I saw *his* eyes too, round, inquiring, fierce with a hunger of observation. He was studying me with a gimlet sharpness such as I had never before been able to perceive.

B
Then we walked out of the shop, and I stepped on to the pavement, which came up and hit me, so that I had to grasp the nearest support—Father's 25 coat. 'Take care, now, take care!' he said indulgently (though he disapproved of all these concessions to physical weakness). 'And mind you don't break them!'

I walked still with some uncertainty, carefully placing my feet and feeling their impact on the pavement, whose surface I could see sparkling like quartz 30 in the lamplight.

The lamplight! I looked in wonder at the diminishing crystals of gas-flame

strung down the hill. Clapham was hung with necklaces of light, and the horses pulling the glittering omnibuses struck the granite road with hooves· of iron and ebony. I could see the skeletons inside the flesh and blood of the   35
Saturday-night shoppers. The garments they wore were made of separate threads. In this new world, sound as well as sight was changed. It took on hardness and definition, forcing itself upon my hearing, so that I was besieged simultaneously through the eye and through the ear.

C

By the time we reached the darker streets near home, my head ached under   40
the burden of too much seeing. Perhaps the grease of the fried fish, and the lateness of the hour, had something to do with the exhaustion that almost destroyed me as we trailed homeward. The new spectacles clung to my face, eating into the bridge of my nose and behind the ear-lobes. I longed to tear them off and throw them away into the darkness. I tried to linger behind, so   45
that at least I might secrete them in the pocket of my blouse.

But before I could further this purpose, something caught my attention. I realised that, after all, the side-streets were not quite dark; that the yellow pools round each gas-lamp, now as clearly defined as golden sovereigns, were augmented, pervaded, suffused by a bluish silver glory. I looked upward,   50
and saw the sky. And in that sky I saw an almost full moon, floating in space, a solid ball of roughened metal, with an irregular jagged edge.

I stopped walking, and stared. I turned up my face, throwing back my head to look vertically into the zenith. I saw the stars, and I saw them for the first time, a few only, for most were obscured by the light of the moon; but   55
those I saw were clean pin-points of light, diamond-hard, standing not upon a velvet surface, but floating in space, some near, some far, in an awe-striking perspective that came as a revelation to my newly-educated eyes.

Answer the following questions in your own words as far as possible. Questions marked with an asterisk (*) should be answered *very briefly*, and in *these* answers complete sentences are not essential. (For instance, an answer may consist of a clause: 'Because ...'). Other questions should be answered in complete and correct sentences.

From Section A:

*(a) Give in a single word or a short phrase the meaning of *two* of the following words *as used in the passage*:
customary (l. 2); approximation (l. 9); surmise (l. 11); intensified (l. 18).

(b) Explain what is meant by the following figurative expressions:
(i) 'an open framework that felt like the Forth Bridge' (ll. 2–3);
(ii) 'studying me with a gimlet sharpness' (ll. 22–3).

(c) Why was the boy 'half-prepared for the surprise' (l. 13)? (Your answer should state why he was 'prepared' and why only 'half-prepared'.)

*(d) In the last paragraph of this section one verb is repeated several times. Which verb is it and why is it repeated?

From Section B:

(**e**) Explain the following expressions, with particular reference to the italicized words:
  (**i**) 'Clapham was hung with *necklaces* of light' (l. 33);
  (**ii**) 'I was *besieged* simultaneously through the eye and through the ear' (ll. 38–9).
(**f**) What are the chief effects, on the boy, of his new ability to see? (Confine your answer to a correct sentence *of not more than 30 words.*)

From Section C:

*(**g**) Give in a single word or a short phrase the meaning of *two* of the following words *as used in the passage:*
      exhaustion (l. 42); secrete (l. 46); further (l. 47); suffused (l. 50); zenith (l. 54).
*(**h**) Why is the moon described as 'a solid ball of roughened metal' (l. 52)?
(**i**) Explain, with particular reference to the words italicized, the expression, 'in an awe-striking *perspective* that came as a *revelation* to my *newly-educated* eyes' (ll. 57–8).
*(**j**) In place of the adverbial phrase 'under the burden of too much seeing' (l. 40–1) write an adverbial clause (of the same meaning) making the cause of the headache clear.

From the whole passage:

(**k**) Describe the changes in the boy's mood during the passage. (Do not use more than 30 words.)
(**l**) What are the blessings and what are the drawbacks of the new glasses? (Answer in not more than *two* sentences and using not more than 30 words.)

10:9

The instructions given to candidates before they tackle the questions recognises that some of the answers must be expressed in full sentences but deliberately instructs candidates to answer others (those marked with an asterisk) *very briefly. Normally answers should be in full, accurately written sentences unless you are instructed otherwise.*

To work through this exercise in considerable detail will highlight some of the problems candidates have to face in arriving at, and presenting, their answers and responses.

(i) *The vocabulary question*
The answers should be correctly spelt and should be in the same part of speech as the word used in the passage. It is best to look for a strict synonym; sometimes such a synonym may consist of two words joined together by *and*, but if you use such double-worded synonyms make sure that one part does not invalidate the other: *e.g.* in the worked example set out below, a good synonym for 'customary' would be *usual*; an incorrect answer would be 'usual and ordinary'.

The following lists set out some answers which would be 'acceptable', 'less acceptable', and 'not acceptable'—given the uses of the words in the specific context of the passage:

customary
Acceptable: usual, which was the practice;
Less acceptable: normal, habitual, routine, common, prevalent;
Not acceptable: universal, traditional, orthodox, familiar, regular, ordinary.

approximation
Acceptable: approach, similarity, resemblance, likeness, something near (to);
Less acceptable: imitation, appearance;
Not acceptable: guess, rough answer.

surmise
Acceptable: conjecture, guess, suppose, suspect, have a hunch, divine;
Less acceptable: imagine, fancy, think, foresee, presume, conceive, anticipate;
Not acceptable: dream, speculate, prophesy, predict.

intensified
Acceptable: concentrated, emphasised, heightened, stressed, made clearer (more vivid).
Less acceptable: exaggerated, reinforced;
Not acceptable: added to, augmented, strengthened, enhanced.

(ii) *Figurative expressions*

Normally, those assessing the answers to questions on figurative language look for approximations to basic ideas, such as the following:

(*a*) *An open framework that felt like the Forth Bridge* (lines 2–3): there should be some reference to a similarity of structure (*e.g.* made of bars, strips, etc.); for an additional reward there might be some reference to *heavy, metallic, clumsy*, or a similar idea.

(*b*) *Studying me with a gimlet sharpness* (lines 22–3): there should be some reference to the *piercing* or *intent* quality of the gaze; an additional reward might be given if an additional point is made, *e.g.* the fact that a gimlet is a sharp tool, that his brother was inquisitive, or that the writer had never seen anyone looking at him closely before.

(iii) *Inference question*

The rubric asks students to explain why the writer was 'prepared' and why 'half-prepared'.

Possible answers might be that he was 'prepared' because he had already guessed what the world looked like by screwing up his eyes; he was 'half-prepared' because his impressions had hitherto been only vague ones.

(iv) *Word-recognition and stylistic inference*

The word required presumably is 'saw' or 'to see'. It is repeated because it is central to the meaning of the passage and emphasises the boy's eagerness and his surprise.

The inference is a correct one but the correct expression of the response will determine whether the student is fully rewarded or not.

(v) *Explanation of figures of speech*

(**a**) The comparison with 'necklaces' presumably suggests that the lights curved, were in rows, were bright, and seemed strung together, *i.e.* there are a number of 'meanings' in the use of the single metaphor.

(**b**) The use of 'besieged' suggests that the sights and sounds seemed to press in on the boy and were confusing, threatening, attacking him. The main point presumably about the metaphor here is that the boy felt under attack and unable to free himself easily.

(vi) *Summary of effects*

The rubric also insists that the candidate should use a single correct sentence. This question is, therefore, not only a comprehension test but also a test of grammatical and syntactical skills. Ideas such as triumph, success, difficulty in walking, the sharpness of the sounds, the clarity of details and structures, and the recognition of beauty around him are some of those that the sentence should set out to express.

(vii) *Again, another vocabulary question*

This is similar in kind to (i).

Possible responses might be:

exhaustion *Acceptable:* extreme fatigue (weariness, etc.), state of being worn out;
Less acceptable: fatigue, tiredness, weariness, prostration;
Not acceptable: weakness, feebleness, giddiness, unsteadiness.

secrete *Acceptable:* hide, conceal, put out of sight, stow away;
Less acceptable: bury;
Not acceptable: pocket, put away.

further *Acceptable:* advance, promote, forward, contribute, etc.
Less acceptable: proceed with, help, aid, begin to carry out;
Not acceptable: carry out, fulfil.

suffused *Acceptable:* permeated, overspread, mixed, blended with;
Less acceptable: penetrated, charged, run through, spread, pervaded;
Not acceptable: augmented, coloured.

zenith *Acceptable:* the sky overhead, the point overhead, the highest point in the sky;
Less acceptable: highest point;
Not acceptable: summit, sky, topmost point.

(viii) *A figurative expression*

The moon = *a solid ball of roughened metal* (line 52)

There are three main points in the comparison:

      'solid ball' = it was spherical and dense
      'roughened' = there are marks or patches on it
      'metal' = it was gold or silver in colour

These three aspects of the metaphor would need to be referred to, although not necessarily in a complete sentence.

(ix) *A complex explanation of vocabulary and figurative language*

The italicising of the three words *perspective*, *revelation* and *newly-educated* points the candidate to the explanation required; but clearly this question is not intended to be a vocabulary question of the same order as (i) or (vii). It demands some reference to the contextual use of the words and the sentence-construction and expression are both important here.

perspective:	the stars seemed to stretch away into the distance;
revelation:	it was a view he had not previously seen or expected;
newly-educated:	his eyes had recently been taught by the glasses to see clearly.

It is sometimes hard in questions of this kind for students to know just how much detail to give in their explanations. It is usually advisable to write accurately but concisely; there is no point in writing several lines in response.

(x) *Adverbial phrase/clause*

Under the burden of too much seeing (lines 40–1), an adverbial clause of the same meaning making the cause of the headache clear.

This is a thinly disguised grammatical question as well as a 'vocabulary' one on the phrase 'under the burden of'. Grammatical questions of this kind are less frequently set now.

A possible response might be:

'because it felt the strain of seeing too many things.'

(xi) *Summary of the boy's changing mood*

Clearly the boy undergoes a number of experiences and his mood changes with them. The summary would need to include references to the fact that he was:

astonished, expectant, surprised, triumphant, unsure, wondering, overwhelmed, exhausted, irritated, and amazed at the sky.

(xii) *Summary of the blessings and drawbacks of the new glasses*

Possible responses might include:

blessings:	he can see more clearly; he can enjoy the beauty of the world more fully.
drawbacks:	the glasses are uncomfortable; the sights and the noises make him very tired.

In this question there is an additional demand that the candidate should use not more than two sentences and not exceed 30 words in length.

Multiple-Choice/Objective Tests

10:10

The form of Multiple-Choice Comprehension tests

Most tests consist of between forty and sixty items based on two or three passages or extracts. These passages often represent different kinds of writing selected from fiction, non-fiction, narrative, discursive, factual, and personal writing, but they may also consist of statistical tables, diaries, or dramatic excerpts.

'Questions' on the passages are called *items*, although the form of the introductory statement may be that of a direction or a complete or incomplete remark as well as a direct question; this introductory statement is called the *stem*. The suggested 'answers', usually four or five in number, are called options. Only one of these options, the *key*, is the correct or the best answer to the problem or question posed in the stem. The options other than the key are called *distractors*.

10:11

The areas which can be tested by multiple-choice items include (i) summary; (ii) vocabulary; (iii) inference; (iv) implication; (v) figurative language; (vi) the influence of punctuation on meaning; (vii) idiom; (viii) comparisons; (ix) ambiguities; (x) context—in fact, all the areas tested by the older, more traditional form of tests.

10:12

Multiple-choice testing of comprehension recognises that in English more than one answer might be 'correct' or 'possible' and items can be varied from the *single-response* type (where only one option is required as the key) to *double or multiple-completion* types (where two or more options may be acceptable). In some instances where as many as four options are possibly correct, an item can be devised using an EXCEPT format where candidates have to spot as their key the one option which is wrong. Examples of these three kinds of item based on the passage and its questions, discussed in **10:8,** pages 196–201, are as follows:

(NOTE The keys, or correct responses, are marked by asterisks.)

(i) *Single-response item*
Which *one* of the following words is closest in meaning to 'customary' as used in line 2?

    A Traditional
 ***B** Usual
    C Habitual
    D Normal
    E Universal

Notice that all the options are similar in length, shape, and form; none attracts attention more than the others by its design; a badly constructed item would ignore this requirement.

    e.g. Which one of the following is closest in meaning to 'rodeo' as used in line 200?

        A A fête
        B A sale

C A carnival
D A market
*E A round-up of cattle on a Western American range for branding.

(ii) *A double-completion item*
Which *two* of the following are blessings offered by the new glasses?

1 The boy can see with far greater clarity.
2 They are much more comfortable to wear.
3 The boy can avoid accidents much more easily.
4 They are much more attractive to look at.
5 The boy can appreciate natural beauty more fully.

A 1 and 2 only
*B 1 and 5 only
C 2 and 3 only
D 3 and 4 only
E 4 and 5 only

NOTE All the options are of similar form and length; each of the options appears twice in the final list.

(iii) *A multiple-completion item*
Which *three* of the following are suggested by the comparison of the street lights with 'necklaces' (line 33)? The street lights seemed to be:

1 set out in curved rows
2 bright and very shiny
3 contrasted with the darkness
4 distant and rather small
5 strung together in long lines

A 1, 2, and 3 only
*B 1, 2, and 5 only
C 1, 3, and 4 only
D 2, 4, and 5 only
E 3, 4, and 5 only

(iv) *An* EXCEPT *item*
These items are particularly useful for testing figurative language or summary skills.

  e.g. All the following moods were experienced by the boy in the course of the passage EXCEPT

A astonishment
B surprise
C exhaustion
*D despair
E irritation

In these four kinds of item notice that the *stem* sometimes consists of a direct question and sometimes of an incomplete statement.

10:13

Consider the following passages and the items based on them. Try to decide which skills in comprehension the items are testing. (At the end of the items in each passage the keys and the skills tested are given for you to check against your answers.)

Passage One

Questions **1** to **10** are based on the following passage. Read the passage carefully and then answer the questions. Each question has five suggested answers. Select the best answer to each question.

My Aunt Trix, like St Francis, spoke to the birds. I have seen her at Edinburgh Zoo, addressing cynical macaws who strolled courteously along their perches to listen to her. Herself like some rare bird, with her large prominent eyes, her sharp nose scenting the air, and her fingers clutching at it like restless talons, she spoke to them in high, piercing, affable, pedantic tones   5
until a crowd of curious Scots gathered round her, keeping far enough off to show their superior distain for an eccentric, but sufficiently near to observe if the birds would bite her when she popped chocolates through the bars into their huge, slow, lazy beaks. When birds and Scots were assembled in sufficient numbers on either side of the metal barrier, Aunt Trix would turn to tell their 10
human brethren what the birds were thinking, as if she were the interpreter between two portions of the animal kingdom. At this point, the more prudent citizens of Edinburgh would steal off in some alarm: but others remained, glued to the spot by my aunt's shining eye. After one of these performances I said to my Aunt Trix, 'If you'd lived two hundred years ago, they would have 15
burned you as a witch.' She eyed me with a gay and guileful smile and said, 'I know they would have done, my dear.'

1 The use of 'addressing' (line 2) suggests most strongly that Aunt Trix

    A   whispered quietly to the macaws
    B   idly engaged in chatter with her friends
    C   scolded those who were not paying attention
    D   formally directed her remarks at her listeners
    E   spoke shyly to the unsuspecting birds

2 Which one of the following words is closest in meaning to 'affable' as used in line 5?

    A   Coaxing
    B   Reassuring
    C   Condescending
    D   Friendly
    E   Colloquial

3 The tone of voice in which Aunt Trix spoke to the macaws (line 5) was all of the following EXCEPT

    A   formal
    B   penetrating

C cynical
D courteous
E learned

4 All of the following show that Aunt Trix was an 'eccentric' (line 7) EXCEPT her

    A habit of 'addressing cynical macaws'
    B behaviour and general appearance
    C giving chocolates to birds
    D 'gay and guileful smile'
    E interpretation of the birds' thoughts

5 The crowd watching Aunt Trix was all of the following EXCEPT

    A interested to see what she was doing
    B scornful of her eccentricity
    C interested to see if she would be bitten
    D made up entirely of Scots
    E interested in what the birds thought

6 Which one of the following words is closest in meaning to 'prudent' as used in line 12?

    A Cautious
    B Shocked
    C Frightened
    D Anxious
    E Scornful

7 Some citizens were described as 'prudent' (line 12) because they

    A managed to leave without being noticed
    B were afraid of Aunt Trix
    C could not understand what was happening
    D left before they became involved
    E were quick to see through Aunt Trix

8 Which one of the following words is closest in meaning to 'guileful' as used in line 16?

    A Evil
    B Sinister
    C Twisted
    D Sarcastic
    E Sly

9 Aunt Trix had all the following EXCEPT

    A a pointed nose
    B conspicuous eyes

C a constant smile
D sharp grasping fingers
E a piercing voice

10 The writer's attitude to his aunt is best described as one of

A scorn
B amusement
C embarrassment
D devotion
E superiority

Keys, and skills tested in Passage One

Item   1: Key D; vocabulary and inference.
Item   2: Key D; vocabulary.
Item   3: Key C; summary; EXCEPT format.
Item   4: Key D; summary and inference; EXCEPT format.
Item   5: Key E; summary and inference; EXCEPT format.
Item   6: Key A; vocabulary.
Item   7: Key D; inference/implication.
Item   8: Key E; vocabulary and inference.
Item   9: Key C; summary; EXCEPT format.
Item 10: Key B; summary and response to content and style.

Passage Two

Questions **1** to **15** are based on this passage. Read the passage carefully; then answer the questions.

September is the month of memories. Perhaps this is due to the smell of autumn, half acrid like tanned leather, half of 'mellow fruitfulness', the ghosts of roses and of apples on shelves. And smells are the great conjurors of memories. A whiff of honeysuckle brings back to me, instantly, the garden of my childhood, with the mother of the family standing, water-can in hand,   5
talking to me across a thicket of Michaelmas daisies, with a veil of gnats, playing between us, and the sun flashing on her gold-rimmed spectacles. It is a poignant scene, saved from sadness by being so sacred. All that from a sprig of honeysuckle: the annihilation of over half a century. Or perhaps the right word is not annihilation but distillation; for this process leaves an attar*   10
of time, a tiny phial to be stored in the mind, whence it impregnates the personal universe.

I have just returned from a morning's outing with a grand-daughter who is developing, at an early age, a passion for domestic economy. She insisted, at the open door of my workroom where I had just begun to settle down to   15
the habitual daily output of words, that I should take her out to gather blackberries, because she wanted Cook to teach her how to make bramble jelly. As I have a weakness for this conserve, I was not reluctant to leave pen and paper and submit myself to this diminutive tyrant.

We set off solemnly, with a mother and the grandmother to watch us go   20
down the narrow lane between the honeysuckle hedges. Before we had lost sight of the watchers at the gate, the dachshund came rushing after us,

whimpering with reproach at having been forgotten. He hurled himself along and pulled up gradually in front of us, to open at once into a scheme of investigation, criss-crossing the lane from one hedge to the other with a 25 nervous frequency that must have tested his brakes to the utmost.

At the bottom of the hill we stopped by the dell. We began to pick, but the best berries were too high. I lifted up my grand-daughter, seating her on my shoulders in the manner of a 'flying angel'. From that height she had approach to unlimited hoards of fruit. Cries of exultation came from above 30 my head, and I felt a small pair of legs kick out with excitement, so that I almost stumbled into one of the clumps of bramble and deposited my burden into the middle of it.

Unable to help in the gathering, I furtively picked a vintage berry here and there and popped it into my mouth. At once the taste of childhood came 35 back to me, and I stood there, a beast of burden, but now only about twelve years old, somewhere in the wilds of Hampshire, with my parents and elder brother on the other side of the bush, dressed in out-of-date clothes, exchanging conversation with me. I could hear the loved voices of those vanished dear ones; long since vanished. 40

  * A fragrant oil distilled from roses.

1 Smells are called the 'great conjurors' of memories (lines 3–4) because they

  A change them into something else
  B surprise us with unfamiliar experiences
  C call them apparently from nowhere
  D make them seem like ghosts
  E deceive us by subtle tricks

2 The 'poignant scene' is 'saved from sadness' (line 8) because it is

  A recreated by the smell of honeysuckle
  B associated with memories which he treasures
  C connected vaguely with his religious beliefs
  D linked with the feast of Michaelmas
  E recalled from the very distant past

3 The process, set in motion by the honeysuckle, is called 'distillation' (line 10) because it

  A derives from the scent of the flowers
  B silences everything for half a century
  C lingers unchanged in the author's mind
  D reduces fifty years to their essence
  E brings back things with fragrant memories

4 Which one of the following words is closest in meaning to 'impregnates' as used in line 11?

  A Dominates
  B Pervades

C Conceives
D Shapes
E Disturbs

5 The first paragraph (lines 1–12) is mainly about

A gardens which he remembers
B memories which make him sad
C events which recall his family
D smells which evoke memories
E months which are memorable

6 The author was 'not reluctant to leave pen and paper' (lines 18–19) because he was

A fond of bramble jelly
B too weak to decline
C unable to settle down
D very fond of the child
E submissive to tyranny

7 Paragraph two (lines 13–19) suggests that the author is

A irritable
B timid
C indulgent
D lazy
E insensitive

8 'We set off solemnly' (line 20) most probably because

A the man realised his responsibility
B it was a serious matter for the child
C the author resented the interruption
D they wanted to avoid the frisky dog
E the others were sorry to see them go

9 The 'scheme of investigation' (lines 24–5) was that the dachshund intended to

A explore both sides of the lane
B join the search for blackberries
C discover why he had been left behind
D make sure of the two people
E test his powers of braking

10 The movements of the dachshund (lines 23–6) were characterised by all the following EXCEPT

A inquisitiveness
B great speed

C fearfulness
D constant stopping
E purposefulness

11 Which one of the following words is closest in meaning to 'dell' as used in line 27?

A Stream
B Gate
C Hollow
D Footpath
E Wood

12 There were 'Cries of exultation' (line 30) mainly because the little girl was

A being carried shoulder-high
B terrified of being dropped
C kicking out with excitement
D full of high spirits
E seeing lots of blackberries

13 Which one of the following words is closest in meaning to 'furtively' as used in line 34?

A Frustratedly
B Stealthily
C Delicately
D Largely
E Haphazardly

14 A 'vintage' berry (line 34) is one which is

A suitable for wine-making
B particularly fine in quality
C indicative of a good year
D especially old and glossy
E reminiscent of former fruit

15 Eating a blackberry (lines 34–5) reminds the author of all the following EXCEPT

A his parents and brother
B clothes of long ago
C days spent blackberrying
D carrying gathered fruit
E voices from the past

Keys, and skills tested in Passage Two
  Item 1: Key C; inference and figurative language.

Item 2: Key B; context and inference.
Item 3: Key D; vocabulary and figurative langauge.
Item 4: Key B; vocabulary.
Item 5: Key D; summary.
Item 6: Key A; inference and context.
Item 7: Key C; summary and response.
Item 8: Key B; inference and context.
Item 9: Key A; vocabulary, inference, and context.
Item 10: Key C; summary; *except* format.
Item 11: Key C; vocabulary.
Item 12: Key E; inference.
Item 13: Key B; vocabulary, context, and response.
Item 14: Key B; vocabulary and figurative language.
Item 15: Key D; summary; *except* format.

For further examples of passages and items see pages 216–31; also B. Rowe and R. A. Banks, *Objective Tests in English Language for GCE* (Hodder and Stoughton, 1971); B. Rowe and R. A. Banks, *New Objective Tests in English Language* (Hodder and Stoughton, 1974).

EXERCISES

109   Read the following passage carefully and then answer the questions which follow:

Enjoying as we do the immense superiority of a generation which has devised means of mass destruction more effective even than those inflicted by nature on our ancestors, it is easy and tempting to deride their inability to understand the calamity which has overtaken them. It would, perhaps, be more fitting to wonder at the courage and wisdom of those who saw their   5
civilisation apparently doomed by a hideous and inexplicable calamity and could still observe its development with scientific objectivity, draw reasonable deductions about its habits and likely course and do their best to curb its ravages. It is also sobering to reflect that only within the last century have we learned enough to detect the origins and plot the course of the epidemics   10
and that, even today, quick and expensive action is necessary if they are to be checked before they do great damage. It is much less than a hundred years since the sophisticated and immensely learned Dr Creighton concluded positively that the source of the Black Death lay in the mounds of dead left unburied by successive disasters which had overtaken China. He invoked   15
cadaveric poisoning as the reason for the high death rate amongst priests and monks: priests tended to live near the village churchyard while: 'Within the monastery walls were buried not only generations of monks, but often the bodies of princes, of notables of the surrounding country, and of great ecclesiastics.'   20

Today we smile politely at Dr Creighton's blunders; it is reasonable to wonder whether a hundred years from now the theories of today may not seem equally ridiculous. On the whole it is unlikely that they will. Undoubtedly further discoveries will be made, dark corners illuminated, concepts amended or refined. But the techniques of scientific investigation are now   25
sufficiently evolved to have established as a fact the main elements of the Black Death and to explain authoritatively the cycle of its activity.

That the Black Death, in its original form, was bubonic plague has been correctly accepted for many years. Bubonic plague is *endemic* to certain remote areas of the world. From time to time it erupts there in the form of minor   30
localised *epidemics*. Far more rarely it breaks its bounds and surges forth as one of the great *pandemics*. Unlike influenza, bubonic plague in such a mood moves slowly, taking ten years or more to run its course across the world. When it comes, it comes to stay. The high mortality of its initial impact is followed by a long period in which it lies endemic, a period interspersed with   35
occasional epidemics which gradually die away in frequency and violence. Finally, perhaps several hundred years after the original outbreak, the plague vanishes.

(i)   Explain *in your own words* why 'wonder' would be a more fitting emotion in the situation described in lines 4–9.

(ii) Suggest *two* reasons from the passage why 'today we smile politely at Dr Creighton's blunders' (line 21).

(iii) From the passage what distinctions can you see in the meanings of the following words?

(*a*) *endemic* (line 29);

(**b**) *epidemics* (line 31);

(**c**) *pandemics* (line 32).

(**iv**) Using your own words, explain *in not more than 60 words* the main features of the cycle of the Black Death's activity. (State the exact number of words you use.)

110 Read the following passage and then answer the questions that follows:

'Eliot, we are ready to hear from you now.'

I had expected more of a *preamble*, and I was starting cold. I hadn't got the feel of them at all. I glanced at Brown. He gave me a smile of recognition, but his eyes were *wary* and piercing behind his spectacles. There was no give there. He was sitting back, his jowls swelling over his collar, as in a portrait   5 of an eighteenth century bishop on the linenfold, the bones of his chin hard among the flesh.

I began, carefully *conciliatory*. I said that, in this case, no one could hope to prove anything; the more one looked into it, the more puzzling it seemed. The only thing that was indisputable was that there had been a piece of   10 scientific fraud; deliberate fraud, so far as one could give names to these things. No one would want to argue about that—I mentioned that it had been agreed on, the night before, by Dawson-Hill and me, as common ground.

'I confirm that, Master,' came a *nonchalant* murmur from Dawson-Hill   15 along the table.

Of course, I said, this kind of fraud was a most unlikely event. Faced with this unlikely event, responsible members of the college, not only the Court, had been *mystified*. I had myself, and to an extent still was. The only genuine division between the Court and some of the others was the way in which one   20 chose to make the unlikely seem explicable. Howard's own version, the first time I heard it, had sounded nonsense to me; but reluctantly, like others, I had found myself step by step forced to admit that it made some sort of sense, more sense than the alternative.

I was watching Brown, whose eyes had not left me. I hadn't made them   25 more hostile, I thought: it was time to plunge. So suddenly I announced the second piece of common ground. If the photograph now missing from Palairet's Notebook V—I pointed to the pile in front of the Master—had been present there, and if that photograph had been a fraud, then that, for there would be no escape from it, would have to be a fraud by Palairet.   30

(**i**) From this passage give *two* examples of Eliot's study of his audience.

(**ii**) Set out the main points of Eliot's argument in this passage.

(**iii**) Explain in you own words the meaning in this context of the following words:

(**a**) *preamble* (line 2);

(**b**) *wary* (line 4);

(**c**) *conciliatory* (line 8);

(**d**) *nonchalant* (line 15);

(**e**) *mystified* (line 19);

(**iv**) Examine carefully Eliot's manner of presenting his case here.

111 Read the following passage carefully, and then answer, wherever possible in complete statements and in your own words, the questions that follow.

A marvellous stillness pervaded the world, and the stars, together with the serenity of their rays, seemed to shed upon the earth the assurance of ever-lasting security. The young moon, shining low in the west, was like a slender shaving thrown up from a bar of gold, and the Arabian Sea, smooth and cool to the eye like a sheet of ice, extended its perfect level to the perfect circle of   5
a dark horizon. The propeller turned without a check, as though its beat had been part of the scheme of a safe universe; and on each side of the *Patna* two deep folds of water, permanent and sombre on the unwrinkled shimmer, enclosed within their straight and diverging ridges a few white swirls of foam bursting in a low hiss, a few wavelets, a few ripples, a few undulations that,   10
left behind, agitated the surface of the sea for an instant after the passage of the ship, subsided splashing gently, calmed down at last into the circular stillness of water and sky with the black speck of the moving hull remaining everlastingly in its centre.

Jim, on the bridge, was penetrated by the great certitude of unbounded   15
safety and peace that could be read on the silent aspect of nature like the certitude of fostering love upon the placid tenderness of a mother's face. Below the roof of awnings, surrendered to the wisdom of white men and to their courage, trusting the power of their unbelief and the iron shell of their fire-ship, the pilgrims of an exacting faith* slept on mats, on blankets, on   20
bare planks, on every deck, in all the dark corners, wrapped in dyed cloths, muffled in soiled rags, with their heads resting on small bundles, with their faces pressed to bent fore-arms: the men, the women, the children; the old with the young, the decrepit with the lusty—all equal before sleep, death's brother.   25

A draught of air, fanned from forward by the speed of the ship, passed steadily through the long gloom between the high bulwarks, swept over the rows of prone bodies; a few dim flames in the globe-lamps were hung short here and there under the ridge-poles, and in the blurred circles of light thrown down and trembling slightly to the unceasing vibration of the ship   30
appeared a chin upturned, two closed eyelids, a dark hand with silver rings, a meagre limb draped in a torn covering, a head bent back, a naked foot, a throat bared and stretched as if offering itself to the knife. The well-to-do had made for their families shelters with heavy boxes and dusty mats; the poor reposed side by side with all they had on earth tied up in a rag under   35
their heads.

* They were Mohammedan pilgrims voyaging from the East to Mecca.

(i) 'The assurance of everlasting security' (ll. 2–3). Explain in your own words the meaning of this phrase, and quote from the passage another phrase that has a similar meaning.

(ii) Explain, each in a single or short phrase, the meanings of *four* of the following words as they are used in the passage:
serenity (l. 2); undulations (l. 10); placid (l. 17); exacting (l. 20); decrepit (l. 24); prone (l. 28); meagre (l. 32).

(iii) The sea is said to be like a sheet of ice (l. 5) because both are level, smooth and cool to the eye. Justify in a similar manner the following comparisons:

(**a**) The young moon ... like a slender shaving thrown up from a bar of gold (ll. 3–4);

(**b**) sleep, death's brother (ll. 24–5).

(**iv**) Quote *three* expressions, other than that referred to in question (iii) above, that suggest the calmness of the sea.

(**v**) From the second and third paragraphs quote *three* effective examples of the use of contrast, and show what point they add to the description when they are considered together.

112 Read the following passage (which for your convenience has been divided into three sections) and answer the questions. The narrator, an officer in the Burmese police force when Burma was still ruled by Britain, has been called out to deal with a tame elephant, which has run wild and killed a man.

A

As soon as I saw the elephant I knew with perfect certainty that I ought not to shoot him. It is a serious matter to shoot a working elephant—it is comparable to destroying a huge and costly piece of machinery. Moreover, I did not in the least want to shoot him.

But at that moment I glanced round at the crowd that had followed me.   5
It blocked the road for a long distance on either side. I looked at the sea of yellow faces above the garish clothes—faces all happy and excited over this bit of fun, all certain that the elephant was going to be shot. They were watching me as they would watch a conjuror about to perform a trick. They did not like me, but with the magical rifle in my hands I was momentarily   10
worth watching. And suddenly I realised that I should have to shoot the elephant after all. The people expected it of me and I had got to do it; I could feel their two thousand wills pressing me forward, irresistibly. And it was at this moment, as I stood there with the rifle in my hands, that I first grasped the hollowness, the futility of the white man's dominion in the East.   15

Here was I, the white man with his gun, standing in front of the unarmed native crowd—seemingly the leading actor of the piece; but in reality I was only an absurd puppet pushed to and fro by the will of those yellow faces behind. I perceived in this moment that when the white man turns tyrant it is his own freedom that he destroys. He becomes a sort of hollow, posing   20
dummy, the conventionalised figure of a sahib. For it is the condition of his rule that he shall spend his life in trying to impress the 'natives', and so in every crisis he has got to do what the 'natives' expect of him. He wears a mask, and his face grows to fit it. I had got to shoot the elephant. A sahib has got to act like a sahib; he has got to appear resolute, to know his own mind   25
and do definite things. To come all that way, rifle in hand, with two thousand people marching at my heels, and then to trail feebly away, having done nothing—no, that was impossible. The crowd would laugh at me. And my whole life, every white man's life in the East, was one long struggle not to be laughed at.   30

B

But I did not want to shoot the elephant. I watched him beating his bunch of grass against his knees, with that preoccupied grandmotherly air that elephants have. It seemed to me that it would be murder to shoot him. At that age I was not squeamish about killing animals, but I had never shot an elephant and never wanted to.   35

It was perfectly clear to me what I ought to do. I ought to walk up to within, say, twenty-five yards of the elephant and test his behaviour. If he charged I could shoot; if he took no notice of me it would be safe to leave him until the mahout came back. But I was a poor shot with a rifle and the ground was soft mud into which one would sink at every step. If the elephant 40 charged and I missed him, I should have about as much chance as a toad under a steam-roller. But even then I was not thinking particularly of my own skin, only of the watchful yellow faces behind. For at that moment, with the crowd watching me, I was not afraid in the ordinary sense, as I would have been if I had been alone. A white man mustn't be frightened in front of 45 'natives'; and so, in general, he isn't frightened. The sole thought in my mind was that if anything went wrong those two thousand Burmans would see me pursued, caught, trampled on and reduced to a grinning corpse. And if that happened it was quite probable that some of them would laugh. That would never do. I lay down on the road to get a better aim. 50

C

The crowd grew very still, and a deep, low, happy sigh, as of people who see the theatre curtain go up at last, breathed from innumerable throats.

When I pulled the trigger I did not hear the bang or feel the kick, but I heard the devilish roar of glee that went up from the crowd. In that instant, in too short a time, one would have thought, even for the bullet to get there, 55 a mysterious, terrible change had come over the elephant. He neither stirred nor fell, but every line in his body had altered. He looked suddenly stricken, shrunken, immensely old, as though the frightful impact of the bullet had paralysed him without knocking him down. At last, after what seemed a long time—it might have been five seconds, I dare say—he sagged flabbily to his 60 knees. His mouth slobbered. An enormous senility seemed to have settled upon him. One could have imagined him thousands of years old.

Answer the following questions *in your own words as far as possible*. Questions marked with an asterisk (*) should be answered *very briefly*, and in these answers complete sentences are not essential. (Other questions should be answered in complete and correct sentences.)

From Section A:

* (i) Give in a single word or a short phrase the meaning of any *three* of the following words *as they are used in the passage*:
    garish (l. 7); futility (l. 15); dominion (l. 15); conventionalised (l. 21); resolute (l. 25).
* (ii) Why is killing the elephant 'comparable to destroying a huge and costly piece of machinery' (l. 3)?
 (iii) What in the way the crowd is watching the author reminds him of a conjuror's audience (l. 9)?
 (iv) Why does the author think of himself as 'an absurd puppet' (l. 18)? (Your answer should explain the relevance of both words—'absurd' and 'puppet'.)
 (v) 'He wears a mask, and his face grows to fit it' (ll. 23-4). What does this sentence tell you about the behaviour of white men in the East?

From Section B:

*(vi) What do you understand by the words 'that preoccupied grand-motherly air' (l. 32)?

(vii) Explain why the author does not do 'what [he] ought to do' (l. 36).

(viii) 'I was not afraid in the ordinary sense, as I would have been if I had been alone' (ll. 44–5). (i) Of what was the author *not afraid*, and (ii) of what was he *afraid*?

From Section C:

(ix) Describe *in your own words* how the audience reacted when the author took aim.

*(x) In this Section the author is *twice* surprised by time. (*a*) What surprises him, and (*b*) why does it do so?

(xi) Write a single correct sentence of *not more than 20 words* describing the effects of the bullet on the elephant.

From the whole passage:

*(xii) In describing this episode the author uses many terms taken from the theatre. (*a*) List these briefly, and (*b*) suggest why he uses such terms.

(xiii) Summarise in correct sentences:

(*a*) why the author was unwilling to kill the elephant, and

(*b*) why he was driven to do so.
    (*Do not use more than 50 words on the whole answer.*)

(xiv) In lines 19–20 the author says 'that when the white man turns tyrant it is his own freedom that he destroys'. Explain briefly *in your own words* what he means by this.

113 Questions **1** to **12** are based on the following passage. Read the passage carefully and then answer the questions. Each question has five suggested answers. Select the best answer to each question.

Sweeping, polishing, fetching and carrying, occasionally helping to move a patient, conscious or unconscious, under the sergeant-majorly supervision of Mr Perkins, time passed smoothly. With satisfaction he noticed himself becoming accepted and integrated into the community of the hospital, finding his place in a feudal pyramid-shaped society that brooked no vague- 5
ness as to questions of status. He found this refreshingly different from the world outside; here, there could be no false pretensions, for rank, prestige and privileges were settled automatically. At the top were the doctors; these had their own hierarchy, but it was too distant to be observed from below, and concerned no one but themselves and the few uppermost nurses— 10
Matrons and Sisters—who shared the same status. Next came the nurses in general, again with an elaborate hierarchy from Staff Nurse to Probationer. At the bottom, the broad base of the triangle, came the cooks, technicians, clerical and domestic workers. There was, of course, a rigid line of demarcation between each trade here. Charles found his place somewhere near the 15
bottom. As an orderly he cut rather little ice, being inexperienced and

without knowledge of any technical trade: it was soon discovered that he was of little use at emergency patching up of electrical equipment, plumbing, or any other deep mystery. So he was tolerated and kept busy on humble tasks; which suited him perfectly. Anonymity, obscurity, a relief from strain, the $\qquad$ 20 situation was exactly what he had prescribed for himself. Finally, he found with gratitude that hospital life, being so grotesquely unlike anything in the world outside, did not admit of any of the usual social classifications. It was not considered strange that he should be working at a manual occupation and still sounding his aitches. $\qquad$ 25

1 The writer calls the society of the hospital 'feudal' (line 5) because it

  A   seems like a survival from the Middle Ages
  B   would be difficult to alter in any way its authoritarian character
  C   is class-conscious and oppressive towards the lower orders
  D   has rules that are enforced with military discipline and severity
  E   is based on a scale of fixed and sharply distinguished ranks or positions

2 'A pyramid-shaped society' (line 5) is one in which

  A   the ranks of society are as rigid as in Ancient Egypt
  B   there are hidden snags and rewards
  C   the social ranks are fixed as firmly as a monument of stone
  D   there is a social validity and permanence
  E   the higher the social rank the fewer the people are in it

3 Which one of the following words is closest in meaning to 'brooked' as used in line 5?

  A   Produced
  B   Tolerated
  C   Observed
  D   Suggested
  E   Implied

4 Charles found life at the hospital 'refreshingly different from the world outside' (lines 6–7) because

  A   he was left mainly to his own devices with no-one to bother him
  B   the hospital had a very friendly atmosphere in which he was soon accepted
  C   he preferred to be near the bottom of the social scale
  D   no one could claim to be higher in the social scale than he really was
  E   he found his work a very satisfying form of service to the community

5 The 'rigid line of demarcation' mentioned in lines 14–15 would run between

  A   Charles and a Matron
  B   a Sister and a Staff Nurse
  C   any two doctors

D   an electrician and a probationer
E   a cook and a plumber

6 'He cut rather little ice' (line 16) means that he was not

A   regarded as important or very useful
B   treated respectfully by his fellow-workers
C   admired for speaking correctly and grammatically
D   pulling his weight
E   given a fair chance

7 'Anonymity' as used in the passage (line 20) means that

A   no-one there knew Charles's real name
B   people knew Charles's name but did not address him by it
C   nobody knew that Charles was not really a manual worker
D   Charles was trying to escape detection
E   no-one was interested in Charles as a person

8 Hospital life is said by the author to be 'grotesquely unlike anything in the world outside' (lines 22–3) mainly because

A   clear divisions exist between the different ranks
B   people are very friendly with one another
C   all the lower paid workers speak very correctly
D   status is fixed according to function
E   people can remain unknown and untroubled by their superiors

9 The phrase which best indicates the attitude to Charles of others in the hospital is

A   'under the sergeant-majorly supervision' (line 2)
B   'a feudal pyramid-shaped society that brooked no vagueness' (line 5)
C   'it was soon discovered that he was of little use at emergency patching up of electrical equipment' (lines 17–18)
D   'So he was tolerated and kept busy on humble tasks' (line 19)
E   'hospital life . . . did not admit of any of the usual social classifications' (lines 22–3)

10 Charles enjoyed hospital life for all the following reasons EXCEPT that

A   he was accepted as part of the hospital staff
B   no one was interested in who he was
C   the situation made no demands on his nerves
D   there were none of the usual class-distinctions
E   manual work was the work for which he was really fitted

11 It can be inferred from the passage that Charles took this job because

A   he wanted to be of use to the sick, even in a humble way
B   it was an easy way for an unskilled man to earn money

C no one would ask him any awkward questions
D he wished to study the organisation of a hospital
E he needed to escape from the stresses of the life he had been leading

12 The aspect of hospital life that this passage lays most emphasis on is the

A tedious nature of the work
B range of jobs to be done
C strict scale of rank to status
D difficulty of gaining promotion
E opportunity of public service

114   Questions **1** to **25** are based on the following passage. Read the passage carefully and then answer the questions. Each question has five suggested answers. Select the best answer to each question.

All the men in the boat were silent. There was nothing else that could be done.

'I have been looking at that cliff,' Finn said. 'I think I can climb it. There will be water on the top.'

Roddie's face slowly drew taut and his eyes hardened. 'No one can climb   5
that cliff,' he said to his brother.

'Yes, if you landed me there, I could do it.'

They looked at the black ledge to which he pointed. The water rose to it, then fell down about twelve feet sheer in sucking, greeny-white swirls, and then rose again.   10

'And how would we land you there?' asked Roddie in level mockery.

'If you shifted the anchor over there,' said Finn, 'one of you could pay out rope, while the others brought her in stern first on the oars. When you were close to the rock and the stern rose up, I could jump.'

Roddie said, 'What if the stern hit the rock coming up? What if you   15
slipped? Do you think we could help you then?'

'Someone must take a chance,' said Finn, a flash of colour in his cheek-bones.

'Oh? Why?' demanded Roddie.

'Because if I don't do it now, I won't have the strength to do it tomorrow.'   20
Roddie's tone had whipped him. He shut his mouth to keep more words from boiling out.

In their exhausted, thirst-tormented, overwrought condition, a bout of irritation was understandable enough, but the others felt that the animosity which had flared between the brothers was deeper than irritation. Finn   25
knew what was troubling his brother. Roddie would not like to be the bearer of the tidings of Finn's death to Finn's mother. Something deep inside Finn exulted over Roddie and his bitter predicament.

'Well, boys,' said Roddie quietly, 'I'm willing to listen to you.'
No one spoke.   30

Roddie nodded and looked at the cliffs. 'One of us will try it. Who is it to be?'

'As skipper,' said Rob, 'you can't desert the boat.'

Henry nodded. There was nothing to discuss with a young fellow like Finn in the boat. And it was Finn's idea.   35

There was a minute's long silent conflict in all their minds; then Roddie

pointed to the anchor rope. Finn stripped off his heavy sea clothes, and tied
two bottles round his waist.

Roddie let the anchor down carefully, holding the rope immediately he
felt bottom, and motioned them to row away. With left hand up, Henry   40
guided Roddie's control of the anchor rope, while the two men on the oars
paddled gently. It was a desperate venture, because no two seas behaved
quite alike, and the stern was thrown giddily not only up and down but in a
swaying circular motion. Now the stern began to rush on the cliff-face, then
to sag away, while the water streamed from the rock, from the weed, and   45
boiled underneath in seething froth.

'When she comes up, Finn boy,' said Henry in a hoarse voice.

Up she came, rushing on the rock. Not until she was a foot from the top of
her swinging heave did Finn rise in one swift motion and leap from the
narrow stern-post, and land on toes, knees, and hands, in that order, on the   50
small, rounded, sloping ledge of dark rock.

Down below in the gulf, eyes stared up as Finn began to climb.

The shrieking of the sea-birds became an infernal torment to their ragged
nerves, and when suddenly Rob seemed to go mad in a high-pitched croak,
their hearts leapt as their heads turned—and they saw, choking the rock   55
channel, advancing upon them, a gigantic wall of water. Along the rock
walls it smashed in a roar flinging white arms at crevice and ledge.

Swung seaward on the crest of it, they hung for a dizzying moment on a
level with Finn. He had seen it coming and flattened to the sloping rock,
gripping with fingers and knees and toes. The solid water swept the soles of   60
his feet, but the white spray covered him like a shroud. Down went the boat,
down, down, until tangle, that grew in a sea-green underworld, saw the light
of day, and curved over, and flattened like trees ridden by a hurricane.

And there was Finn, splayed black against the rock.

At first the climbing was not difficult, because there was a distinct ridge   65
sloping steeply up the face of the rock for all the world like a narrow, tumbled,
broken path. On his left hand the cliff rose sheer, and on his right it fell sheer
into the sea. But now Finn reached a wall, little more than twice his own
height, but to his eyes unclimbable.

All at once, as he looked up, his vision darkened and his heart began   70
beating at a tremendous rate. He had lived and moved these last seconds
beyond his exhausted strength. His skin went cold all over and his flesh
started to quiver and tremble in a sickening manner. He lay against the rock,
face in, until the silent buzz of the darkness in his head began to subside and
his vision to clear. The whistling of his breath made his mouth so much dryer   75
than it was, that, when he closed it, it stuck, and came apart again painfully.

Deliberately he let his mind sink down in him as if he were going to sleep.
For panic was near. They would be watching him, wondering why he was
taking so long, as if he were playing with their nerves, particularly with
Roddie's. Well, let them! So long as the panic stings kept off. For about half   80
a minute, he was invaded by a delicious feeling of languor. He let it soak into
his limp tissues. He felt cradled in an eagle's eyrie.

Arising, he looked at the rock. In front of him and on the inward side it
was flawless and impossible, but on the outward edge it was notched and in
two places riven to miniature ledges. Without giving himself time for thought,   85
he reached up his right hand and gripped a boss.

They watched him from the boat. There were moments when the slowness

of his movements had, for Roddie, the element of extreme horror that is
found in nightmares.

But Finn was still on the rock. And the rock was not his danger, as he 90
knew. He loved the perilous cleanness of height. He could go as carefully here
as if he were crossing stepping-stones in a stream. What he feared was his
staying power, the trembling fingers.

He rounded the desperate corner, fingers pressing on the ledge above, toes
on the ledge below, and suddenly found that he had rounded the real danger. 95
His spirit lifted in a rush, in a silent cry. The rock leaned back. His toe came
up searching for a purchase, found it, felt all round it, gripped; his right hand
moved up and got a hold he could have swung on; his left hand, his left foot;
slowly, with a certainty of care; up, up over, until he lay on his stomach in
safety, with a laughing ecstasy in his heart. 100

Roddie, unknown to himself, groaned and sagged, completely exhausted.
He had plumbed depths of fear and terror that Finn knew nothing of.

1 From the description of the water at the black ledge (lines 8–10) it is clear
that

A   there was a large swell on the sea
B   great waves were pounding the rock
C   the water was splashing twelve feet into the air
D   the sea was at high tide
E   water was siphoning up from beneath the rock

2 Which one of the following expressions best explains the meaning of 'level'
as used in line 11?

A   In an accusing voice
B   Looking him straight in the eyes
C   In a calm, even tone
D   Pretending to agree with him
E   In an indifferent manner

3 Roddie's question in line 11 was mocking because it suggested that Finn
was

A   too inexperienced to attempt such a feat
B   showing off in front of the others
C   careless of the danger to the others
D   not thinking of the obvious initial difficulty
E   too young to tell the skipper what to do

4 Roddie opposed Finn's proposal for all the following reasons EXCEPT that
he

A   considered that the cliff was unclimbable
B   feared that Finn would be killed
C   realised the danger of approaching the rock
D   resented Finn's challenge to his authority
E   believed that Finn had not foreseen all the hazards

5 There was 'a flash of colour' in Finn's face (line 17) because he was

    A   eager to start his climb up the rock
    B   amazed at his own daring
    C   angered by Roddie's mocking opposition
    D   ashamed of his brother for being afraid
    E   embarrassed to be quarrelling openly with Roddie

6 Finn is said to have been 'whipped' (line 21) by Roddie's tone most probably because it

    A   frightened him
    B   depressed him
    C   confused him
    D   angered him
    E   punished him

7 Finn wanted to make his attempt at once because he

    A   was afraid he might soon lose his nerve
    B   felt sure that the weather was slowly getting worse
    C   believed that he could distinguish himself in front of the crew
    D   knew that he was gradually becoming weaker
    E   was confident of his ability to climb the cliff

8 Which one of the following phrases best explains the meaning of 'bout' as used in line 23?

    A   Short contest
    B   Slight rage
    C   Bitter conflict
    D   Sudden climax
    E   Brief spell

9 The word 'predicament' (line 28) indicates that Roddie had to

    A   make a difficult choice
    B   decide quickly
    C   accept the situation
    D   take the consequences
    E   admit he was defeated

10 For which *two* of the following reasons was it agreed that Finn should be the one to climb the cliff?

    1 Roddie could not leave the boat.
    2 Finn had originated the plan.
    3 Henry was needed to guide the boat in.
    4 Everyone else was exhausted.
    A **1** and **2** only
    B **1** and **3** only

C **2** and **3** only
D **2** and **4** only
E **3** and **4** only

11 Finn tied two bottles round his waist (lines 37–8) in order to

    A help him survive during his exhausting climb
    B keep him afloat if he slipped into the sea
    C bring back water from the cliff-top
    D balance him as he sprang on to the rock
    E sustain him if the rock proved to be waterless

12 Roddie held the rope 'immediately he felt bottom' (lines 39–40) because

    A the taut rope was to be used to control the movement of the boat
    B he was in a hurry to proceed with the risky part of the scheme
    C a loose rope could easily become entangled in the rocks
    D if too much rope was let out, they might lose the anchor
    E they needed to know just how deep the water was at that point

13 The spray is compared to a shroud (line 61) for all the following reasons EXCEPT that it

    A covered Finn's body from sight
    B was white in colour
    C suggested Finn's nearness to death
    D was fine and moist
    E had no distinct shape

14 Which one of the following is closest in meaning to 'tangle' as used in line 62?

    A Coarse seaweed
    B Submarine creatures
    C Twisted ropes
    D Shore vegetation
    E Underwater coral

15 The word 'splayed' (line 64) suggests that, against the rock, Finn was

    A fastened
    B stretched
    C silhouetted
    D wedged
    E camouflaged

16 During his climb, Finn dispelled the danger of panic by

    A not giving himself time for thought
    B ignoring the people in the boat
    C splaying himself against the rock

D refusing to hurry in his climbing
E forcing himself to relax mentally

17 Which one of the following is closest in meaning to 'languor' as used in line 81?

    A Comfortable yearning
    B Sudden ecstasy
    C Easy nonchalance
    D Drowsy lassitude
    E Quiet security

18 When the rock is described as 'flawless and impossible' (line 84) the writer means it was

    A perfect and unreachable
    B solid but dangerous
    C unbroken and unclimbable
    D peerless but forbidding
    E indescribable and treacherous

19 Finn did not give himself time for thought (line 85) probably because

    A he had to hurry before his strength gave out
    B it was essential to complete his mission quickly when so much depended on it
    C he knew he could depend on his instinctive skill as a rock-climber
    D if he had stopped to think, the climb would have seemed too dangerous
    E he was by nature a hasty and impetuous person

20 Finn's movements reminded Roddie of the horror of a nightmare (lines 88–9) because

    A there was nothing he could do to help
    B he could not believe that it was really happening
    C the motions of the climber seemed so long-drawn-out
    D he felt that Finn would never reach the top
    E it seemed that Finn was far off in a mist

21 Which one of the following words is closest in meaning to 'purchase' as used in line 97?

    A Fissure
    B Opportunity
    C Projection
    D Hold
    E Ledge

22 The expression 'laughing ecstasy' (line 100) implies that Finn was

    A mocking Roddie's fears
    B amused by his predicament
    C exhilarated by his success
    D very close to tears
    E becoming rather hysterical

23 All of the following are particularly critical moments in Finn's venture EXCEPT the

    A leap from the boat
    B coming of the great wave
    C climb to the foot of the wall
    D pause at the foot of the wall
    E turning of the corner of the rock

24 In the passage, Roddie displays all the following qualities EXCEPT a

    A skill in manoeuvring the boat
    B willingness to listen to others
    C sense of responsibility towards his crew
    D resentment of his brother's initiative
    E readiness to act on a decision

25 The closeness of the relationship between the two brothers is suggested by all the following EXCEPT

    A Roddie's unwillingness to let Finn make the climb
    B Finn's understanding of the reasons for Roddie's attitude
    C Roddie's feelings of horror as he watches the slow climb
    D Finn's sense of triumph on reaching the top of the cliff
    E Roddie's exhaustion when the climb has been accomplished

115   Questions **1** to **24** are based on the following passage. Read the passage carefully and then answer the questions. Each question has five suggested answers. Select the best answer to each question.

    It was at the Mechanics' Institute that I met George Thompson, three years older than I, and he impressed me as soon as I saw him. Most of the students were artisans bent on improving themselves. We were a very humble lot, content, even grateful to take what the lecturers told us as gospel; and the lecturers were pretty perfunctory. For the most part, the instruction   5 consisted of the lecturer dictating to us while we, always a sentence behind, laboriously wrote down the lecturer's words as faithfully as we could remember them.

    Naturally, I saw nothing wrong with this method of teaching at all: the lecturers knew, and they were telling us. I was ready to venerate them as   10 men of knowledge: they were, in fact, school-teachers whose fate it was to teach during evenings in the same horribly dark, dingy, overcrowded class-rooms they taught in during the day. The rest of the class hated George: he

broke up the even flow of dictation. As one man grumbled to me: 'How can
the teachers get through the syllabus if that Thompson keeps on interrupt-   15
ing?' For George would jump up amid the lecturer's droning and say, 'Sir, I
don't see that'; or, 'The experiment quoted doesn't prove the law,'—once,
even, at the end of one demonstration, 'I did not understand that. Could you
please repeat the experiment?' and then it was perfectly plain that the
lecturer had made a botch of his demonstration, knew he had, and was   20
trying to fob us off with a faulty display. George would have none of it; and
I watched him with wonder as he rose from his desk, short, though not as
short as I, but with very broad shoulders and his great domed head and
rock-like jaw. I watched him, as I say, with fear and trembling, for to me the
teachers represented not only knowledge but also authority; they were little   25
gods, and George was defying them.

I had been attending these evening classes four weeks before he spoke to
me. He kept himself to himself; indeed, he walked and talked in a manner so
brusque that he seemed to be brushing people aside. When he did speak to
me it was in characteristic fashion. At the end of the class he walked across   30
the room to me and said: 'Ashted, join me in a pie at Boswell's.' I was taken
aback. Here was no tentative fumbling towards acquaintanceship, but something that was half-way between an order and a challenge.

He led the way to Boswell's I had not been there before, for I was still boy
enough to regard it as grand and sophisticated beyond me. It was famous for   35
its hot meat pies, as I appreciated when, timidly, I followed George to a
zinc-topped table in the far corner. One sat marooned as it were in mingled
odours that had the density and palpability of fog. Steam, through which
loomed vaguely the great copper coffee and tea urns on the counter and the
figures of men at other tables, was the solvent in which these odours were   40
borne, and the odours were those of tobacco pipes, wet macintoshes, and
bubbling hot meat pies. It was a pleasing blend of smells that titillated the
nostrils and made the mouth water, for dominant all the time was the savour
of the pies. It promised richness and succulence, a tenderness of meat, a
consistency of gravy-soaked pastry, unsurpassed. I sat down with George   45
and knew I wanted one of those pies more at that moment than anything in
the world.

Nothing was said by either of us until the coffee and pies arrived. We fell
on them as though starving. When we were finished, George said: 'Boswell's
pies are *good*,' and then he quite confounded me by adding: ' "If a man write   50
a better book, preach a better sermon, or make a better mousetrap than
his neighbour, though he build his house in the woods, the world will
make a beaten path to his door." ' He stared at me. 'Who said that?' he demanded. I did not know. 'Emerson. Ralph Waldo Emerson. You must read
him.'   55

George looked at me: 'That night school! I wonder if it's ever struck you
how very shoddy it is, how incompetent the teaching. You may take my
word for it, Ashted: what we are given there is a parody of knowledge. And
why? Because our betters still believe that anything is good enough for
working people, the likes of you and me. Yet even that is progress, Ashted,   60
because only a few years ago nothing, not anything, was good enough for us.
So we mustn't be indignant, or rather we must keep our indignation for more
serious things and try and use the third-best that's thrown to us in such a
way as to give us an inkling of the first-best. It can be done.'

He paid for the pies and coffee and went. I might have run after him and   65 caught him and accompanied him on his way, which was also mine; but I was shy. I felt he wanted to be alone now. I was shy for another reason too: I wanted to be alone; not to think, but to feel, to indulge in the luxury of rejoicing. I had a friend. For the first time in my life, I had a friend.

1 It is true to say that most of the students

    A   considered the lecturers to be inefficient
    B   felt great respect for the lecturers
    C   were embarrassed by the lecturers' failures
    D   thought the copying of notes to be boring
    E   were ashamed of their own ignorance

2 The attitude of most of the students towards the teaching they received at night school can best be described as

    A   undiscriminating
    B   unsatisfied
    C   uninterested
    D   unsystematic
    E   unconventional

3 When George jumped up and said, 'Sir, I don't see that' (lines 16–17) he was signifying that

    A   he was tired of listening to the lecturer's droning voice
    B   he wanted to show that he knew more about the subject than the lecturer did
    C   there was something unfair or dishonest about the lecturer's procedure
    D   the lecturer had made a slip in the experiment which he was demonstrating
    E   he was not clear about some point the lecturer had made

4 The account of George's behaviour in class is meant to suggest that he was

    A   contemptuous of the other students
    B   unable to understand the lessons
    C   determined to learn the subject properly
    D   fond of the sound of his own voice
    E   trying to dominate the lessons

5 All of the following contributed to the poor quality of the education available at the night school EXCEPT the

    A   lecturers' lack of interest in their work
    B   interruptions of the teaching by George
    C   unsuitable accommodation
    D   teaching methods employed
    E   students' attitude towards the lecturers

6 Compared with Ashted, George Thompson was all of the following EXCEPT

    A less shy
    B older
    C more critical
    D smaller
    E better read

7 The narrator watched George 'with fear and trembling' (line 24) because he was

    A scared of George's aggressive manner towards everyone
    B shocked at George's unnecessary rudeness to the lecturers
    C afraid that George would interfere with the teaching
    D aghast at George's audacity in challenging the lecturers
    E frightened that George would be expelled from the class

8 The lecturers in the Mechanics' Institute are referred to as 'little gods' (lines 25–6) because the students regarded them as all the following EXCEPT

    A symbols of wisdom and power
    B subjects for respect and obedience
    C holders of a divine mission
    D possessors of superior knowledge
    E beings incapable of making mistakes

9 George's invitation to Ashted (line 31) can best be described as

    A curt and assured
    B strange and frightening
    C moody and insolent
    D rude and aggressive
    E cynical and unfriendly

10 In the passage, the statement that George's manner was 'brusque' (line 29) means that he was

    A rude and impolite
    B blunt and abrupt
    C hostile and domineering
    D casual and ill-bred
    E bold and determined

11 Which one of the following is closest in meaning to 'tentative' as used in line 32?

    A Hesitant and exploratory
    B Clumsy and awkward
    C Friendly and attentive

D Inexperienced and unsophisticated
E Lukewarm and off-hand

12 The author had not been to Boswell's before because he

    A was too young to enter
    B was unable to afford it
    C did not know the way
    D did not like the atmosphere
    E was over-awed by it

13 The word 'marooned' (line 37) is used to suggest that at the tables one felt

    A lost in the crowd of people
    B hidden from sight in a fog
    C overwhelmed by odorous waves
    D isolated in a sea of smells
    E abandoned to one's own devices

14 The steam is called a 'solvent' (line 40) because

    A all the smells seem blended and suspended in it
    B it is so thick it seems to dissolve the outlines of objects
    C all the narrator's nervousness is melted away by it
    D it is as soaked in flavour as the pies themselves
    E it acts like an aerosol to purify the air

15 The statement that the smell 'promised richness and succulence' (line 44) means that it suggested that the pies would be

    A nourishing and satisfying
    B full of flavour and juicy
    C expensive and luxurious
    D hot and spicy
    E stuffed with meat and vegetables

16 The lines of Emerson quoted by George (lines 50–3) are best summarized as meaning

    A good authors, preachers and inventors are hard to find
    B people will travel a long way to see a novelty
    C something first-class is bound to be recognised
    D some people try to hide their talent and achievements
    E craftsmen and scholars have a duty to society

17 Thompson's comments on the night school were

    A uninformed
    B commendatory
    C irrational

D   discerning

E   irrelevant

18 The statement that 'nothing, not anything, was good enough for us' (line 61) means that in the past, the working people had been given

   A   the best education available

   B   only a third-rate education

   C   an education befitting their position

   D   a better education than now

   E   no education at all

19 George objected to the night school for all the following reasons EXCEPT that

   A   the teachers tried to cover up any mistakes they made

   B   it was impossible to gain there any idea of the really first-rate

   C   the lecturers were poor at demonstrating and speaking about their subjects

   D   those in authority thought anything would do for working people

   E   the education given there was an inferior imitation of the real thing

20 By the way in which he spoke to Ashted about the night school, Thompson showed that he was

   A   better educated than the teachers

   B   fond of interrupting the lessons

   C   supercilious about working people

   D   critical of those who were indignant

   E   ready to make the best of what was offered

21 At first, Thompson says 'we mustn't be indignant' (line 62) because

   A   nothing was good enough for them

   B   anything was good enough for them

   C   educational facilities had improved

   D   teachers were doing their best

   E   they all had an inkling of the first-best

22 Which one of the following is closest in meaning to 'inkling' as used in line 64?

   A   Sight

   B   Taste

   C   Hint

   D   Impression

   E   Dislike

23 In his attitudes to night school and to Boswell's, the narrator showed that at that time he was, respectively

 A bored at night school and unsophisticated about Boswell's
 B appreciative at night school and indifferent to Boswell's
 C attentive at night school and impressed by Boswell's
 D critical at night school and enthusiastic about Boswell's
 E conscientious at night school and disparaging about Boswell's

24 Before his meeting with Thompson, we may assume that Ashted had been

 A conformist
 B bored
 C ignorant
 D popular
 E perceptive

11
Figures of Speech

11:1

It is one thing to recognise figures of speech and another to use them effectively in writing. They may be classified in six categories according to the effect they have within the text where they are used or the way in which they are internally organised:

1 *Comparison:*   Metaphor, Personification, Simile; Allegory, Fable, Parable
2 *Contrast:*   Antithesis, Oxymoron, Paradox
3 *Word-arrangement:*   Apostrophe, Chiasmus, Climax and Anti-climax, Epigram, Hypallage, Pleonasm, Syllepsis, Zeugma
4 *Word-association:*   Metonymy, Prolepsis, Pun, Synecdoche
5 *Suggestion:*   Burlesque, Parody, Mock-heroic, Euphemism, Hyperbole, Innuendo, Irony, Litotes, Sarcasm
6 *Sound:*   Alliteration, Onomatopoeia

Comparison

11:2

(i) *Metaphor* (French word in origin *métaphore*, from Greek *metaphora:* 'transfer')

A metaphor is a comparison between two or more things fundamentally unlike but alike in the one respect in which they are being compared; in a metaphor the comparison is usually implicit.

e.g. He is a pig.

In a *simile* (see (iii) below) the comparison would be explicit and introduced by 'like' or 'as'.

e.g. He is like a pig.

It is usually considered confusing to mix a number of metaphors in the same sentence or paragraph.

(ii) *Personification* (probably from French *personifier*, from Latin: 'to make into a person')

This is a special kind of metaphor where a personal form, or nature, or characteristics are attributed to a thing or an abstract idea.

e.g. Disease *ran riot* through the village.
The ship *made her way* into the harbour.

(iii) *Simile* (Latin word in origin, *similis*: 'like')

This, like metaphor, is a comparison between two or more things fundamentally unlike, but alike in the one respect in which they are being compared; in a simile the comparison is explicit and is introduced by 'like' or 'as'.

e.g. She sang *like a nightingale*.
He looked *like a pig*.

Allegory, *Fable*, and *Parable* are forms of extended metaphor.

(iv) *Allegory* (Greek word in origin, *allegoria*: 'speaking otherwise')

Normally this is a story in verse or prose which operates on at least two levels of meaning, one literal or superficial and the other using symbolism and much deeper.

Allegories in English include John Bunyan's *Pilgrim's Progress* and George Orwell's *Animal Farm*. In both stories there is a narrative line but beneath this narrative level there are levels of deeper meaning: *e.g.* the progress of the Christian through life from damnation to salvation; the nature of political power and its corruption.

(v) *Fable* (French word in origin, *fable*, from Latin *fabula*: 'a story')

A fable is a short narrative, often in which animals or birds or even non-living objects represent human beings, with a moral at the end.

The earliest collection of fables is attributed to Æsop, a semilegendary person; the collection dates from the sixth century BC. Phaedrus, a Thracian slave, collected some Latin fables during the reign of Caesar Augustus (63BC–14AD). Later La Fontaine (1621–95) in France and Rudyard Kipling (1865–1936) in England also produced work on fables, sometimes based on those of earlier writers.

Some well-known examples of fables are: *The Fox and the Crow*; *The Hare and the Tortoise*; *The Town Mouse and the Country Mouse*. See, too, Kipling's *Just So Stories* (1902).

(vi) *Parable* (Greek word in origin, *parabole*: 'a side-throw')

A parable is a short story, often with a moral.
It is related, therefore to both 'allegory' and 'fable'. It is distinguished from 'fable' by being a term usually restricted to moral stories found in the Bible.

e.g. *The good Samaritan* (Luke, 10); *The Prodigal Son* (Luke, 15); *The Five Wise and the Five Foolish Virgins* (Matthew, 25)

Contrast

11:3

(i) *Antithesis* (Latin word in origin from Greek *antitithemi*: 'set against')

This is a figure of speech in which one word is set off against another:

e.g. 'More haste, less speed.' (NOTE The word 'speed' here means 'success', from the Old English *spēd*.)
'To err is human, to forgive divine.'

(ii) *Oxymoron* (Greek word in origin, *oxy+moros*: 'pointedly foolish')

This is a figure of speech where contradictory or incongruous words are used in combination to produce a special effect.

e.g. He had to be *cruel* to be *kind*.
He found the taste of success *bitter-sweet*.

(iii) *Paradox* (Greek word in origin, *paradoxos*: 'contrary to accepted opinion')

A paradox is a statement or a proposition which on the face of it seems to be self-contradictory or at variance with common sense; on investigation, or when explained, however, it may prove to be well-founded.

e.g. 'The child is father to the man.'
'He that believeth in me though he were dead yet shall he live.' (John 11: 25)
'For whosoever will save his life shall lose it: but whosoever will lose his life for my sake shall save it.' (Luke 9: 24)

Paradox and *oxymoron* are very closely related.

Word-arrangement

11:4

(i) *Apostrophe* (Greek word in origin, *apostrophos*: 'turning away')

A figure of speech, by which a writer suddenly stops in his line of writing and turns to address, in a pointed way, a person or thing, present or absent.

e.g. 'Milton, thou shouldst be living at this hour.'
'O ye gods, ye gods, must I endure all this?'

(ii) *Chiasmus* (Greek word in origin, *chiasma*: 'a cross-shaped mark', like the Greek letter χ)

A balancing of two contrasted phrases, where the order of words in one phrase is reversed in the other.
  (This is a highly contrived figure and is not often used.)

e.g. It's easy to ask but to answer is hard.

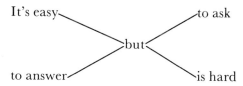

(iii) *Climax and Anti-climax* (Greek words in origin, *climax*: 'a ladder'; *anti*: 'opposed to')

Climax: A figure in which a number of ideas or items are set out in an ascending order of importance.

e.g. Because of his stupidity he lost his car, his house, his job, and his wife and family.

Anti-climax (sometimes called *Bathos*, a word of Greek origin meaning 'depth'): A figure in which a number of ideas or items are set out in an ascending order of importance but where the last idea or item, instead of heightening the effect, suddenly lowers it or makes it ludicrous.

e.g. 'Because of his stupidity he lost his car, his house, his job, his wife and family, and his hat.'

(iv) *Epigram* (French word though Latin in origin, ultimately from Greek, *epigramma*: 'inscription')

A pointed, brief, and witty statement; it often contains an element of surprise.

e.g. 'The Golden Rule is that there is no Golden Rule.' (G. B. Shaw)
'No man can be a pure specialist without being in the strict sense an idiot.' (G. B. Shaw)
'Fortunately in England, at any rate, education produces no effect whatsoever. If it did, it would prove a serious danger to the upper classes.' (Oscar Wilde)

(v) *Hypallage* (Greek word in origin, *hypo*: under + *allassein*: 'to exchange')

(Sometimes hypallage is referred to as 'transferred epithet'.)
A figure of speech in which an adjective belonging to one noun is transferred to another to which it does not properly belong.

e.g. A *sleepless* night. (It is the person in bed who is *sleepless*—not the night.)

A *condemned* cell. (The cell is not *condemned* but the person in it is.)
Sad news. (The news is not *sad* but the person who receives it is.)

(vi) *Pleonasm* (Greek word in origin, *pleonasmos*: 'superfluity')

An unnecessary, redundant use of words. It may not repeat the sense exactly but it adds little of any importance.

e.g. In this day and age = 'now', 'today'.
He was wearing a beret *on his head*.
He investigated the *surrounding* circumstances.

(vii) *Syllepsis* (Greek word in origin, *syn*: together + *lambanein*: 'to take')

Compare Zeugma (below).
A figure of speech in which a word has the same syntactical relation to two or more words but has a different sense in relation to each.

e.g. He lived in Edinburgh and in sin.
She lost her heart and her handbag at the dance.
She caught the aeroplane and a cold.

(viii) *Zeugma* (Greek word in origin *zeugnynai*: 'to yoke together')

A figure of speech in which an adjective or a verb is applied to two nouns but, strictly speaking, can apply to one of them only.

e.g. With eyes and ears pricked up, the dog waited for his master.
(Here *pricked up* refers strictly only to 'ears', not 'eyes'.)

Word-association

11:5

(i) *Metonymy* (Greek word in origin, *metonymia*: 'name-change')

The substitution for the name of a thing the name of an attribute of it or of something closely related to it.

e.g. 'The House' for *Parliament*;
'The Crown' for *the Queen*;
'Shakespeare' for *the works of Shakespeare*.

(ii) *Prolepsis* (Greek word in origin, *prolepsis*: 'taking in advance')

A figure of speech in which a matter is stated in a brief manner, before being set out in detail.

e.g. The murderer, now a *dead* man, rose to receive his sentence.

It is also a term used to cover the situation in a debate where supposed arguments are raised and disposed of before they have been actually put in full:

e.g. 'Some will argue that . . .'

(iii) *Pun* (a late-seventeenth-century word whose origin is unknown; Italian *puntiglio*, 'a fine point' has been suggested)

A play on words where a word is used in such a way as to suggest two or more meanings or associations simultaneously.

e.g. *Epitaph on a Brewer*

Here lies poor *Burton*;
He was both hale and *stout*;
Death laid him on his *bitter bier*.
Now in another world he *hops* about.

(iv) *Synecdoche* (Greek word in origin, *synekdoche*: 'taking together')

A figure of speech where a comprehensive term is used for a less comprehensive one or vice-versa; *i.e.* a whole for a part or a part for the whole.

e.g. The school won the tennis tournament. (The school = the school's tennis team; *i.e.* the whole for a part.)
'Give us this day our daily bread.' (Bread = food; *i.e.* part for the whole.)

Suggestion

11:6

(i) *Burlesque* (Italian word in origin, *burlesco*, from *burla*: 'a joke')

The term is usually restricted to a form of theatrical entertainment, where a serious work of literature or music is imitated in a derisive or amusing manner; a grotesque imitation of what is, or is intended to be, dignified in action, speech, or manner.

The musical *O, What a lovely War!* showed the life of carefree Londoners during the First World War whilst at the same time the serious and devastating numbers of casualties in the battles in France were shown on a backdrop; the serious was made to seem unimportant (*burlesque*) and an intrusion in order to make a powerful point about both the losses and about the utter waste of life.

Mock-heroic works in the opposite way; it takes a trivial topic and elevates it into very serious action. For example, in 'The Rape of the Lock' Alexander Pope took a trivial incident (a young man cuts a lock of hair from a girl's head at a party) and raises it in tone and by language to the level of heroic warfare, similar to an incident in one of the great epics *The Iliad* or *The Odyssey*.

(ii) *Parody* (Greek word in origin, *paroidia*: 'mock-song') ·

A composition in prose or verse in which the characteristic turns of thought and phrase in another work or kind of work are imitated in such a way as to make them appear ridiculous, especially by applying them to ludicrously inappropriate subjects.

The Greeks used parody; Cervantes' *Don Quixote* parodied medieval romances; *Hamlet* contains a parody of the exaggerated verse in the plays of Shakespeare's contemporaries. Lewis Carroll's 'Father William' from *Alice's Adventures in Wonderland* (1865) parodies a ballad by Robert Southey, 'The Old Man's Comforts' (1799).

The Old Man's Comforts
AND HOW HE GAINED THEM

You are old, Father William, the young man cried,
    The few locks which are left you are grey;
You are hale, Father William, a hearty old man,
    Now tell me the reason, I pray.

In the days of my youth, Father William replied,
    I remember'd that youth would fly fast,
And abused not my health and my vigour at first,
    That I never might need them at last.

You are old, Father William, the young man cried,
    And pleasures with youth pass away;
And yet you lament not the days that are gone,
    Now tell me the reason, I pray.

In the days of my youth, Father William replied,
    I remember'd that youth could not last;
I thought of the future, whatever I did,
    That I never might grieve for the past.

You are old, Father William, the young man cried,
    And life must be hastening away;
You are cheerful, and love to converse upon death,
    Now tell me the reason, I pray.

I am cheerful, young man, Father William replied,
    Let the cause thy attention engage;
In the days of my youth I remember'd my God!
    And He hath not forgotten my age.

Robert Southey

Father William

"Repeat '*You are old, Father William*'," said the Caterpillar.
Alice folded her hands, and began:

> "*You are old, Father William,*" *the young man said*
>   "*And your hair has become very white;*
> *And yet you incessantly stand on your head—*
>   *Do you think, at your age, it is right?*"
>
> "*In my youth*", *Father William replied to his son,*
>   "*I feared it might injure the brain;*
> *But, now that I'm perfectly sure I have none,*
>   *Why, I do it again and again.*"
>
> "*You are old,*" *said the youth, "as I mentioned before.*
>   *And have grown most uncommonly fat;*
> *Yet you turned a back-somersault in at the door—*
>   *Pray, what is the reason of that?*"
>
> "*In my youth*", *said the sage, as he shook his grey locks,*
>   "*I kept all my limbs very supple*
> *By the use of this ointment—one shilling the box—*
>   *Allow me to sell you a couple?*"
>
> "*You are old*", *said the youth, "and your jaws are too weak*
>   *For anything tougher than suet;*
> *Yet you finished the goose, with the bones and the beak—*
>   *Pray, how did you manage to do it?*"
>
> "*In my youth*", *said his father, "I took to the law,*
>   *And argued each case with my wife;*
> *And the muscular strength, which it gave to my jaw*
>   *Has lasted the rest of my life.*"
>
> "*You are old,*" *said the youth, "one would hardly suppose*
>   *That your eye was as steady as ever;*
> *Yet you balanced an eel on the end of your nose—*
>   *What made you so awfully clever?*"
>
> "*I have answered three questions, and that is enough,*"
>   *Said his father, "Don't give yourself airs!*
> *Do you think I can listen all day to such stuff?*
>   *Be off, or I'll kick you down-stairs!*"

"That is not said right," said the Caterpillar.

"Not *quite* right, I'm afraid," said Alice, timidly: "some of the words have got altered."

"It is wrong from beginning to end," said the Caterpillar decidedly, and there was silence for some minutes.

Lewis Carroll

(iii) *Mock-heroic* (Mock-epic)

For a discussion of *mock-heroic*, see (i), under *Burlesque*.

(iv) *Euphemism* (Greek word in origin, *euphemismos*: 'fair speech')

The substitution of a pleasant word or expression for one of far less pleasant associations.

e.g. *To pass away* for 'die'.
A *clean bomb* for 'a bomb with minimum amounts of radioactive fall-out, but one which still kills thousands'.

Euphemism should not be confused with 'Euphuism', which is the use of ornate, flowery, and very elaborate language of the kind used by John Lyly in his work *Euphues*, published in 1578–80.

(v) *Hyperbole* (Greek word in origin, *hyperbole*: 'overshooting, overthrowing')

An exaggerated or extravagant statement made for emphasis, but not expected to be taken literally.

e.g. She was *as old as the hills*.
He went on talking *for ever*.
She has *hundreds of dresses*.

(vi) *Innuendo* (Latin word in origin, *innuendo*: 'by nodding at'; used in old legal terminology, where this word introduced an additional explanation)

An oblique hint or an indirect suggestion, usually of a depreciatory nature; at first glance it may seem inoffensive.

e.g. 'I hear that George is ill.' 'Nothing trivial, I hope.'
'Surely he can't be as stupid as that!'

(vii) *Irony* (Greek word in origin, *eironeia*: 'dissimulation')

A figure of speech in which the intended meaning is the opposite of that expressed by the words actually used; it often takes the form of sarcasm or ridicule couched in language which seems to be full of praise.

e.g. In Mark Antony's speech after the murder of Julius Caesar he ultimately condemns Brutus, Cassius and the other conspirators by repeating again and again the idea: 'Brutus is an honourable man'; 'So are they all, all honourable men!'

This whole speech of Mark Antony is based on irony:

> 'Yet Brutus says he (Caesar) was ambitious;
> And, sure, he is an honourable man.
> I speak not to disprove what Brutus spoke ...'

Without saying a word against Brutus and Cassius but, on the contrary, by praising them Antony persuades the crowd to rise and seek revenge on Caesar's murderers. (See pages 133–4.)

(viii) *Litotes* (Greek word in origin, *litos*: 'single, simple, meagre')

An understatement used for emphasis, often with a negative.

e.g. Not bad.
She's not stupid.
He can't half run.

This figure of speech is the opposite of hyperbole (see **11:8** (v), page 240).

(ix) *Sarcasm* (Latin word from Greek in origin, *sarcasmus*; Greek *sarkazein*: 'to tear flesh like dogs')

This is a figure of speech, often close to irony, but the attack is usually more obvious. A sharp, bitter, cutting remark or expression.

e.g. 'She was a real beauty.' (meaning 'She was very ugly.')
'Thank you. You are a great help.' (meaning 'Your help is useless.')

Sound

11:7

(i) *Alliteration* (Latin word in origin, *ad + litera*: 'playing on the same letter')

A figure of speech where the sounds at the beginnings of successive words or words in close proximity are repeated.

e.g. 'Apt alliteration's artful aid.'
'He cast one longing, lingering, look behind.'

This figure was used extensively in Old English verse and in some later medieval poetry. It is often found in tongue twisters, where slight changes to break the alliterative pattern make the words difficult to pronounce.

e.g. Still the sinking steamer sank.

(ii) *Onomatopoeia* (Greek word in origin, *onomatopoeia*: 'name-making')

The making of a word to imitate a sound.

e.g. 'cuckoo', 'fizz', 'plop', 'quack'.

EXERCISES

116 Write sentences in which the following nouns are used metaphorically:

1 book;	**2** cage;	**3** door;
4 fruit;	**5** key;	**6** mountain;
7 night;	**8** road;	**9** sea;
10 thirst.		

117 Write sentences in which the following verbs are used metaphorically:

1 borrow;	**2** drag;	**3** eat;
4 fill;	**5** give;	**6** launch;
7 pierce;	**8** ripen;	**9** sink;
10 taste.		

118 Give *two* current expressions using similes which often accompany each of the following adjectives; (*e.g. thick*: as thick as a post; as thick as thieves):

1 black;	**2** clear;	**3** dead;
4 easy;	**5** good;	**6** happy;
7 mad;	**8** old;	**9** poor;
10 straight.		

119 Use each of the following figurative expressions in a sentence of your own to show that you understand its meaning and its use:

1 bury the hatchet;	**2** catch a cold;	**3** fall on one's feet;
4 give one the slip;	**5** hit the target;	**6** lose the thread;
7 pass the buck;	**8** shut the door;	**9** strike oil;
10 sweep the board.		

120 There are at least *ten* figures of speech used in the following dialogue. Find them, describe them, and say what are their effects:

A What did you say he lost at the party? His wallet and his voice?

B Everything!

A The more I tell him, the more he ignores what I say. First his hat, then his book, then his gloves, and now this!

B 'There's no fool like a young fool,' as they say, but he's not as daft as he seems.

A You could have fooled me. He seems round the bend half the time, although I must admit I have seen him serious on two occasions.

B What can I do? Who needs enemies with friends like that?

121 Explain the meanings of the following pairs of expressions which make use of figurative expressions:

1 (*a*) an apple-pie bed;	(*b*) apple-pie order;
2 (*a*) chance one's arm;	(*b*) lay down one's arms;

3 (*a*) to keep a dog and bark oneself;   (*b*) to bark up the wrong tree;
4 (*a*) to have one's cake and eat it;   (*b*) to go like hot cakes;
5 (*a*) to let the cat out of the bag;   (*b*) like a cat on hot bricks;
6 (*a*) to play second fiddle;   (*b*) to fiddle the books;
7 (*a*) to split hairs;   (*b*) without turning a hair;
8 (*a*) strike while the iron is hot;   (*b*) having too many irons in the fire;

9 (*a*) to stand on one's own legs;   (*b*) without a leg to stand on;
10 (*a*) to know the ropes;   (*b*) to give one enough rope.

122

1 Find current *euphemisms* to express the following ideas:
   (*a*) he died;   (*b*) she was ill;   (*c*) he stole the money;
   (*d*) she was very ugly;   (*e*) he was a liar.
2 Identify the figures of speech used in the following sentences and explain their effects:

   (*a*) He had tons of luck and was as rich as Croesus.
   (*b*) The hand that rocks the cradle rules the world.
   (*c*) Greed stalked the land and claimed its prey.
   (*d*) There is always a Judas lurking in the garden.
   (*e*) She made a leap in the dark, took him at face value, and accepted his proposal of marriage.

123   Re-express literally the sense of the following sentences which contain figurative language:

1 He soon came down to earth when confronted by the truth.
2 You will go through the roof when you get to the bottom of it.
3 With a head as big as that he thinks he'll set the Thames on fire.
4 People living in glass houses shouldn't throw stones.
5 If you remain hand in glove with them you'll finally fall between two stools.
6 If you accuse me of burning the candle at both ends, it will be a clear case of the pot calling the kettle black.
7 He was so full of himself he could barely see the wood for the trees.
8 Believing that possession was nine tenths of the law, he decided to put all his eggs in one basket.
9 He drew a red herring across the trail by beating about the bush.
10 He threw cold water on the proposal, although he was living in a fool's paradise.

124   With the help of a good dictionary or a book such as *A Dictionary of Phrase and Fable* by E. C. Brewer, explain the meaning and trace the origin of the following current English expressions:

1 To blow hot and cold.
2 To call (or haul) someone over the coals.
3 To nail one's colours to the mast.

4 To cross the line.
5 The hair of the dog that bit you.
6 To fall foul of someone.
7 It was all Greek to me.
8 To wash one's hands of the situation.
9 To stretch a point.
10 A red-letter day.

125 Write sentences of your own containing figures of speech as follows:

1 *Anti-climax* to produce humour.
2 A *metaphor* to suggest fear.
3 *Irony* to emphasise a point.
4 A *simile* to stress natural beauty.
5 *Hyperbole* to impress.
6 *Paradox* to make a fundamental truth more arresting.
7 *Onomatopoeia* to suggest the noises at a party.
8 *Euphemism* to avoid embarrassment.
9 *Metonymy* to convey a general truth convincingly.
10 *Oxymoron* in order to sharpen a contrast, or even paradoxical, idea.

12
Common Errors

In 1646 Thomas Browne, a Norfolk doctor, wrote a book called *Vulgar Errors* (*Pseudodoxia Epidemica*). It dealt with some common beliefs of the time which were, in fact, totally wrong: *e.g.* that an elephant has no joints; that snails have no eyes, that crystal is congealed ice; that men have one rib fewer on one side of the body than the other (because a rib was taken from Adam to form Eve).

Common errors grow up and are popularly maintained. Of course, in language if the 'error' becomes so dominant and is accepted into educated speech or writing, it becomes 'correct'. For example, during the Renaissance a *b* was added to the spelling of the words of French origin *dette* and *doute* because of the false assumption that they had come directly into the language from the Latin *debitum* and *dubitum*. The modern spellings *debt* and *doubt* are the correct ones (although the pronunciation of both words refuses to acknowledge the *b*).

Vocabulary

12:2

Confusion between Words

acetic: adj. vinegar-like, sour;
ascetic: adj. austere, abstinent, self-disciplined.

advice: n. counsel, information, skilled opinion;
advise: v.i. and t. give counsel, information, skilled opinion (to).

affect: v.t. to influence, to act upon; to have a liking for;
    v.i. to incline, to tend;
effect: n. result of an action; goods, property;
    v.t. to bring about, to accomplish.

assurance: n. confidence, feeling of certainty; security; an insurance against
    something which is assured (certain): *e.g.* death;
insurance: n. a sum paid in return for premiums paid in the event of a *possible*
    or *likely* occurrence taking place: *e.g.* an accident, fire, illness.

between: prep. usually used to refer to *two* items only;
among: prep. usually used to refer to three or more items.
    (This distinction is being rapidly eroded in current usage.)

complement: n. that which completes or fills up; that which completes a verb of incomplete predication (*e.g. to be, become, seem, appear, grow* or *turn* when they mean 'become'); a ship's crew;

compliment: n. an expression of regard or praise; delicate flattery; a present.

comprise: v.t. to contain, to include, to consist of (NOTE: this verb is used without *of*);

consist (of): v.i. to be composed (of), to be made up (of).

continual: adj. always going on, frequently;

continuous: adj. unbroken and uninterrupted.
> (This distinction is being eroded. *Chambers Twentieth Century Dictionary* defines *continual*: 'without interruption' and *continuous*: 'joined together without interruption'. Some, however, try to distinguish *continual* = 'repeated regularly at frequent intervals' and *continuous* = 'going on without a break'; *i.e.* compare tapping with a ruled straight line.)

co-respondent: n. a man or woman cited in a divorce petition as the person with whom the respondent (husband/wife) has committed adultery;

correspondent: n. a journalist employed to send in reports; a person with whom one exchanges letters.

council: n. an assembly called together or elected for deliberation, advice, or administration;

counsel: n. consultation, deliberation, advice, plan, purpose; one who gives counsel: *e.g.* a barrister or advocate; *v.* to advise.

delusion: n. an act of deceiving or a state of being deceived; a false impression or opinion;

illusion: n. an impression made on the senses, especially the sense of sight, which is false.
> (NOTE This distinction is being eroded: *e.g. Chambers* defines *illusion* as 'delusion'. In the expressions 'he saw an illusion' or 'he suffered from delusions' the words are not yet interchangeable in usage.)

allusion: n. reference (usually indirect).

demur: v.i. to object, to hesitate because of uncertainty; to make problems over; *n.* objection;

demure: adj. sober, grave, coy, reserved.

derisive: adj. conveying ridicule or mockery (*e.g.* The crowd's cheering of the despised politician was *derisive*).

derisory: adj. inviting ridicule or mockery (*e.g.* 'The employer's offer of a one per cent annual increase in salary was a *derisory* one').

detract: v.t. and i. to take away (something) from a whole;

distract: v.t. to divert or draw away (attention, etc.) from; to bewilder; to drive mad or infuriate.

disinterested: adj. without bias, impartial;

uninterested: adj. not personally concerned. (*e.g.* A judge should be disinterested but not uninterested in a case.)

exceptional: adj. unusual; forming an exception;
exceptionable: adj. open to objection; objectionable.

few/fewer: adj., pron. small in number/smaller in number;
little/less: adj., pron. small in size or quantity/smaller in size or quantity.

hang: v.t. and i. to suspend, to exhibit;
 The 'strong' form of the verb (*hang/hung/hung*) is used in all senses of the
verb; the past participle of the 'weak' form (*hang/hanged/hanged*) is normally restricted to the act of judicial hanging.
 e.g. The picture was hung on the wall.
  The murderer was hanged on the gallows.

incredulous: adj. not believing, sceptical;
incredible: adj. hard to believe in; surprising.

infer: v.t. deduce, conclude;
imply: v.t. express indirectly, insinuate, hint, suggest.
 e.g. 'Am I to infer (*i.e.* 'deduce') that you are implying (*i.e.* 'suggesting')
  that I am a fool?'

ingenuous: adj. open, frank, free from deception;
ingenious: adj. clever, skilful, well-contrived.

its: poss. adj. or pron. belonging to it;
it's: pers. pron. + *is* (*it + is*)

licence: n. an authorisation, a permit;
license: v.t. to authorise, permit.
 (NOTE: 'an off-licence' but 'off-licensed premises')

lie: v.i. a 'strong' verb (*lie/lay/lain*): to be in or assume a horizontal position;
 e.g. 'the boy *lay* down'.
 v.i. a 'weak' verb (*lie/lied/lied*): to tell an untruth;
lay: v.t. a 'weak' verb (*lay/laid/laid*): to set down, to cause to lie. *e.g.* 'The
hen laid an egg'.

practicable: adj. feasible, able to be carried out or followed;
practical: adj. useful, concerned with practice or conditions or usefulness,
efficient; inclined to action rather than to theory.
 (This distinction is becoming less strictly maintained. *Chambers Twentieth
Century Dictionary* gives as a definition of *practical*: 'workable'. G. H.
Vallins in *Good English*, 1951, comments: 'In ... *practical* and *practicable*,
the force of -*al* and -*able* is difficult to define; but in general, *practical* is
the opposite of *theoretical*, while *practicable* means 'able to be put into
practice'. Fowler in *Modern English Usage*, 1926, states warningly, 'Each
word has senses in which there is no fear that the other will be substituted
for it.')

practice: n. action, performance, custom, repeated performance to acquire
a skill;
practise: v.t. to perform, to carry out, to do on a regular or habitual
basis.

principal: n. head of college, business etc.;
    adj. first, main;
principle: n. fundamental truth, theoretical basis, source.

prophecy: n. prediction, statement of what will happen in the future;
prophesy: v.t. and i. to foretell future events.

raise: v.t. to lift, to elevate, to rouse, to build, to erect, to call up, etc. (a
    'weak' verb: *raise/raised/raised*);
rise: v.i. to get up, to stand up, to return to life, to increase, etc. (a 'strong'
    verb: *rise/rose/risen*).

respectable: adj. worthy of respect;
respectful: adj. showing respect;
respective: adj. relating to a group, person(s), or item(s) already mentioned.
    e.g. The footballer, the athlete, and the swimmer spoke about their
    respective sports.

revenge: v.t. to inflict injury as a retribution for; to avenge + a reflexive
    pronoun;
    v.i. to take vengeance;
    n. an act done vindictively;
avenge: v.t. inflict retribution on behalf of
    (the corresponding noun is *vengeance*).
    (NOTE The distinction between *revenge* and *avenge* as transitive verbs is
    not always observed—or clear.)

sensual: adj. of the senses, but often connected with the gratification of
    sexual or gluttonous appetites;
sensuous: adj. of the senses but without any suggestion of carnal appetite.

sceptic: n. an agnostic, one who doubts;
septic: adj. infected, contaminated by putrefaction.

stationary: adj. not moving, remaining in one place;
stationery: adj. related to the stationer: *i.e.* one who sells writing materials,
    etc.
    n. writing materials: *e.g.* paper, envelopes, ink, writing pads, etc.

storey (plural *storeys*)*: n.* a part of a building divided horizontally, a tier, a
    floor of the same building;
story: n. a narrative.
    (NOTE Current usage accepts *story/stories* as alternatives to *storey/storeys*,
    but not vice versa. *Story/stories* are the usual spellings for *storey/storeys* in
    American English.)

their: poss. adj. belonging to them;
there: adv. in that place;
they're: a contracted form of *they + are.*

whose: possessive form of *who*;
who's: contracted form of *who + is.*

12:3

Meanings and Forms

agenda: this word is plural etymologically, from Latin, and means 'things to be done'. As a programme of business for a meeting present-day English usage often treats it as a singular.

aggravate: there are two current uses of this word. The first follows the etymological meaning 'make more serious', 'make worse'; the second has established the meaning of 'tease' or 'annoy', which has developed from the first. In informal, colloquial modern usage the noun *aggro* = aggression, violence, may be associated with the second use of *aggravate*.

Etymological meanings are not necessarily the more acceptable and may easily lead to non-tenable assumptions about the language. Jeremy Warburg (in a supplement to R. Quirk, *The Use of English*) has pointed out:

It would make the correct meaning of *style* 'a pointed instrument' and the correct meaning of *like* 'body'; and, one might add, it would make the correct meaning of *nice* 'silly' and the correct meaning of *silly* 'happy' or 'blessed'.

all right/alright: most major dictionaries do not accept the form *alright* as an alternative to *all right*. Chambers *Twentieth Century Dictionary* says it is 'an unaccepted spelling'. The form *alright* presumably arises by analogy with *already, although, altogether*.

alternative: when *alternative* is used as an adjective it often means 'different', 'other':

e.g. Please give an alternative colour, in case the one you have ordered is not available.

Alternative as a noun bearing its etymological meaning should strictly refer to the second from a choice of two (Latin *alter:* one of two). Therefore 'two alternatives' or 'the only alternative' are tautologous (unnecessarily repetitive) expressions. If three or more options are available many careful writers would prefer the word 'choice(s)' to 'alternative(s)'. Current usage, however, is gradually breaking down this narrow, if etymologically correct, restriction on the use of alternative when it functions as a noun. *Chambers Twentieth Century Dictionary* insists on the strict use of the word, nevertheless.

among/amongst: Both words are used as alternative prepositions; *amongst* is possibly less frequently used but Fowler (*Modern English Usage*) suggests that this word is preferred immediately before words beginning with vowels.

backward/backwards: Both forms of the adverb are accepted in current usage. The form 'backwards' has retained the Old English adverbial ending *-es* in a contracted form.

centre around: Centre on or *centre in* are more acceptable to careful users to avoid the difficulty of picturing the idea of something centred around something else. 'Centre around' is common in colloquial speech and may have been formed by analogy with 'revolve/turn around'.

due to/owing to: The distinction in meaning and use between these expressions is clear enough:

owing to: a complex preposition, equivalent to 'because of'; 'owing to' + a noun phrase can replace an adverbial clause:

e.g. He returned home
$$\begin{cases} \text{because his father was ill.} \\ = \text{because of his father's illness.} \\ = \text{owing to his father's illness.} \end{cases}$$

due to: 'due' here is an adjective and is used to limit a noun or pronoun:

e.g. The subsidence *due* to the rain made the house collapse.

War is *due* to man's greed.

Due to is becoming increasingly used for *owing to* as a complex preposition. Such usage may cause confusion and is, therefore, best avoided:

e.g. The Black Death spread rapidly during the Hundred Years' War *due to* man's thoughtlessness.

Here it is not clear whether man's thoughtlessness caused the war or the rapid spread of the disease. The use of *owing to* would have made it more likely that man's thoughtlessness caused the spread of the plague rather than the war.

However, usage seems to be in the process of allowing the two phrases to become interchangeable.

hopefully: This word has been used increasingly in British informal language to mean 'it is hoped'; this use is derived from American English.

Originally the word meant 'in a manner full of hope' and functioned as an adverb to limit a specific verb: *e.g.* 'to travel hopefully is better than to arrive' (R. L. Stevenson). The meaning 'it is hoped' is now accepted by *Chambers Twentieth Century Dictionary* to mean 'if all goes well'.

literally: This word has assumed the role of reinforcing or stressing a statement:

e.g. She was literally rushed off her feet.

The word essentially carries the meaning of 'according to the letter', 'not figurative or metaphorical'. It is literally impossible to be 'rushed off one's feet'; this emphatic use of *literally* is, however, common in informal speech.

must of: This is sub-standard English for 'must have':

e.g. He *must of* been waiting a long time.

nice: Few words in a language have been so consistently condemned as 'nice'. Fowler blames women for the abuse of the word:

'It has been too great a favourite with the ladies, who have charmed
out of it all its individuality and converted it into a mere diffuser of
vague and mild agreeableness.'

The fact is that *nice* has been needed in the language to express pleasure,
'agreeableness', joy, in a way that other words cannot. In spite of learned
attacks on it the word remains strongly in current use. It is hard to think
of a synonym which would fulfil its all-purpose function. Roget's *Thesaurus* lists, among others, *pleasing, agreeable, attractive, enjoyable, tasteful,
proper, genteel.*

There are, of course, a number of very specific meanings carried by
'nice' itself outside the meaning of 'generally pleasurable'. It means also
*finely sensitive, deft, requiring precision or tact or discrimination; fastidious, dainty,
hard to please.*

not only . . . but also: The most common error here is to forget that the words
following *not only . . . but also . . .* must be grammatically balanced: *e.g.*
nouns, or adjectives or clauses, etc.

> *e.g.* She had not only a Rolls Royce but also a Bentley. (Nouns)
> She was not only beautiful but also greedy. (Adjectives)
> She not only ran the church choir but also arranged the flowers
> every Sunday. (Clauses)

Sometimes *also* can be separated from *but* and placed at the end of the
sentence for greater emphasis:

> *e.g.* She had not only a Rolls Royce but a Bentley also.

plurals of nouns ending -um: A number of nouns derived from Latin end in
the singular in *-um: curriculum, gymnasium, referendum, stadium, stratum.* The
plurals of these words are often given in their Latin forms: *curricula,
gymnasia, referenda, stadia, strata,* but by analogy the plurals of such nouns
are being formed by adding a final *-s* to the singular. (The Greek word
phenomenon, however, still carries its plural as *phenomena,* but the plural
form is sometimes used as a singular.)

Two words, *agenda* and *data* are strictly plurals of *agendum* ('that which
has to be done') and *datum* ('that which is given). Increasingly both
agenda and *data* are used as singular nouns with singular verbs:

> *e.g.* Is the agenda ready?
> What data is needed?

psychological moment: This phrase is now commonly used to mean 'at exactly
the right moment', 'in the nick of time'.

H. W. Fowler attributes its origin to German, where the word *Moment*
means 'momentum' rather than a point in time. In German, therefore,
the phrase meant 'the psychological drive'. French misinterpreted the
word *moment* and English imported it with its current meaning.

It is interesting to observe how a living language, such as English, will
borrow phrases from another and give the phrase its own meaning.
Another example is 'a forlorn hope'. During the Boer War a band of

soldiers sent out on a dangerous mission was called the 'verloren Hoop' or 'the lost band' (Dutch *hoop* = 'band', 'troop'). The anglicised version of 'hoop' as *hope* and of 'verloren' as *forlorn* gave rise to the modern meaning of the phrase in English.

syndrome: This word became fashionable during the 1960s and 1970s. It is of Greek origin and is used in medicine to denote a characteristic pattern or group of symptoms belonging to an illness. The essential point about the word, however, is that of 'pattern' or 'group' or 'assembly' rather than 'disease'.

Current usage of the word, nevertheless, outside medicine puts the emphasis on 'disease' or 'disorder': *e.g.* 'the political syndrome'. It is often used in a pejorative (disparaging) context and lacks precision.

'time' words:

> *e.g.* *tonight/that night;*
> *tomorrow/the next day;*
> *yesterday*
> *the day before;*
> *now/then.*

It is a frequent error where writers carelessly forget to adapt 'time' words when they are using a narrative presented mainly in the past tense or when they are using reported speech:

e.g. He came *now* to the inn and said that he would leave *tomorrow; yesterday* he had been a thousand miles away.

instead of

> He *then* came to the inn and said that he would leave *the next day; the day before* he had been a thousand miles away.

Occasionally the use of *now* rather than *then*, for example, can be dramatically effective, if used judiciously.

unique: this word is sometimes unnecessarily qualified: *e.g.* 'more unique', 'very unique', 'quite unique', etc. Such qualification is unnecessary since *unique* means 'single, sole, one and only, unparalleled, having no like or equal' (*Shorter Oxford English Dictionary*).

viable: This is another word which became fashionable during the 1960s and 1970s. Its original meaning, used in science, was 'capable of living, surviving, germinating, hatching' (*Chambers Twentieth Century Dictionary*) from French *vie* (Latin *vita*): 'life'.

It has now come to mean 'feasible', 'workable', 'possible'.

wake/waken/awake/awaken: the meanings and forms of these verbs are hard to distinguish in current usage:

		Past Simple	**Past Participle**
wake:	*v.t.* to rouse from sleep *v.i.* to be awake, to be roused from sleep	*woke* or *waked*	*waked, woken* (sometimes *woke*)

waken:	*v.t.* to rouse from sleep *v.i.* to be awake, to be roused from sleep	*woke* or *waked*	*waked, woken* (sometimes *woke*)
awake:	*v.t.* to rouse from sleep *v.i.* to cease sleeping	*awoke* or *awaked*	*awaked, awoke* (sometimes *awoken*)
awaken:	*v.t.* to rouse from sleep *v.i.* to cease sleeping	*awoke* or *awaked*	*awaked, awoke* (sometimes *awoken*)

Fowler in *A Dictionary of Modern English Usage* argues:

'*Wake* is the ordinary working verb ... *wake* alone has the sense of *be* or *remain awake* ... *awake* and *awaken* are usually preferred to the others in figurative senses ... *waken* and *awaken* tend to be restricted to the transitive sense ... in the passive, *awaken* and *waken* are often preferred to *awake* and *wake*.'

These four words have survived from early English in spite of their similarities and despite the confusions between them. It is rare for a living language to tolerate such a multiplicity of such close forms for such a long period.

12:4

Some Words commonly Misspelt

accelerate
accommodate
accurate
acknowledge (but
acknowledgement or
acknowledgment)
acquire
aeroplane
all right
amongst
appalling
beautiful
beginning
benefited
business
ceiling
cheque
chief
colourful
conscientious, conscience
conscious
deceive
decision
describe
develop, developed

diphthong
disappear
disappoint
dissatisfy
environment
fascinate
fulfil, fulfilment, fulfilled
exaggerate
exercise
existence
excitement
gaol, jail
government
grammar
gramophone
gypsy, gipsy
harass
humorous (but *humour*)
imagery
imaginary
immediate
immensely
independent
instal, installation
interruption

its (=belonging to it)	*resources*
it's (=it is)	*rhyme*
jewellery, jewelry	*rhythm*
knowledge	*satellite*
likable or *likeable*	*scene*
lose (confused with *loose*)	*secretary*
manoeuvre	*seize*
medieval or *mediaeval*	*separate*
mischievous	*silhouette*
mistakable	*sincerely*
necessary	*skilful*
noticeable	*solemn*
occur, occurrence, occurring	*successful*
panic, panicked, panicking	*sufficient*
paraffin	*suppress*
parallel, paralleled	*surprise*
peaceable	*temporary*
possess	*till* (but *until*)
privilege	*tongue*
professor, professional	*tyre* (American *tire*)
proffer, proffered	*trolley* or *trolly*
psychiatrist	*unnecessary*
psychology	*unnoticed*
questionnaire	*waggon* or *wagon*
queue, queueing	*weird*
receive	*woollen*
recur, recurring	

12:5

Malapropisms

For a full discussion of malapropisms see **7:11**, pages 140–1.

Grammar

12:6

Adjectives

(i) *Comparatives and superlatives*

The comparative form is used to compare two items within a group or set; the superlative form is used to compare three or more. See **5:31–5:35**, pages 68–70, for a discussion of uses of these forms.

Therefore, it is best to avoid constructions such as 'This is the *best* of two'; '*these are the three best pupils*'. Only one pupil can be 'best' but it is possible to have a first or 'best group of three pupils so that the idea would be more accurately expressed as: '*these are the best three pupils*'.

(ii) *Misrelated ('unattached') participles*

See **5:52** (v), page 87, where it was emphasised that the -*ing* participle when used adjectivally should relate to the correct noun or pronoun:

> *e.g.* *Walking* down the street, the house came in sight. (Incorrect)
> *Walking* down the street, I saw the house. (Correct)

(iii) *Adjectival forms used wrongly as adverbs*

Some words have the same forms for both adjectives and adverbs: *e.g. fast, ill,* etc. but usually they are easily distinguishable since the adverb often takes an -*ly* suffix: *e.g. sad/sadly, happy/happily.* The correct form will be dictated by the sense; consider, for example, the difference in meaning between:

> (*a*) He returned *sad.* (Adjective)
> (*b*) He returned *sadly.* (Adverb)

(*a*) suggests that he was 'sad' when he returned; (*b*) suggests that the *way* in which he returned was 'sad'. Although such differences in meaning are readily distinguishable, it is a marked feature of sub-standard English for adjectives to be used where adverbs (with correct adverbial forms) are undoubtedly required:

> *e.g.* He was *quick* to run through the village. (Correct)
> He ran through the village *quick.* (Incorrect)

(iv) *Demonstrative adjectives*

Demonstrative adjectives should agree in number with the nouns they limit:

> *e.g. That sort* of book interests me.
> *These kinds* of chairs are modern in design.

(v) *Distributive adjectives (each, every, either, neither)*

Care needs to be exercised to ensure that when these words are used as adjectives they are used with singular nouns:

> *e.g. Each* girl was offered a present.
> *Either* way of presenting it is acceptable.

When *either* or *neither* are used as correlating conjunctions they may, of course, be followed by plural nouns:

> *e.g. Either boys* or *girls* may attend but not both.

(vi) *Due* (to)

The confusion of this adjective + *to* with the compound preposition *owing to* is fully discussed in **12:3**, page 250.

12:7

Conjunctions

(i) *Like/as*

G. H. Vallins in *Better English*, 1953, says that *like* for *as* as a conjunction is an Americanism. In British English it is still preferable in educated usage to distinguish *as* (a subordinating conjunction introducing an adverbial clause of manner) from *like* (a preposition introducing a noun phrase):

> *e.g.* The athlete ran *as* he usually does. (Conjunction)
> The schoolboy ran *like* his hero. (Preposition)

The second of these examples means: 'His hero ran and so likewise did the schoolboy' rather than 'The schoolboy ran in the same manner as his hero'. The distinction is being eroded by the use of *like* as a synonymous conjunction to *as*. The loss of such a distinction might have arisen by the ellipsis of the adverbial clause:

> *e.g.* He ran *as* usual. (Correct)
> He ran *like* usual. (Incorrect)

(ii) *Than/as*

In sentences such as
> She is cleverer than I
> *or* He is not so clever as she

it may be seen that *than* and *as* are conjunctions introducing the clauses 'than I am' and 'as she is' respectively. In informal uses of English, however, it would be more usual to find:
> 'She is cleverer than me'
> *and* 'He is not so clever as her'

where *than* and *as* are used as prepositions introducing noun phrases. Modern usage permits both sets of constructions to express the ideas, but the first is more formal (and may be seen by some to be pedantic), whilst the second is certainly the form used in spoken English.

(iii) *Because/that*

In sentences such as:
> The reason he came was *that he was invited*

the italicised clause is a complement of the verb *was* and not an adverbial clause of reason.
In sentences such as:
> He came *because he was invited*

the italicised clause is an adverbial clause of reason.
In the first the clause is correctly introduced by *that* and the second by the conjunction *because*. In the construction 'The reason ... is *that* ...', the use of *because* is unacceptable in educated usage.

(iv) *Neither ... nor*

Care should be taken that *nor* is used (not *or*) together with *neither* as correlatives:

> *e.g.* I saw *neither* the traffic lights *nor* the policeman on duty.

The phrases which follow *neither* and *nor* should be accurately balanced as grammatical equivalents.

(v) *While*

While is often used ambiguously. Consider the sentence:
> He wrote the lyrics *while* she played the piano.

Here it is not clear whether the two situations are being contrasted or whether they are being conducted simultaneously. The context would normally establish the sense more precisely, but the ambiguity might have been partly or wholly avoided by the use of a different conjunction (*e.g. after* which, *during* which, *but*).

12:8

Verbs

(i) *Concord*

Verbs should agree in number and in person with their subjects. Sometimes, however, the number may prove difficult to establish. The following examples will suggest some of the major areas of difficulty:

(*a*) Each of the boys *was* late. ('Each' is singular.)
(*b*) A bunch of flowers *costs* one pound. (The 'head' word in the subject is 'bunch' not 'flowers'.)
(*c*) Sausage and mash *is* my favourite dish. ('Sausage and mash' may be seen as a single dish here but a plural verb would undoubtedly be required in a construction such as 'Sausages and steak *are* both sold by the butcher'.)
(*d*) The band *plays* in the park every Sunday. ('The band' is a collective noun seen here as a single unit. For a full discussion of collective nouns and their number see **5:3** (ii), page 47.)

(ii) *Sequence of Tenses*

For a discussion of sequence of tenses see **5:43** (v), page 75.
The basic principle is that present tenses should follow present tenses and past tenses past tenses:

> *e.g.* He *says* that he *is* the driver.
> He *maintained* that he *was* the owner.

(iii) *Infinitives*

It is sometimes argued that split infinitives (*i.e.* where the marker *to* is separated from the infinitive form of the verb) should be avoided at all costs.

Modern usage, however, sometimes tolerates split infinitives to avoid all ambiguities or loss of emphasis:

> *e.g.* To knowingly sell stolen property is an offence.

Usually, however, the splitting of infinitives is clumsy and can easily be avoided.

(iv) *The -ing* participle: gerunds/verbal nouns

For a discussion of the *-ing* participle see **5:52**, pages 86–7.
A distinction in meaning may be made between the following sentences:

(**a**) I dislike John singing like that.
(**b**) I dislike John's singing like that.

(*a*) means 'I dislike *John* because he sings like that' *or* 'I dislike him when he sings like that'; (*b*) means 'I dislike the *singing* done by John'.
The sharpness of this distinction is rarely made in informal speech but careful users of the language would normally take care in written English to preserve the distinction between the use of noun + *-ing* participle and noun in the genitive + *-ing* participle.

12:9

Prepositions

(i) There is no reason why a preposition should not end a sentence if this is the obvious and clear position for it. To avoid such a use can lead to immense clumsiness. Sir Winston Churchill is reputed to have deliberately ridiculed those who sought to avoid using prepositions at the ends of sentences at all costs by saying, 'This is the sort of English up with which I will not put.'

Sir Ernest Gowers in *Plain Words*, first edition, 1948, quotes an amusing pair of stanzas written by an American, Morris Bishop:

> I lately lost a preposition;
> It hid, I thought beneath my chair
> And angrily I cried, 'Perdition!
> Up from out of in under there.'

> Correctness is my *vade mecum*,
> And straggling phrases I abhor,
> And yet I wondered, 'What should he come
> Up from out of in under for?'

(ii) A number of nouns, verbs, adjectives, and adverbs are associated with particular prepositions used to follow them:

> *e.g.* complain *about* (a problem);
> congratulate someone *on* (his success);
> different *from* (although 'different *to*' is common);
> dislike *of*;
> influence *on/over* (but note 'an influence *for* good');
> liable *to*;

proud *of*;
sympathise *with*.

12:10

Pronouns

For the use of pronouns see **5:8–5:20**, pages 48–62.

(i) *Relative pronouns*

Who/whom sometimes produces difficulties; *who* is the subject form; *whom* is the object form:

> *e.g.* *Who* is there?
> This is the man *who* did it.
> To *whom* did you go?
> This is the man *whom* you saw.

In informal speech the distinction occasionally breaks down, especially in questions involving the use of prepositions:

> *e.g.* *Who*(*m*) did you give the book to?

(ii) *Number*

The number of pronouns sometimes raises problems:

> *e.g.* Anyone can park *his* or *her* car there. (Correct)
> Anyone can park *their* car there. (Incorrect)
>
> *Anyone, each, everyone* are regarded as singular; *all* is regarded as plural.

> *e.g.* *All* are to apply, but few will be chosen.

NOTE *None* is strictly singular (= not one) but occasionally (and some would argue, incorrectly) it takes a plural verb, *e.g.* when it is followed by a preposition and a plural noun:

> *None* of the soldiers *were* injured.

Allowing the verb to be attracted into the plural because of the close proximity of a plural noun (*soldiers*) is best avoided. Most careful users of the language would prefer:

> *None* of the soldiers *was* injured.

(iii) *Case of personal pronouns*

NOTE the following:

> Let *you* and *me* join the party. (*You* and *me* are the objects of the verb 'let'.)
> *Between you and me* (see **5:8** NOTE (*a*), page 49).
> It is *I/me* (see **5:8** NOTE (*b*), page 49).

12:11

Adverbs

See **5:55–5:66**, pages 89–94, for a discussion of the regular and irregular use of adverbs.

(i) *The position of adverbs helps determine meaning*

For example, compare the sense of the following sentences:

> (*a*) He wanted his car repaired *badly*.
> (*b*) He *badly* wanted his car repaired.

> (*c*) He wanted his dinner cooked *immediately*.
> (*d*) He *immediately* wanted his dinner cooked.

> (*e*) *Only* he saw the girl yesterday.
> (*f*) He *only* saw the girl yesterday.
> (*g*) He saw *only* the girl yesterday.
> (*h*) He saw the *only* girl yesterday.
> (*i*) He saw the girl *only* yesterday.
> (*j*) He saw the girl yesterday *only*.

(ii) *Double negatives*

In early English the more negatives a sentence contained the more negative the idea became. In modern educated British usage double negatives are seen to cancel each other out:

> *e.g.* 'He didn't want nothing' = 'He wanted something.'

The argument runs as follows: one must presumably want nothing or want something—no other possibility exists; therefore, if one does not want nothing, one must want something. However, in sub-Standard English the double negative is used in colloquial varieties as an emphatic negative still. It is best avoided totally in written English and formal uses of the language.

12:12

Style and Expression

In December, 1981, two pounds of best, ripe, Lancashire tripe were awarded to the booby-prize winners in the Plain English Awards, 1981, Competition organised by the Plain English Campaign and the National Consumer Council. *The Daily Telegraph* published some of the 'winning' entries, amongst which were the following:

(*a*) *British Rail 'Travellers-Fare' explaining to a passenger why a train had no restaurant car:*

Whilst I can readily appreciate your frustration at the loss of breakfast, since in the circumstances you describe it is unfortunately true that in many cases where a catering vehicle becomes defective and both stores and equipment need to be transferred into a replacement car, this can only be done during the train's (*sic*) journey.

It is not of course possible to make the transfer whilst vehicles are in the sidings and the intensity of coach working is such that the train sets are not available to be put into a platform at other times to enable the transfer to be carried out. We are very concious (*sic*) of the need to reduce instances of failure and provide the advertised service to a minimum, and each case is recorded and the reasons closely scrutinised in an effort to avoid a repitition (*sic*).

(**b**) *A letter from the Travellers' Insurance Association*

We would advise that our policy does exclude a contingency consequent upon a condition which is receiving or awaiting treatment at the date of issue of the policy.
We would therefore advise that the person who had a heart operation in 1963 is not receiving any of the forementioned as she will be covered for that condition under the policy.
If the lady is receiving any of the aforementioned the policy only excludes her for a contingency consequent upon that particular condition.
We still wish to offer her the cover of the rest of the policy including medical and other expenses and the cancellation or curtailment due to any unforeseen condition for which she is not receiving any medication or treatment for.* We hope that this clarifies the situation.

It is hard to think that the last sentence is completely free from irony. Nevertheless, examples such as these demonstrate the need to avoid the following if they impede clear communication:

clichés; jargon; irrelevance; verboseness; turgidity, *non-sequiturs*; clumsy structures.

* NOTE this unnecessary preposition at the end of the sentence.

EXERCISES

126   The sentences which follow contain 'faults' not normally acceptable in current educated written English. Rewrite them to remove these errors:

   1 He asked who's this coat was.
   2 In the bookshop there were less books available than last year.
   3 Neither the Rolls Royce or the Bentley impress them.
   4 He could not tolerate those kind of errors.
   5 The current practise of licencing supermarkets to sell alcoholic drinks robs public houses of their profits.
   6 In paying her a complement, the relationship between them seemed even more incredulous.
   7 The reason I came was because you invited me.
   8 Chased by the bear, he ran like he had never run before.
   9 He relied on the fact that the man must of changed his mind hopefully.
   10 He could literally have fallen through the ground when she not only praised him but gave him a present.

127   The sentences in this exercise contain possible ambiguities in expression. Rewrite them to remove these ambiguities:

   1 The other driver changed his mind at the last minute and so I had to hit him.
   2 Would you rather the train took you or the mini?
   3 I should like to try on that dress in the window.
   4 He collided with a stationery car coming the other way.
   5 The jockey broke his leg when the horse fell at the first fence and had to be destroyed.
   6 Correct also the following sentences in a similar manner.
   7 His foot touching a slipper, he bent his head down to see what it was and kicked it under the table.
   8 Why be disappointed with foreign cars? Buy British.
   9 He assured his friend he had never bought his wife an expensive present.
   10 My first name and surname begin and end with the same letters.

128   Rewrite each of the following sentences *twice*, placing the word in brackets in two different places to give two distinct meanings.

   1 He paid eighty pence for all that rubbish. (*almost*)
   2 She lost her purse just before Christmas. (*unfortunately*)
   3 The woman bought some tomatoes in the market last week. (*only*)
   4 He worked on the question into the night. (*hard*)
   5 It is hard to believe that you sent me that parcel. (*especially*)
   6 The girl understood that his promise would be carried out. (*immediately*)
   7 There was no sign that he would do anything. (*obviously*)
   8 He was convinced that what he had committed himself to was now lost. (*totally*)
   9 They stood in the fields in the cool evening air. (*still*)
   10 He denied that he had ever made such serious allegations. (*emphatically*)

129   The following are jumbled sentences. Rewrite them with the words arranged correctly and without ambiguity. (NOTE Some of the sentences are capable of being arranged in more than one way to make good sense.)

   1 gentlemen some old the gave venerable good the advice boy.
   2 it sobbed the done you how tears her have through could girl.
   3 ago same me do year the lent which you you a have about book.
   4 off to driver at the was raced by car its the bend but stop a first brought.
   5 buy the from beach the was crowded to through too ice-cream sand the walking an pedlar.
   6 touching sang the written the ballad sincerity choir a seventeenth and in simplicity century the with.
   7 able enthusiastically and all teacher since well to listen to to class the the ready was was teach learn.
   8 him the apprehended protested the spite the criminal of against his policeman who innocence given evidence in.
   9 lane negligible the traffic had in the the in eastbound westbound that at miles tail-back of a least two was but.
  10 raged the on to hours the the of morning great the the residents into local of annoyance disco early.

130   Write the following sentences in good, correct English; give reasons for any changes you make:

   1 Between you and I, the party was hardly a success.
   2 He was so overwhelmed by sleep that he laid down on the couch.
   3 No-one can argue that they know everything.
   4 We had three weeks holiday last year.
   5 This car needs repairing badly.
   6 The acquirements of the regulations were waved, although his answers were barely comprehensive to the examiners.
   7 I have always and always shall be interested in English.
   8 Drinking heavily is both bad for yourself and for others.
   9 The preacher took as his text the two first verses of the chapter.
  10 He was one of those drivers who takes unnecessary risks.

Selected Bibliography

Clearly a book of this kind is deeply indebted to major reference works in the subject:

The Oxford English Dictionary
Chambers Twentieth Century Dictionary
Collins English Dictionary

BAUGH, A. C. *A History of The English Language* (second edition, revised), Routledge and Kegan Paul, 1959.

CLOSE, R. A. *A Reference Grammar for Students of English*, Longman, 1975.

FOWLER, H. W. *A Dictionary of Modern English Usage*, Oxford University Press, 1926; second edition, revised by SIR ERNEST GOWERS, Oxford University Press, 1965.

QUIRK, R. and GREENBAUM, S. *A University Grammar of English*, Longman, 1973.

VALLINS, G. H. *Spelling*, revised by D. G. SCRAGG, Andre Deutsch, 1965.

Other important works have offered attitudes, approaches, and descriptions which have conditioned many of those used in this book:

JESPERSEN, O. *Growth and Structure of the English Language*, Blackwell, 1948.

QUIRK, R. *The Use of English*, Longman, 1962, with supplements by A. C. GIMSON and JEREMY WARBURG.

VALLINS, G. H. *Good English*, Pan, 1951; *Better English*, Andre Deutsch, 1955.

WRENN, C. L. *The English Language*, Methuen, 1949.

KEY TO THE EXERCISES

Exercise 2 (no. 3)

The original passage from Laurie Lee's *Cider with Rosie*, 1959, Chatto and Windus, p. 73, was punctuated as follows:

He'd been coming from milking; it was early, first light, and he was just passing Jones's pond. He'd stopped for a minute to chuck a stone at a rat—he got tuppence a tail when he caught one. Down by the lily-weeds he suddenly saw something floating. It was spread out white in the water. He'd thought at first it was a dead swan or something, or at least one of Jones's goats. But when he went down closer, he saw, staring up at him, the white drowned face of Miss Flynn. Her long hair was loose—which had made him think of a swan—and she wasn't wearing a stitch of clothes. Her eyes were wide open and she was staring up through the water like somebody gazing through a window. Well he'd got such a shock he dropped one of his buckets, and the milk ran into the pond. He'd stood there a bit, thinking, 'That's Miss Flynn'; and there was no one but him around. Then he'd run back to the farm and told them about it, and they'd come and fished her out with a hay-rake. He'd not waited to see any more, not he; he'd got his milk to deliver.

Exercise 4

Some possible ways of punctuating the sentences:

1 He says, 'I am to sing the second verse.'
  I ask, 'Why?'
  'He says I am to sing the second verse?' I ask. 'Why?'
2 The film she saw was a strange one.
  The film, she saw, was a strange one.
  The film, she saw was a strange one.
3 The house I had seen that night was clearly haunted.
  The house, I had seen that night, was clearly haunted.
  The house, I had seen, that night was clearly haunted.
4 Everyone ran to the houses, collapsed in a heap. I heard the hurricane vanishing into the distance.
  Everyone ran to the houses. Collapsed in a heap, I heard the hurricane vanishing into the distance.
5 'I can describe to you my—'
  'Rubbish!' he replied. 'I don't want to know!'
  'I can describe to you my rubbish.'
  He replied, 'I don't want to know!'
6 'Higginbottom, the lawyer! You know—the man I saw.'
  'Higginbottom, the lawyer you know.'
  'The man I saw?'
7 'Can you give me the details I need to know? For my work, you see?'
  'Can you give me the details? I need to know for my work, you see.'
  'Can you give me the details I need to know for my work? You see?'
8 'How fast did the rabbits run?'
  'In the field by the hedge or near the trees?'

'How fast did the rabbits run in the field?'
'By the hedge or near the trees?'
9 'Off you go! Quickly, before I see you! Never cheat!'
'Off you go quickly, before I see you never cheat.'
10 'Can you do it at once? If I pay you six pence, I believe. You said so.'
'Can you do it at once, if I pay you six pence? I believe you said so.'
'Can you do it at once, if I pay you? Six pence, I believe you said. So.'

Exercise 5

Consider the meanings of the sentences punctuated in the following ways:

1 I assure you, it is true I am never wrong.
2 John, the baker's son Fred, and I saw it. Before it blew up, it was a fantastic sight.
3 He thought he saw her. Getting off the bus, he looked once more but she had gone.
4 What is it? That you never understand the purpose of life is obvious.
5 We went to the Safari Park before—last Wednesday, to be precise.
6 What more is there to say? Now that I have admitted it, Brown must be involved.
7 If we offend, it is with our good will
That you should think we come—not to offend—
But with good will to show our simple skill:
That is the true beginning. Of our end
Consider then: we come—but in despite
We do not come—as minding to content you;
Our true intent is all for your delight.
We are not here that you should here repent you;
The actors are at hand and, by their show,
You shall know all that you are like to know.
8 Would you prefer the soldier to kill you? Or the general?
9 'How can you believe that?'
'There are fairies at the bottom of your garden, I assure you.'
'There are not!'
10 I finished my work and returned. The day after, I intended to go on holiday.

Exercise 6

Jean Rawlings, the headmaster's secretary, is sitting at her desk. A knock is heard. As a nervous little boy enters, hidden behind a huge pile of exercise books, he stammers almost inaudibly, asking whether he can see the headmaster. He nearly falls over the carpet.

'No, you can't at the moment. He is busy.'
'Er—when—can I see him? You mean...?'
'What for, Jenkins?'
'The prefect sent me with these books to show him.'
'They are a disgrace.'

'I think he is always picking on us for no reason at all. He tells us off whenever he can.'

'All right! If you want, leave them there where you can see a space. I'll make clear that's all you want, if you can come back tomorrow when the headmaster is free. He will want to see you to . . .'

'Thank you.'

'And watch how you go!' (*as the boy falls over the carpet and upsets the pile of books*).

Exercise 14

manoeuvre; practise; machinery; committee; government; humorous; occurrence; principal; silhouette; harassed; embarrassed; separated; auxiliary; mischievous; woollen; beginning; chaos; exaggerated; lose; unnecessary.

Exercise 15

1 (*a*) *benefited;* (*b*) *focused;* (*c*) *panicked;* (*d*) *profited;*
   (*e*) *referred.*

2 (*a*) *acquiring;* (*b*) *beginning;* (*c*) *controlling;* (*d*) *occurring;*
   (*e*) *singeing;* (*f*) *queueing* (or, more rarely, *queuing*).

Exercise 16

1 *genius, jealous, wondrous;* 2 *leisure, seize;*
3 *occurring; tunnelling;* 4 *argument; mistakable; smoky.*

Exercise 17

1 *calories;* 2 *chimneys;* 3 *heroes;* 4 *intricacies;*
5 *pianos;* 6 *picnics;* 7 *prophecies;* 8 *roofs;*
9 *status* (with a long ū, rarely used); 10 *tomatoes.*

Exercise 19

suc*cess*ful; auth*or*; achi*ev*ements; negl*igi*ble; rec*ei*ved; incred*ible*; sur*prise*; correspond*ence*; complimentary; encyclop*ae*dia.

Exercise 20

1 din*ghy*; 2 *chasm*; 3 syn*chro*nise; 4 kno*wl*edgeable;
5 dip*hthong*; 6 negl*igi*ble; 7 exa*gg*erate; 8 forf*ei*t;
9 super*sede*; 10 par*allel*.

Exercise 22

The living language is as people speak it; and the spelling is required to be a sensible way of transferring that usage to paper by the use of phonetic bricks called letters, in some sensible and fairly consistent way. It is not at all necessary, as some spelling reformers have thought, that there should be as many letters, like *ch* or *sh* to represent a sound not given by any single letter. In the case of vowels we have seen that this method has very great advantages over having as many different vowel letters as there are vowels; for by giving *different* ways of spelling the same sound it enables us to distinguish, on paper, different things whose names bear the same pronunciation.

Exercise 23

1 Sandra (*proper*); sun-lotion (*common*); bikini (*common*); air-bed (*common*); holiday (*common*); Costa Brava (*proper*); dream (*common*).
2 Truth (*abstract*); politics (*abstract*); path (*common*); politicians (*common*).
3 church (*collective*); bricks (*common*); mortar (*common*); people (*common*); ideals (abstract).
4 herd (*collective*); cows (*common*); living-room (*common*); furniture (*common*); peace (*abstract*); afternoon (*common*).
5 disco (*common*); lights (*common*); people (*common*); sweat (*common*); din (*common*); chaos (*abstract*).

Exercise 25

1 *warfare; pacifism; treachery; womanhood; childhood.*
2 *ability; lightness; safety, safeness; ferocity, fierceness; truth, trueness; strength; quietness, quietude; vanity, vainness* (rare); *anxiety, anxiousness; loyalty.*
3 *collision; solution; departure; employment; occurrence; determination; judgement, judgment; deliverance; refusal; arrangement.*

Exercise 27

(The list below indicates some of the possibilities.)

1 *... he ... it ... ours (his) ...*
2 *You ... him (her, them, mine, ours) ... you ... us ... me (us) ... His ... it ...*
3 *... you ... Those ... They ...*
4 *She ... them (him, her) ... she ... They ...*
5 *They (Those) ...; they ... I ... It ... you (one) ... them.*

Exercise 28

1 *... myself ... myself ...*
2 *... each other ... themselves ...*
3 *Who (What) ... whose ...*
4 *... one another ... itself.*
5 *What (Whatever) ... itself* (or *ourselves*, depending on the sense).

Exercise 29

1 *... nothing ...; something ... One ...*
2 *... many ... Everything ... The former ... the latter ...*
3 *... few ... some ...*
4 *... none ... Most ...*
5 *Anybody ... such ...*

Exercise 30

1 *that* (*which*) **X**. 2 *that* (*which*). 3 *that* (*which*) **X**.
4 *whose.* 5 *who . . . that* (*which*) **X**. 6 *who . . . . which.*
7 *whose.* 8 *whom.* 9 *which* (*that*) **X**.
10 *which.*

Exercise 31

1 *successful* (boy) 2 *involved* (person) 3 (book) *on the table.*
4 *inconvenient* (moment) . . . (one) *chosen by him to call.*
5 *more elegant* (solution) 6 *winning* (car).
7 *very distinguished* (philosopher) *in his own field.*
8 *really devastating* (remark). 9 (noise) *throbbing from the disco.*
10 *very old* (cat).

Exercise 32

1 *attractive;* 2 *circular;* 3 *cultural;* 4 *dangerous;*
5 *dusty;* 6 *friendly;* 7 *heroic;* 8 *readable;*
9 *useful;* 10 *woollen, woolly.*

Exercise 33

1 *disbelieving, unbelieving;* 2 *undisciplined;* 3 *unlawful;*
4 *illegible;* 5 *illimitable;* 6 *unlucky;*
7 *immoral;* 8 *imperceptible;* 9 *implausible;*
10 *irresponsible.*

Exercise 34

1 *Worse, worst;* 2 *Cleverer, more clever; cleverest, most clever;*
3 *farther, further; farthest, furthest;* 4 *funnier, more funny; funniest, most funny;*
5 *better, best;* 6 *smaller, smallest;*
7 *more real, most real;* 8 *more regular, most regular;*
9 *more reluctant, most reluctant;* 10 *more wonderful, most wonderful.*

Exercise 35

1 *Adverb* (manner). 2 *Adjective.*
*3 *Adverb* (place)—where the table was made; *Adjective*—which table is referred to.
4 *Adverb* (manner). 5 *Adverb* (place).
*6 *Adverb* (manner)—how he saw the man; *Adjective*—the man who was better.
*7 *Adjective*— but it may limit either 'she' or 'ward'.
8 *Adverb* (time). 9 *Adverb* (manner).
10 *Adjective* (the word 'hard' here functions as an objective complement—see **5:86** (ii)).

(* The sentences marked with an asterisk are ambiguous; the grammatical function of words determines meaning.)

Exercise 37

1 *was running;*   2 *was carrying, was limping;*   3 *had been stealing;*
4 *were tracking;*   5 *were trying;*   6 *was leaping;*
7 *were streaking;*   8 *was turning;*   9 *were bounding;*
10 *has been paying.*

Exercise 38

1 *has listened;*   2 *had sung, had come;*   3 *have not been able to understand, has done;*
4 *had offered;*   5 *had (never) heard;*   6 *have slept, had mentioned;*
7 *has been;*   8 *has been;*   9 *have found;*
10 *had slipped; had found.*

Exercise 39

1 The dinner *was cooked* by me today (or *that day*, depending on the sense).
2 The potatoes *were burnt* by me and the meal *was eaten* by the cat.
3 My husband came in and the gas *was turned* off by him.
4 What was left *was eaten* by us with little enthusiasm.
5 The next meal *will be cooked* by me (myself) without listening to any advice.
6 The broth *is spoilt* by too many cooks.
7 I *am helped* more by him reading the newspaper in the armchair.
8 Nevertheless, he is still adorable, although I *am annoyed* by him.
9 The car *is repaired* well by him and some money *is saved* by us that way.
10 The car *was painted* bright mauve by him the other day to the amusement of the neighbours.

Exercise 40 (see **5:41** and **5:44**)

1 *may, can, must;*   2 *must, shall;*   3 *can, will;*
4 *can, will;*   5 *could;*   6 *should, must;*
7 *could, dared;*   8 *should, could;*   9 *needs, should, must;*
10 *ought.*

Exercise 41

1 *did . . . see* (trans.): the dog on the corner.
2 *could . . . miss* (trans.): him, a dog that size.
3 *was . . . doing* (trans.): what.   4 *was . . . bounding* (intrans.).
5 *Did*(n't) *. . . object* (intrans.).   6 *got* (intrans.).
7 *should have controlled* (trans.): it.   8 *came* (intrans.); *called* (trans.): them.
9 *walked* (intrans.); *arrived* (intrans.).10 *knew* (trans.): what to do.

Exercise 42

1 *was:* green with envy;   2 *became:* angry;
3 *seemed:* far too expensive;   4 *sounded:* powerful;
5 *be:* so objectionable;   6 *remained:* unconcerned;
7 *are:* impossible;   8 *looked:* calm;
9 *grew:* more and more interested;   10 *are:* absolute beasts.

Exercise 43

1 *began, begun;*   2 *bought, bought;*   3 *cast, cast;*   4 *did, done;*
5 *dreamed* or *dreamt, dreamed* or *dreamt;*   6 *hurt, hurt;*
7 *laid, laid;*   8 *lay, lain;*   9 *shut, shut;*
10 *smelled* or *smelt, smelled* or *smelt.*

Exercise 44

1 *shall* for *will* (future tense, auxiliary); *will* may be left if it is a modal expressing volition.
2 *is* for *are.*
3 *had been* for *have been* (sequence of tenses).
4 *typing* is a misrelated participle: change to a construction such as, *when they are typing up notes ...*
5 *lie* for *lay.*
6 *should* may be left if it is a modal expressing obligation.
7 *were* for *was.*
8 *take* for *takes* (*who,* the subject of *takes,* refers to 'people').
9 *let* for *lets* (subjunctive needed).
10 *were* for *was.*

Exercise 45

1 *were:* past, active, subjunctive; *should ... do:* past, active, subjunctive (see **5:44** (v) NOTE, page 77).
2 *Shut:* present, active, imperative; *is:* present, active, indicative.
3 *'ll see:* future, active, indicative; *Wait:* present, active, imperative; *goes:* present, active, indicative.
4 *join:* present, active, imperative; *let:* present, active, imperative; *see:* present, active, infinitive.
5 *knew:* past, active, indicative; *tried:* past, active, indicative; *scraped:* past, active, indicative.
6 *may go:* present, active, subjunctive.
7 *'ve had:* present perfect, active, indicative; *'m going to get:* future, active, indicative.
8 *'ll make:* future, active, indicative; *keep:* present, active, subjunctive.
9 *Try:* present, active, imperative.
10 *'s doing:* present, active, indicative.

Exercise 46

1 *... so that he could see her* (purpose).
2 *... that he left in despair* (result).
3 *... because she had a date* (reason).
4 *... so that he would understand* (purpose).
5 *... that he swore vengeance* (result).
6 *... so that he could make a date, too* (purpose).
7 *... since she was in the bath* (reason).
8 *... so that he could ask her out* (purpose).

9 *...because the constant ringing of the door bell got her out of the bath* (reason).
10 *...that she slammed the door in his face* (result).

Exercise 47

1 *...as soon as he could·...* (time).
2 *As he approached the house ...* (time).
3 *...although he could not see much in the dark* (concession).
4 *If he had stopped to think ...* (condition).
5 *As he was on his own ...* (circumstance).
6 *Unless he was disturbed ...* (condition).
7 *...where a log lay across his path* (place).
8 *As he stumbled ...* (time).
9 *...as if he were in a dream* (manner).
10 *...when he realised his predicament* (time).

Exercise 48

1 *busily;*   2 *coolly;*   3 *friendlily;*   4 *well;*   5 *happily;*
6 *publicly;*   7 *quickly.*   8 *scientifically;*   9 *strangely;*   10 *wrongly.*

Exercise 50

Some examples
1 *upward(s); downward(s); sideward(s); skyward(s); leeward; outward(s); inward(s); windward; seawards; homeward; northward(s); westward(s); southward(s); eastward(s).*
2 *business-wise; money-wise; weather-wise; crosswise; lengthwise; dress-wise; school-wise; depth-wise; quality-wise; age-wise.*

Exercise 52

1 *very*: degree, limits 'dangerously'; *dangerously*: manner, limits 'drove'.
2 *already*: time, limits 'was ... reluctant'.
3 *in the middle of the high street*: place, limits 'saw'.
4 *Where*: interrogative (place), limits 'can meet'.
5 *uneasily*: manner, limits 'moved'; *in a swirl of mist*: manner, limits 'moved'.
6 *somewhat*: degree, limits 'tired'.
7 *the week before*: time, limits 'had read'.
8 *never*: time, limits 'would admit'.
9 *hopelessly*: degree, limits 'irresponsible'.
10 *just*: time, limits 'had arrived'.

Exercise 53

1 *down*: fell ... the stairs.   2 *without*: a green hill ... a city wall.
3 *between*: lost ... us.   4 *by*: what train ... did (you) go.
5 *but*: all these ... the one you wanted.
6 *to*: paid no attention ... her question.
7 *for*: to answer ... her crime.   8 *except*: was nobody ... me.

9 *per*: fifty pence ... pound.
10 *From*: which direction ... did (you) come.

Exercise 57

1 averse *to*;	2 conscious *of*;	3 due *to*;	4 experienced *in*;
5 guilty *of*;	6 proud *of*;	7 satisfied *with, by*;	8 sensitive *to*;
9 separate *from*;	10 useful *for*.		

Exercise 58

Some examples: there are other possibilities.

1 *neither ... nor* (co-ordinating); 2 *when* (subordinating);
3 *unless* (subordinating); 4 *until* (subordinating);
5 *Although* (subordinating); 6 *but* (co-ordinating);
7 *that* (subordinating); 8 *and* (co-ordinating);
9 *if* (subordinating); 10 *because* (subordinating).

Exercise 59

1 ... *where no-one could follow him* (adverbial, time).
2 ... *how I had done it* (noun, object).
3 ... *when we had to act* (adjectival, limits 'moment').
4 ... *where the girl had gone* (noun, object).
5 ... *why anyone had left the scene* (noun, object).
6 ... *because he suspected we were all guilty* (adverbial, reason).
7 ... *that the stolen goods were hidden behind the sofa* (noun, object).
8 ... *before we gave ourselves away* (adverbial, time).
9 ... *where we had put them* (adverbial, place).
10 *After the police arrived* ... (adverbial, time).

Exercise 61

1 *the dog* (direct).
2 *the neighbour* (indirect); *the letters* (direct).
3 *him* (indirect); *danger money* (direct).
4 *another attempt* (direct); *him* (indirect); *the same treatment* (direct).
5 *the Head Postmaster* (indirect); *what had happened* (direct).
6 *the owner* (indirect); *a telephone message* (direct); *the postman* (indirect); *I'll send the owner a telephone message* (noun clause, direct object of 'promised').
7 *his ears* (direct).
8 *his wife* (indirect); *Mabel, have you heard this?* (noun clause, direct object of 'asked'); *him* (direct).
9 *the milkman* (indirect); *a nasty turn* (direct).
10 *the GPO* (direct object of preposition 'to'); *something to say to the GPO* (direct object of '(ha)ve'); *me* (indirect); *my pen* (direct).

Exercise 62

1 ... *if my apply trees had much fruit on them* (direct object of 'asked').
2 *'I suppose so'* ... (subject of 'was').

3 ... *he wanted some* (subjective complement of 'seemed').
4 ... *what would happen to the fruit* (direct object of 'asked').
5 *That he had asked me at all* ... (subject of 'was').
6 ... *that I would give him some* (direct object of 'promised').
7 *'Let me help you pick them'* ... (subject of 'was').
8 ... *they were not yet ripe* (direct object of 'said').
9 ... *that I had given him an immediate offer* (subjective complement of 'seemed').
10 *'Where shall we start?'* (direct object of 'shouted').

Exercise 63

1 ... *if I came to the disco often* (noun, direct object of 'asked').
2 ... *I gave her* (adjectival, limits 'reply').
3 ... *whether you do come often* (noun, direct object of 'to know').
4 ... *which was both ingenuous and yet sincere* (adjectival, limits 'insistence').
5 *What you suspect* ... (noun, subject of 'is').
6 ... *what I suspect* (noun, direct object of 'do ... know').
7 ... *that you suspect something* (noun, direct object of 'tell').
8 ... *which I can't follow* (adjectival, limits 'riddles').
9 *What I do* (noun, subject of 'doesn't matter').
10 ... *if I would like to dance* (noun, direct object of 'don't ... ask').

Exercise 74

The King, coming up to Alice, and looking at the Cat's head with great curiosity, asked her whom she was talking to. Alice replied that it was a friend of hers, a Cheshire Cat, and offered to introduce it. The King said that he didn't like the look of it at all but declared, however, that it might kiss his hand if it liked. The Cat remarked that it would rather not. The King told the Cat not to be impertinent and not to look at him like that. He had got behind Alice as he had spoken. Alice said that a cat might look at a king. She had read that in some book but didn't remember where. The King said very decidedly that nevertheless it must be removed and he called to the Queen who had been passing at that moment. He addressed her endearingly and said that he wished she would have that cat removed! The Queen had only one way of settling all difficulties great or small and, without even looking round, ordered his head to be taken off.

Exercise 77

The tumult died down.
Napoleon called upon the four pigs, 'Confess your crimes.'
Without further prompting they confessed, 'We have been secretly in touch with Snowball since his expulsion and have collaborated with him in destroying the windmill and entered into an agreement with him to hand over Animal Farm to Mr Frederick. Snowball has privately admitted to us that he has been Jones's secret agent for years past.'
The dogs promptly tore out their throats.
Napoleon demanded, 'Has any other animal anything to confess?'
The three hens came forward. 'Snowball appeared to us in a dream,' they said, 'and incited us to disobey Napoleon's orders.'

They, too were slaughtered. A goose came forward and confessed.

'I secreted six ears of corn during last year's harvest and ate them in the night.'

A sheep confessed, 'I urinated in the drinking pool.'

Two more sheep confessed, 'We murdered an old ram by chasing him round and round a bonfire whilst he was suffering from a cough.'

They were all slain on the spot.

Later Boxer said, 'I don't understand it. I should not have believed that such things can happen on our farm. It must be due to some fault in us ourselves. The solution, as I see it, is to work harder. From now onwards I shall get up a full hour earlier in the morning.'

Exercise 78

1 The girl argued, 'It is not my fault if the old lady left her front door open. It simply invited me to go in.'
2 The policeman said, 'I cannot accept that. I shall arrest you for the theft of five pounds and a china dog.'
3 The girl protested, 'I am innocent. The old lady gave me the money and the dog as presents.'
4 Of course, the old lady affirmed, 'I have done no such thing. The dog is precious to me, as my dead husband gave it to me as a birthday present.'
5 The policeman declared, 'I have heard enough. I shall take this girl to the police station and charge her. I remind you, Madam, that you may be required to give evidence later.'
  'Of course,' the pensioner agreed.
6 The girl protested that she had told him she hadn't done it and wondered why it was that nobody would believe her.
7 PC Jones merely stated that he had heard enough and warned that anything she then said would be taken down and might be used in evidence later against her.
8 WPC Atkinson asked her at the police station where she lived. She said that the girl knew that her parents would need to be informed.
9 The girl asked why they had to be brought into it and said that, in any case, they wouldn't care; they never cared about her. The girl broke down in tears.
10 Jones told the WPC to make a note of her details and to find out where she lived. Then he would call round to see the parents.

Exercise 83

(Some possible antonyms are given here; there are others, but the closest antonym will depend on the use of the original word in its own defining context.)
1 *achieve*: fail, miss, miscarry.
2 *credulous*: sceptical, doubting, distrustful (of), suspicious (of).
3 *dear*: cheap, inexpensive, economical; hated, despised, unloved, disliked, obnoxious, offensive, disagreeable.
4 *hinder*: aid, assist, help; rescue, support, benefit.

5 *loss*: gain, profit, acquisition.
6 *loud*: silent, quiet, hushed, soft.
7 *obstacle*: aid, assistance, help; co-operation.
8 *permanent*: impermanent, transient, transitory, transitional, ephemeral, changing.
9 *pleasure*: pain, suffering, ache, anguish, agony, torment; adversity, misery.
10 *reluctance*: willingness, readiness, acquiescence; eagerness.

Exercise 88

1 To go away without giving notice.
2 A stale joke.
3 To leave the accepted, normal way of behaving; to fail to work properly.
4 Gibberish; incomprehensible jargon.
5 To behave in a furtive, inconsistent, and unreliable manner.
6 One way or the other.
7 To pay each one for himself or herself.
8 Intolerable; unacceptable; not to be endured.
9 To feel unwell; to be drunk. (*cf. to feel off colour*)
10 One drink too much.

Exercise 90

1 *indelible*: incredible; 2 *irreprehensible*: incomprehensible;
3 *impound*: compound; 4 *progeny*: prodigy; 5 *illicit*: elicit;
6 *deprived*: derived; 7 *calendar*: colander; 8 *dissolve*: resolve;
9 *proscription*: prescription; 10 *averse*: adverse.

Exercise 113

1 *E.*   2 *E.*   3 *B.*   4 *D.* 5 *E.*   6 *A.*   7 *E.*   8 *D.*
9 *D.*   10 *E.*   11 *E.*   12 *C.*

Exercise 114

1 *A.*   2 *C.*   3 *D.*   4 *D.*   5 *C.*   6 *D.*   7 *D.*   8 *E.*
9 *A.*   10 *A.*   11 *C.*   12 *A.*   13 *D.*   14 *A.*   15 *B.*   16 *E.*
17 *D.*   18 *C.*   19 *D.*   20 *C.*   21 *D.*   22 *C.*   23 *C.*   24 *D.*
25 *D.*

Exercise 115

1 *B.*	2 *A.*	3 *E.*	4 *C.*	5 *B.*	6 *D.*	7 *D.*	8 *C.*
9 *A.*	10 *B.*	11 *A.*	12 *E.*	13 *D.*	14 *A.*	15 *B.*	16 *C.*
17 *D.*	18 *E.*	19 *B.*	20 *E.*	21 *C.*	22 *C.*	23 *C.*	24 *A.*

Exercise 118

Some examples
1 As black as your boots; as black as thunder.
2 As clear as crystal; as clear as mud.
3 As dead as the dodo; as dead as a door nail.
4 As easy as pie; as easy as jumping off a cliff.
5 As good as gold; as good as one's word.
6 As happy as the day is long; as happy as a sandboy.
7 As mad as a hatter; as mad as a March hare.
8 As old as the hills; as old as Methuselah.
9 As poor as a churchmouse; as poor as Lazarus.
10 As straight as an arrow; as straight as a die.

Exercise 120

he lost his wallet . . . and his voice: syllepsis
Everything!: hyperbole.
The more . . . the more he ignores what I say: antithesis
First his hat . . . now this!: climax
There's no fool . . . young fool: epigram
. . . as daft as he seems: simile
You could have fooled me: metaphor
. . . round the bend: metaphor
. . . half the time: hyperbole
. . . I must admit . . . serious on two occasions: irony
What can I do?: rhetorical question
Who needs enemies with friends like that?: rhetorical question; metaphor

Exercise 122

Some examples
1 (*a*) He passed over; he kicked the bucket; he went for a Burton; he went to his maker; he is no more with us.
  (*b*) She was under the weather / below par / off colour / not herself.
  (*c*) He borrowed what was not his; he put his hand in the till.
  (*d*) She was nothing to write home about; she had an inner beauty; she was not the most beautiful of creatures.
  (*e*) He spoke less than the truth; he could not distinguish fact from fiction.

2 (*a*) hyperbole;   (*b*) synecdoche;   (*c*) personification;
  (*d*) personification;   (*e*) metaphor.

Exercise 126

1 *who's* / whose;　　　　2 *less* / fewer;　　　　3 *or* / nor;
4 *those* / that or *kind* / kinds;　　5 *practise* / practice, *licencing* / licensing;
6 *complement* / compliment, *incredulous* / incredible;
7 *because* / that;　　　　8 *like* / as;　　　　9 *must of* / must have;
10 *literally* / figuratively, *not only ... but ... also* / not only ... but also ...

Exercise 128

1 *almost* paid; *almost* eighty pence; *almost* all.
2 *unfortunately* lost; *unfortunately* just before.
3 *only* woman; *only* some; *only* market; *only* last week.
4 worked *hard*; the *hard* question; *hard* into the night.
5 *especially* hard, *especially* sent; *especially* me; parcel *especially*.
6 *Immediately* the girl; *immediately* understood; *immediately* carried out.
7 *obviously* no sign; *obviously* do; anything *obviously*.
8 *totally* convinced; *totally* committed; *totally* lost.
9 *still* stood; stood *still*; *still* fields; *still* cool; *still* evening air.
10 *emphatically* denied; *emphatically* made; *emphatically* serious.

Exercise 130

1 *Between you and* **me** ... (Between is a preposition and takes the object form of the personal pronoun. See **5:75**, page 96.)
2 *laid* / **lay** (See **5:47** (ii), page 81.)
3 *No-one* / **he** or **she** (See **12:10** (ii), page 259.)
4 *weeks* / **weeks'** (See **3:7** (i), page 20.)
5 *badly* misrelates to 'repairing' and causes ambiguity; the sentence needs rephrasing.
6 *waved* / **waived**; *comprehensive* / **comprehensible**.
7 *been* omitted after 'I have always ...'
8 *both* is misplaced; it should follow the word 'bad'; alternatively, the word 'bad' may be repeated before the phrase 'for others'. The correlation of ideas is then strictly observed.
9 *two first* / **first two**. Sense demands the change.
10 *takes* / **take**. Sense demands the change and **take** has a subject 'who' which has as its antecedent the plural noun 'drivers'; the verb needs to be plural, therefore, to maintain the correct agreement of subject and verb.

Index

Bold type indicates a main entry

active voice, *see* voice
adjectives:
  attributive, 87
  comparatives, superlatives, 68–70
  confusion with adverbs, 255
  demonstrative, **62–3,** 126, 255
  distributive, **63–5,** 255
  finite, 71
  formation of, 68
  identifying, 66
  indefinite, **63–5,** 255
  interrogative, **51,** 63
  non-finite, 71
  numerical, 66
  possessive, **62,** 84
  predicative, 87
  quantifying, 66
adjective 'equivalents', 67, 79, 84, 88, 95,
  97, 102, 104
adjuncts, 102; *see* adverbs
adverbs, 75, 85, 86, **89–94,** 95, 96, 102,
  103, 104, 121, 127, 255, 258, 260
  comparatives, superlatives, 90–1
  concession, 91
  condition, 97
  degree, 89, **92–3**
  formation of, 89
  frequency (relative time), 92
  interrogative, 93
  manner, 89, **90–1,** 97
  negative condition (*unless*), 97
  place, 89, **91–2,** 97, 127
  purpose, 97
  reason, 97
  relative (conjunctive), 93–4; with pre-
    positions, 258
  result, 97
  sentence, 94
  time, 89, **91,** 97, 127

adverb 'equivalents', 89, 97
affixes, *see* prefixes and suffixes
aggravate, 249
-al(1), 42
all, 53, **55–6**
allegory, 233
alliteration, 241
alternative, 249
American English, 42, 53, 248
anti-climax (bathos), 235
antithesis, 234
antonyms, 138
any, 53, **54** (*pron.*); 64 (*adj.*)
anybody/anyone, 53, **57**
anything, 53, **57**
apostrophe, 49–50 (*punctuation*); 234
  (*figure of speech*)
appropriateness, 3ff; *see also* registers,
  levels of meaning, directed writing
auxiliaries, 72, **73,** 74, 83, 101, 121, 126;
  see verbs

because/that, 256
between, 49, 245
both, 53, 55–6 (*pron.*); 65 (*adj.*)
burlesque, 237

-ce/-se, 42, 139, 245, 247
chiasmus, 235
climax, 235
colloquial (non-formal), 121–2
common errors, 245–61
comparatives, superlatives, 254; *see* adjectives, adverbs
complements, 79, 83, 86, 98; 101, 103
  (*subjective*); 102, 104 (*objective*); *see*
  copulas
complex structures (hypotaxis), 7–9
composition, *see* essays

compound words, 2, 48, 57, 123
comprehension, 194–210
conjunctions, 97–8; 97, 99–100 (*subordinating*); 97, 99–100, 257 (*co-ordinating*)
copulas, **79,** 83, 98; *see* complements
'correctness', 3ff; *see also* registers, levels of meaning, directed writing

defective verbs, 81–2; *see* verbs
defining phrases/clauses, 9, 16, **60–2,** 84
definite article, 53, 63, **66,** 86
determiners, *see* adjectives, definite article
diaries, 145
dictionaries, 137, 140
direct objects, 48, 61, 85, 90, 98, 100, **102,** 103, 104, 121, 124
direct questions, 51–2, 63, 85, **105–7,** 124
direct speech, 124–7
directed writing, 145, **156–7;** *see* summary, summary and directed writing
due to/owing to, 250, 255

each, 53, 56 (*pron.*); 65 (*adj.*)
-ed participle, 71, 74, **87–8**
either/neither, 53, **56–7** (*pron.*); 65 (*adj.*)
ei/ie, 41ff
epigram, 235
essays, 145–57
  descriptive, 152–3
  discursive, 153–4
  dramatic writing, 154–6
  narrative, 148–52
  planning, 146–7
euphemism, 240
everybody/everyone, 53, **57**
everything, 53, **57**
exclamations, 125

fable, 233
few/fewer/fewest, 53, **54,** 247 (*pron.*); **64,** 247 (*adj.*)
figurative language, 194, **199–200,** 202, **232–41**
finite verbs (clause structures), 71, 101, **103–4**
(the) former ... (the) latter, 58–9 (*pron.*); 66 (*adj.*)
-ful(1), 42

gender, 84

gerund, 87, 94, 258
grammar, 45–118

hang/hung, 81
head words, 100, 102
homographs, 138–9
homonyms, 138
homophones, 139
how (*interr. adv.*), 93
hyberbole, 240
hypallage (transferred epithet), 235

idiom, **123–4,** 195, 202
imperatives, 76, 99, 125
impersonal verbs, 86
implication, 195, 199–200, 202
indefinite article (*a/an*), **66–7,** 86
indicative mood, 76
indirect commands, 125
indirect objects, 48, 95, 98, **102,** 125
indirect questions, 51–2, 63, **105–7,** 124
indirect (reported) speech, 75, **124–7**
inference, 195, **199–200,** 202
infinitives, 71, 72, 76, **88–9**
-ing participle, 71, 74, **86–7,** 258
innuendo, 240
intonation, **105–7,** 120
intransitive verbs, **78–9,** 85, 86, 103
invitations, 166–8
irony, 240
irregular verbs, 81–2

jargon, **122–3,** 261

less/least, 53, **54** (*pron.*); 64–5 (*adj.*)
letters, 157–66
  business/formal, 163–6
  personal, 157–62
levels of meaning, 5, **137–41,** 194, 199–200; *see* registers
lexis, 137, 139
lie/lay, 81, 247
like/as, 256
litotes, 241
'Living English', 1, 11, 30

Malapropisms, 140–1
many, 53, **54** (*pron.*); 64 (*adj.*)
metaphor, 232–3
metonymy, 236
misrelated participles, 87, 121, 255
mock-heroic (mock-epic), 237

modals, **71-2,** 78, 101, 121, 126; *see* verbs
mood, 75-6
more/most, 53, **54** (*pron.*); 64 (*adj.*)
morphemes, 139
much, 53, **54** (*pron.*); 64 (*adj.*)
multiple choice, 196, **201-10**

negatives, 121, 260
neither ... nor, 257; *see* conjunctions:
    co-ordinating
neologisms (new words), 2
nobody, **53,** 57
none, 53, **54**
non-finite verbs, 71, 257-8
no-one, 53, 57
not only ... but also, 251
nothing, 53, **57**
nouns, 46-8
    abstract, 47
    collective, **47,** 60, 83
    common, 46-7
    compound, 48
    infinitive as noun, 85
    proper, 46, 51
noun 'equivalents', 50, 70, 94, 97, 100,
    101, 102, 103, 104
number, **83-4,** 259

objective tests, 196, **201-10**
Old English (Anglo-Saxon), 1, 53, 138
Old Norse, 2, 138
one (you/they), 53
one (*numerical pron.*), 58
only, 94
onomatopoeia, 241
oxymoron, 234

pace (tempo), 107, 120
parable, 233
paradox, 234
paragraphs, 147-8
paralinguistic (non-verbal) features,
    119-22
parody, 238-9
passive voice, *see* voice
person, *see* verbs
personification, 232
phrasal verbs, 85-6
pleonasm, 236
plurals, **35-6,** 83, 84
précis, 179-87
predeterminers, 55; *see also* prefixes,
    adjectives

predicate, 70, 86, 99, **103-4**
prefixes, **37-41,** 68, 90
prepositional verbs, 85
prepositions, 48, 60, 85, 86, **94-6,** 102,
    125, 258-9
principal/principle, 248
prolepsis, 236
pronouns, **48-62,** 100, 125, 259
    demonstrative, **50,** 126
    distributive, 52, 53, **56**
    emphatic, **50-1,** 84
    identifying, 58-9
    impersonal, 49, **52-3**
    indefinite, 49, **53**
    interrogative, 51-2
    numerical, 58
    partitive, 52, 53, **56**
    personal, **48-9,** 84, 125, 259
    possessive, **49-50,** 84
    quantifying, 58-9
    reciprocal, 51
    reflexive, **50-1,** 84
    relative, **59-62,** 124, 259
    universal, 56
propaganda, 195
pun, 237
punctuation, 9-10, **15-33,** 195, 202
    apostrophe, 20-1
    brackets, 21-2
    capital letters, 28-9
    colon, 18-19
    comma, 16-18
    dash, 22-3
    double dash, 21-2
    exclamation mark, **20,** 107
    full-stop, 15-16
    hyphens, 26-8
    indenting, 29-30
    inverted commas, **23-5,** 124
    italics, 26
    paragraphing, 29-30
    parentheses, 21-2
    question mark, 19
    quotation marks, **23-5,** 124
    semicolon, 18

qualifying (non-defining) phrases/
    clauses, 9, 16, **61-2,** 84
quantifiers (identifying and indefinite),
    65
questions, 99, **105-7**
    negative and affirmative, 106

registers, 5, 120, 139–40
reports, 145, **168–9**
relative (conjunctive) adverbs, 93–4
relative constructions:
    defining (restrictive), 60, **61–2,** 84
    quantifying (non-defining, non-
        restrictive), **61–2,** 84
reported speech, 75, **124–7;** *see* indirect
    speech
rhythm, 107

sarcasm, 241
-self/-selves, 50
sentence adverbs, 94
sentences, 97, **98–105**
    simple, **99,** 103, 104, 121, 123
    double, 97, **99,** 121, 123
    compound/multiple, 97, **99,** 121
    complex, 97, **100,** 104, 121, 123
sequence of tenses, **75,** 257
several, 53, **54** (*pron.*); 64 (*adj.*)
simile, 233
simple structures (parataxis), 7–9
singulars, 83–4
slang, 122
some, 53, **54** (*pron.*); 64 (*adj.*)
somebody/someone, 53, **57**
something, 53, **57**
spelling, **34–42**
    American, 42
    consistency, 34
    conventions, 34–5
    ei/ie, 41
    errors, 253–4
    plurals of nouns, 35–6
    prefixes and suffixes, 37–41
    'rules', 35
spoken English, 84, **119–36**
stress/accent, 57, 107, 120
strong verbs, 79–81
structures, 7–9, 97–100, **100–5,** 120
    simple, complex, 7–9
style, 260–1
subjects, 48, 51, 61, 70, 83, 84, 85, 86, 98,
    99, **100–1,** 103–4, 121, 125, 257
subjunctives, 76–7
subordinate clauses, **98,** 100
such, 58 (*pron.*); 66 (*adj.*)

suffixes, **37–41,** 48, 52, 63, 68
summary, summary and directed writ-
    ing, **179–87,** 194, 195, 201, 202
syllepsis, 236
synecdoche, 237
synonyms, **137–8,** 140

tag-questions, **106,** 121
tagmemes, 139
tenses, **73–5,** 86, 87, 92, 126
than/as, 256
Thesaurus, 138
transitive verbs, **78–9,** 85, 104

verbal nouns, **86,** 87, 258
verbs, **70–89,** 98, 101, 257–8
    auxiliaries, 73
    defective, 81–2
    impersonal, 86
    infinitives, **71,** 257–8
    intransitive, **78–9,** 103–4
    irregular, 81–2
    modal, 71–2
    mood, 75–6
    person, number, gender, 82–4
    phrasal, 85–6
    prepositional, 85
    strong, 79–81
    tenses, 75
    transitive, 78–9, 103–4
    voice, 77–8
vocabulary, 6–7, 121, **137–41,** 195, 197,
    198–9, 201–2, **245–53**
voice, *see* verbs
    active, 77
    passive, **78,** 101

weak (regular) verbs, 79–81
wel(l)-, 42
when, 93
whence/wherefore, 93
where, 93
which, 60
who/whom, 59–60
whose, 59 (*relative*); 93 (*interrogative*)
why, 93

zeugma, 236